JAPAN:
Super Economic Power

JAPAN:
Super Economic Power

Editors

K V.S Rama Sarma
V.D Chopra

GYAN PUBLISHING HOUSE
NEW DELHI-110002

JAPAN: Super Economic Power

Economics, Industry, International Affairs

ISBN: 81-212-0600-6

Published in 1998 in India by
Gyan Publishing House
5, Ansari Road
New Delhi-110002

Laser Type Setting at : R Computer Services, Delhi

Printed at : Mehra Offset Press, New Delhi

Contents

List of Tables

Preface

We have endeavoured to present in this volume how Japan has emerged as one of the most important centres of the world economy during the last five decades. After World War II, Japan once again has caught the attention of world by her ability to achieve a high rate of economic growth. In the new historical conditions when the centre of gravity of international economy has shifted from Europe to the Asia-Pacific region, it has become an important actor in the drama of the new economic relations, which are developing in this region. Within two decades of the war, Japan was able to realise her national aspirations of catching up with a western nations, by achieving gross national product, second to the United States. After the 70s, Japanese economy came out of its old grooves of concentrating its socio-economic energies to the internal economic development. During the last two to three decades, the socio-economic process in Japan took a new turn and it started asserting itself in the international economy, including its economic relations with the United States. This is confirmed by the facts that after the United States, it is Japan which has the highest direct investments in other countries. The two other industrialise countries United Kingdom and Germany come next to it. Japan's direct investments in other countries in 1975 stood at 8.3 billion US dollars and 1994 it increased to 275.6 billion US dollars, the highest rate of growth in the foreign investments. What is new in the situation is that Japan's Bilateral Official Development Assistance to the Asian countries has already become a key factor. In 1995 for instance Japan's Bilateral Official Development Assistance to 10 major Asian countries including China, Indonesia, Thailand, India, and Pakistan amounted to 5152 US million dollars. These statistics peak for themselves and reflect the weightage of Japan on the Asian economy.

This is further substantiated by the fact that when a lack of trade finance paralyzed Thai exporters in 1997, neither their government nor multinational lending institutions could lend a hand. Rescue eventually arrived in the form of the Industrial Bank of Japan (IBJ), which provided the funds that allowed the firms to keep trading. That instance was a typical example of how Japanese banks have played a key role in bringing capital to developing Asia. IBJ organised a 500 million dollars capital-raising for Thailand's export-import bank, which then lent the funds to cash-strapped Thai businesses. Despite their straitened circumstances, it was also a cheap deal for the Thais. In fact, they paid so little for their new funds that American banks—governed by strict criteria for returns on capita—stayed out of the loan syndicate altogether. The contrast between Japanese banks' traditional emphasis on relationships and the Americans' sharp focus on profits couldn't have been more stark. Over the years, Japanese money has not only financed countless companies across the region but has also financed the projects that make growth possible, from Hong Kong tycoon Gordon Wu's Pagbilao power plant in the Philippines to Indonesia's first build-operate-transfer generating plant at Paiton.

"Anything from 40 per cent to 60 per cent of the money for Asian project finance in the mid-90s came from Japan," calculates Frank Packard, managing director and head of project finance for Bank of America in Hong Kong "Many deals wouldn't get done without the Japanese. And now we have to ask: What happens when there is a party and the Japanese do not come?"

That scary scenario may soon become reality as the Japanese economy falters and the yen weakens. The deals that made Asia's high-flying growth possible are quickly becoming rarer. As the cost of capital skyrockets, partly because of down-grades from international ratings agencies, many Japanese banks can no longer afford to spread cheap money around the region. "A weak yen is the worst case for Asia", says Shigeki Makino a fund manager with Fidelity investments in Hong Kong. This underlines that both the internal economy of Japan and its foreign investment policy will be a key factor for the development of the economies of Asian countries in the end of the present century and the beginning of the next century.

In this research-based book, we have attempted to analyse Japan's economic growth with a multidimensional approach—historical, internal and external dynamics.

Though a large number of books on Japan have been written, it is perhaps the first attempt by Indian researchers to critically examined Japan's economic growth on the basis of objective reality. The main merit of this book is that it has analysed the specific features of Japan's economic development based on the ground reality in the country and not on the models of other industrialise countries. Japan has industrialized, modernized its economy and adapted technological revolution to its own specific conditions. That is why it will not be incorrect to say that Japan has evolved its own model of development. In this sense Japan has modernized itself without following the western models. This has its own lesson for other Asian countries.

We must also express our gratitude to the Japanese scholars. We have examined their studies, both published and unpublished to compile this book. We hope that this book will attract the attention of scholars and book lovers in India, Japan and in other Asian countries and in all the developed countries.

New Delhi
July 30, 1998

K V S RAMA SARMA
V D CHOPRA

Introduction

Two countries which performed a truly economic miracle in the post World War II period were the Federal Republic of Germany (West Germany) and Japan. Both these countries were in virtual ruin at the end of the war in which they fought the rest of the world. While in the case of Federal Republic of Germany, the Marshall Aid provided the necessary assistance for reconstruction, in the case of Japan a combination of factors, including the reforms introduced by the United States Administration and the Korean War paved the way for the resurgence of a new and modern nation. It is remarkable that in a span of a decade or so, the popular image of Japan had changed from that of a struggling nation debilitated country depending upon U.S. economic help to that of a leading economic power.

Japan emerged from ashes to become the world's third largest industrial nation in less than 25 years. In just five years, from 1965 to 1970, it doubled its industrial capital stock, a feat never before accomplished by any advanced industrial nation. In international trade, Japan transformed itself from being a mere producer of labour intensive products such as textiles, light machinery, pottery and Christmas trees, ornaments, etc. to be the world's leading exporter of steel, ships, electronic equipment, motor cars, communication systems and heavy machinery, etc. Similarly, this South-East Asian nation was able to change its weak international balance of payments position into one of the strongest, thus transforming itself from a borrower in the international money market into a leading lender to many countries. One important reason for this unique economic miracle that lifted the standard of living of its people and enhanced its prestige is that Japanese culture and traditions impose no barriers to change, as may be the case with other countries. On the contrary, the Japanese ethos stimulated change in a manner perhaps unknown anywhere in the world. Throughout the history Japanese have shown a tremendous capacity to assimilate and adopt new ideas to their particular cultural climate. The Japanese developed institutions, customs and characteristics that have given them a strong sense of national identity and a common sense of purpose.

It was in the late 19th century, the Japanese rejected an outdated feudal system to embark upon the road to modernisation and later, in mid-20th century, having learnt a lesson, which they will perhaps never forget, from the tragic experience of World War II, decided to create a new society dedicated to peaceful cooperation and a democratic way of life. These two significant developments in the recent history of Japan brought about a revolutionary change in both political and social structure, without harming the traditional roots and age-old customs that bound the nation together throughout its long history. It is indeed amusing that the Japanese society always remained homogeneous, accepting the best of external influences and retaining both the form and substance of the indigenous culture. Japan is perhaps one of the few nations outside Europe and America which have not been totally influenced by Western culture. Not endowed with any natural resources, this nation has always had to depend on its own ingenuity to survive with pride. It has always been willing to take technical innovations from others and would send its technicians, academicians and skilled labour to far away lands in search of modern ideas. These ideas are then given the "Japanese touch" in implementation.

That is why it would not be wrong to say that though Japan is modernised in terms of industry, it is not westernised in terms of culture. However, in tune with its tradition of acquiring the best, the Japanese have taken to the Western culture and music in a manner few other nations have done. Tokyo is perhaps the only city in the world which has six symphony orchestras.

GEOGRAPHY

Area

Four main islands—Hokkaido, Honshu, Shikoku and Kyushu, besides thousands of smaller islands of which Okinava is one constitute Japan. The archipelago, lying off the eastern coast of the Asian continent, stretches in an arch, 3800 km. long. It covers an area of 377,435 sq. km. Japan's total area is about 125th of that of the United States, one-ninth that of India and one and half times as big as that of the United Kingdom. In terms of world land area, Japan occupies less than 0.3 per cent. Its population is 111 million.

Climate

Climate is generally mild, although it varies considerably from place to place and the four seasons are clearly distinct. Except in northern Japan, winter is mild. Rainfall is abundant, ranging from 1000 mm to 2500 mm a year. In northern parts of the country, snow is heavy and this provides excellent sites for winter sports. The combination of plentiful of rainfall and a temperate climate produces rich forests and a luxurious vegetation.

Topography

About 72 per cent of Japan's total land area is covered by mountains. More than 580 of these mountains are over 2000 metres high and the highest is the famous Mount Fuji whose snowcapped perfect cone rises some 3776 metres. Mount Fuji is said to be a dormant volcano, its last eruption being in 1107. Japan, known for its volcanoes, has 196 of them, of which 30 are still active. These volcanoes provide the nation with mineral hotsprings which are tapped more for recreation than for medical purposes. Flora and fauna along with the snowcapped mountains, innumerable lakes, rocky gorges and turbulent rivers and graceful waterfalls attract millions of foreign tourists, bringing considerable foreign exchange in the country every year.

History

The origin of the Japanese race is yet to be established, but experts maintain that the early inhabitants of this chain of islands migrated from various parts of East Asia and the South Pacific Islands. It is generally believed that the ancestors of the Japanese were an ethnic group, now known as the Yamato race, whose elders are accepted as the ancestors of the Japanese Imperial family. The Japanese came in contact with the kingdoms on the Korean Peninsula by the end of the 4th century A.D. It was through Korea that industrial arts such as weaving, metal work, taming and shipbuilding which had been highly developed in China under the Han dynasty, were introduced into Japan. In this period, Japanese derived inspiration for fine arts from China and Korea. Confucianism and Buddhism were introduced in Japan in 533 A.D. Japan's first permanent capital was in Nara at the beginning of the 8th century A.D. and remained so far more than 70 years.

A new capital was built in 794 A.D. in Kyoto and was modelled on the Chinese capital. Kyoto remained the city of imperial power for nearly one thousand years. In 1192, Yoritomo established the Shogunate or military government at Kamakura, near what is today known as Tokyo. This is considered to be a turning-point in the Japanese history. In this period Japanese art flourished. Another turning-point in Japan's history was when Ieyasu founded his Shogunate in Edo, as Tokyo was known in 1603. By this time the first westerners, the Portuguese traders had reached the shores of Japan. They landed on a small island in south-west of Japan in 1543. They introduced firearms into the country and also brought the Japanese in touch with Europe which was on the threshold of an industrial revolution. The arrival of Europeans had a great impact on Japan. The Shogunate felt that Christianity brought by Missionaries from Europe in their nation could be a danger and hence Christianity was denounced and the entry of all foreigners banned except for a handful of Dutch and Chinese traders. It was later in the late 18th century and beginning of 19th century that pressure began mounting in Japan for opening up its shores to the outside world once again. In 1853, Commodore Matthew C. Perry of the United States entered Tokyo Bay with a fleet of four ships. He persuaded the Japanese to conclude a treaty of amity with his country. This was followed by Japan entering into similar treaties with Great Britain, Russia and the Netherlands.

This indeed marked a milestone in the history of Japan. One of the most remarkable periods in the Japanese history was the Meiji (1868-1912). Emperor Meiji set out to achieve in a few decades what had taken centuries to develop in the West—the creation of a modern nation, with modern industries and institutions and patterns of society. Before the end of the 19th century, Japan involved in a war with China from 1894-95 and a decade later, in 1904-05 in the Russian-Japanese war. Japan emerged victorious from both. By the end of the World War I, which Japan entered under the provisions of the Anglo-Japanese Alliance of 1902, Japan was recognised as one of the world's great powers. Emperor Taisho, who succeeded Emperor Meiji, was in turn succeeded by the Emperor His Majesty Hirohito in 1912. It was in this year the present era—Shoba—began and this period marked the virtual destruction of the Japanese political institutions which was partly responsible for the outbreak of the Pacific war in 1941. Thoroughly demoralised and its economic structure reduced to ashes, Japan accepted the surrender terms of the Allied powers and by Imperial Edict the people laid down their arms.

That was the end of the chequered history of the people who have exhibited fantastic ethnic unity, tremendous courage and great pride but little political wisdom. That was also the beginning of a new Japan that set out to develop itself on modern lines and in tune with democratic norms. In September 1951, Japan signed the Peace Treaty at San Francisco with 48 nations and regained its sovereign independence in April 1952 when the treaty came into effect. Within a year, Japan had joined all the specialised agencies of the United Nations and in December 1956 it was admitted as a member of the U.N. Thanks to the United States of America, the acceptance of Japan into the comity of nations helped boost the morale of the Japanese.

Economic Recovery

In the early post-war period, there were great doubts about resurgence of Japanese economy. Political, economic and social conditions remained rather bad, till the end of fifties. The average annual growth rate of Japan's gross national product (GNP) from the start of the Meiji period to just prior to the World War II, stood at an estimated 4 to 5 per cent in real terms. The post-war American administration took a series of measures to rationalise and modernise political as well as economic policies. The Bretton Woods Agreement came into force, accompanied by the establishment of the International Monetary Fund (IMF) which laid the foundation for the development of free international trade. In Japan, there were the demilitarisation of the nation, the dismantling of the pre-war "Zaibatsu" financial powers, land reforms and the democratisation of labour. These measures were taken to establish an economic democracy. But the pressing need was to fight destitution and inflation. The price level in December 1945 was about the double of the August level when the war had ended; the next year it even rose to triple that level. According to Mr. Tatsuro Uchino, Councillor of the Economic Planning Agency of Japan, "there were many reasons for this galloping inflation." "First, the latent monetary purchasing power which had accumulated during the years of past military expenditure, surfaced suddenly with the end of the war. Second, continuous and large scale financial deficits were brought about by swollen budgets to pay war industries indemnities and supplementary allowances and to defray the expanses of the occupational forces. Third, the production was at a dangerously low level, because the past inter-relationships of industry had been dismantled and shortages of materials and capital were acute. Industrial output was at its lowest, less than 20 per cent of what it had been in pre-war days." On top of this, 1945 witnessed the failure of agricultural crops. The anti-inflationary campaign began with a series of emergency measures decreed by Shidehara Cabinet on February 16, 1946, including the Emergency Monetary Measures Act, the Bank of Japan Note Deposit Act, the Emergency Food Measures Act and the Price Control Act. Same year the Economic Stabilisation Board was set up as a comprehensive planning authority to stabilise the economy and a price agency subordinate to the Board was established to administer price policies. The Emergency Monetary Measures Act proved to be effective only temporarily and failed to control inflation in order to increase production. It was not until the "priority production system" was put into effect in the autumn of 1946 that the wheels of post-war economic stabilisation and recovery began to turn.

It was a programme meant to restore full scale production by means of graded priorities in allocating the limited availability of resources. The coal mining industry received top priority in the use of steel materials and the increased production of coal was channelled back to the steel industry. The target of coal production in fiscal year 1947 was 30 million tonnes. When the Katayama Cabinet assumed office in May 1947 it used the Priority Production System as the main instrument to fight off the economic crisis. It also formulated what was called the July Price System which, coupled with the Priority Production System was intended to simultaneously achieve expansion of production and control of inflation. The Economic Stabilisation Board played an important role in carrying out this uphill task. At one time the number of items under price control totalled 64,506. The breakthrough was provided, as expected, by the Priority Production System. Mining and manufactured goods production went up by 35 per cent in the fiscal year 1947 and by 50 per cent the following year compared with the respective previous fiscal years. The level of production recovered to about 60 per cent of the pre-war level average (1932-36) in 1948. Inflationary pressures showed a downward trend as the supply-demand gap narrowed. The production of rice returned almost to the pre-war level in 1948, although the population had increased by about 16 per cent in the intervening period. However, material scarcities continued to be the basic problem. As the economic reconstruction programme progressed, some controversy arose on how to further tame inflation and boost production.

This was resolved by the "Nine Economic Principles" put forward by the U.S. Government in 1948. The principles included restraint on fiscal spending, and balanced budget planning, through-going tax collection, restraint on industrial financing, rationalisation of wage stability and improvement of trade and foreign exchange structures. Together they were geared to the prime objective of establishing a single exchange rate. This plan was known as "the Dodge Line", named after its author, Joseph Dodge, who was also the architect of the monetary measures taken to stabilise the economy of the Federal Republic of Germany after the World War II. At the basis of this plan was ruthless financial tightening, accompanied by reduction or elimination of price control, compensation payments and suspension of recovery financing. Both were related to the extreme balanced budget philosophy for the fiscal year 1949. These measures, implemented with great determination, produced substantial progress in the struggle against inflation with rationing and price controls moving out of sight. For the first time, in more than 10 years since war-time controls started, Japanese economy returned to a free state and establishment in April, 1949 of the single exchange rate of $ 1.00 - Y 360. This had a significant effect on the economy. As inflation decelerated by 1950, the Korean War broke out ushering in a domestic economic boom for Japan. America began buying large quantities of goods from Japan.

The scale of the economy in the fiscal year 1951 as compared with that in the fiscal year 1948 was double in terms of mining and manufacturing production, 2.7 times in terms of labour productivity in the manufacturing industry and 4.8 times in terms of export volume. The balance of payments also more or less achieved equilibrium. The United States discontinued economic aid to Japan at the end of June 1951. This was the end of the first phase of the economic reconstruction of Japan. The Economic Stabilisation Board was wound up in July 1952.

Technological Revolution

The war caused an enormous technological gap and to bridge the gap, the industry undertook to introduce imported technology on a wide scale and then moved ahead to develop a unique technology of its own. "This not only brought about a sophistication of Japan's industrial structure through the elevation of labour productivity in those sectors where foreign technology was introduced, but it also stimulated further equipment investment, thus providing a major impetus to the rapid growth of the economy, especially in the late 1950s and 1960s.

In this process, technological interchange between Japan's large enterprise and those of medium and small-scale grew rapidly on the domestic scene, while, internationally, Japan gradually came to export its own technological advancements to other nations.

In the fiscal year 1974, payments of royalties for imported technology amounted to $ 718 million, while the total value of Japanese technology exported was $ 113 million. The ratio of Exports to imports was 0.157, with the corresponding figures being10.0 for the United States, 1.0 for the United Kingdom and 0.4 for the Federal Republic of Germany.

Simultaneously, efforts were stepped up to enlarge production facilities in order to seek advantages on a large scale, against the background of a growing labour shortage and progress in trade and capital liberalisation. Technological innovations and investments to save labour and promote automation made rapid headway. Research and development gained momentum and newly-developed techniques in one field induced and multiplied technological innovations in others.

Shortly after the Peace Treaty, the Japanese economy ran into a serious foreign currency shortage. The nation's foreign currency holdings dwindled sharply to $ 790 million at the end of April, 1954 from $ 1,140 million at the end of 1952, and this led the nation to turn to the IMF for its first loan. The reserve crisis could be traced, among other causes, to the internationally high level of Japanese product prices that emerged in the wakes of the Korean war boom. Contributing factors were the positive industrial expansion policy coupled with the worldwide slump that occurred close on the heels of the Korean war and the increased import of food to make up for poor harvests at home. The crisis was eventually weathered by a severe tightening of the fiscal and monetary reins, and this set the pattern of a 'stop-and-go' policy, based on the balance-of-payment status under the mandate to maintain the exchange rate of 360 yen to the dollar.

It was apparent that if the Japanese economy was to overcome its internationally high price levels and attain the capacity to sustain itself, the only fundamental answer was to elevate the productivity of the national economy as a whole and thus to lower production costs. To this end, the lag in industrial technology development since the war years had to be corrected and superannuated production facilities had to be modernised. A number of programmes aimed at modernizing key industries were launched in the 1950s: the first and second steel industry rationalisation programme, the five-year electric power development programme, the three-year coal-industry rationalisation programme, the five-year ammonium sulphate industry rationalisation programme and the programme for strengthening synthetic-fibre production. Such programmes for industrial modernization were supported by legal, financial and tax privileges. The fiscal 1956 Economic White Paper, published in the second year of the Economic Planning Agency, stated:

> We are no longer in the post-war period. Future growth will be sustained by modernization. We must adapt quickly to the ever-progressing technology and environment of the world. Is it not our most urgent task for the moment to board the train of global technological innovation and commence the business of building a new Japan?

The Japanese phrase for technological innovation *(gijutsu kakuchin)* was coined by this white paper and it became a catch-phrase symbolising the subsequent period and fanning an industry-wide zeal for technological development. Waves of innovation swept through the economy from the latter half of the 1950s, leading to improved production processes, the birth of new products and industries, modernisation of transportation and communication and new developments in the energy sector.

Against this background an income-doubling plan was conceived. One characteristic of the 10-year period from 1955 was that economic plans came to assume the nature of policy guidelines for the Cabinet, especially after the Hatoyama Cabinet. The idea of income doubling had come to the minds of policy makers before the birth of the Ikeda Cabinet in such concepts as "wage doubling" and "Monthly income doubling", but it was Prime Minister Ikeda himself who pushed for the incorporation of the idea in an economic plan. This plan was officially recommended by an advisory council to the government in November, 1960, and its target was to achieve an annual economic growth rate of 9 per cent during the first three years, thereby doubling the size of the national economy in a 10-year period. In parallel with the plan, a "Comprehensive National Development Plan" was formulated.

The actual performance of the economy through the fiscal year 1970, the target year of the income-doubling plan, averaged 9.7 per cent in real annual GNP growth, considerably better than the 7.8 per cent envisaged by the income-doubling plan. The composite price index also advanced at an average annual rate of 5.1 per cent during the period, but high-tempo economic growth was visible beyond doubt. With the rate of wage increase accelerating against the background of labour shortage, and with considerable differences in the levels of productivity between big and small businesses, productivity-gap inflation inevitably set in, pushing up consumer prices in particular. Such an increase in consumer prices against the essential stability of wholesale prices emerged as Japan's unique pattern of price trends.

Scientific Research

The greatness of the Japanese planning lay in fixing correct priorities and pursuing them relentlessly. Both fundamental and applied research received proper attention. No wonder scientific research has made substantial progress over the past decades in Japan. The lead role in basic scientific research in Japan is played by universities and their research institutes. Administrative management of basic research in natural science is the responsibility of the Ministry of Education and that of research in applied science and technology is under the jurisdiction of the Science and Technology Agency of the Prime Minister's Office. The Council for

Science and Technology was established in the Prime Minister's Office in 1959 as an advisory body to the Prime Minister on policy matters in the field of science and technology.

The Science Council, an advisory organisation to the Minister of Education, submits reports and recommendations to the minister on policy matters on science. In 1974, the Council had six special committees on space science, nuclear fusion, life science, international scientific exchange, patents and scientific research organisations. In 1974, national universities had 63 research institutes of their own in the field of natural science, with four research institutes under the direct control of the Ministry of Education, which are for the joint use of several universities. One such example is the National Laboratory for high Energy Physics in Tsukuba New Town for Research and Education, north of Tokyo. Altogether there were 893 scientific and technical research institutes in Japan as of April, 1974, including 714 national, prefectural and special statutory establishments and 179 private ones. Besides these independent institutes, large public organisations and private enterprises have their own research departments.

There were also some 239,200 professional researchers in science and technology. This represents 22 researchers in natural science for every 10,000 persons in Japan. The ratio compares with 26 for the U.S., 14 for the erstwhile Federal Republic of Germany, 11 for France and 31 for the then USSR. At all levels of the educational system, scientific and technical education is an important part of the school curriculum. More than 30 per cent of all university students specialise in some branch of the natural sciences. Japan's three outstanding leaders in the field of physics, Dr. Hideki Yukawa, Dr. Sin-itiro Tomonaga and Dr. Leona Esaki were awarded Nobel Prizes in 1949, 1965 and 1973 respectively. Japan has been active in international cooperation in the field of scientific research through bilateral arrangements and multilateral organizations, including the Association for Science Cooperation in Asia.

Labour Supply

The availability of a large well-trained and well-disciplined labour force contributed immensely to the reconstruction of the economy and its subsequent growth. In the course of Japan's rapid economic development after the war, the demand for labour rose sharply. At the same time, the supply of new labour increased with the expansion of the population of productive-age and much greater labour mobility. A major contributory factor to the supply of labour in those years was the widespread and heavy outflow of the agricultural population to industry. The Japan of Today, published by Ministry of Foreign Affairs provides the following data :

Trends in Employment
(annual average)

Year	*Working population (Million)*	*People with jobs (Million)*	*Unemployment rate per cent*	*Unemployment insurance beneficiaries*
1984	59.3	57.7	2.7	850
1985	59.6	58.5	2.6	639
1986	60.2	58.5	2.8	660
1987	60.8	59.1	2.8	672
1988	61.7	60.1	2.5	565
1989	62.7	61.3	2.3	516
1990	63.8	62.5	2.1	484
1991	65.1	63.7	2.1	486
1992	65.8	64.4	2.2	544
1993	66.2	64.5	2.5	667
1994	66.5	64.5	2.9	773
1995	66.7	64.6	3.2	825
1996	67.1	64.9	3.4	—

Source: Ministry of Labour, Rodo hakusho (White Paper on Labour,) 1996.

In recent years, however, a growing shortage of labour has appeared, especially of young workers, as a result of the post-war decline in the birth rate and a rise in the ratio of secondary school graduates advancing to institutions of higher learning. Thus Japan's advantage in labour supply is being gradually lost. On the contrary unemployment rate has been increasing over the last one decade.

The prolonged economic downturn that took hold after the collapse of the bubble economy has caused companies to make major adjustments in their employment practices. Since 1992 the unemployment rate has continued to increase. The rate of 3.4 per cent in 1996 was the highest since statistical records began in 1953. A Ministry of Labour survey of trends in the labour market found that 30 per cent of 5,359 enterprises employing 30 or more workers had implemented employment adjustment measures between July and September 1995, such as restriction of overtime, in-house transfers, transfers to affiliated firms and encouragement of voluntary retirement.

Japan's labour market has continued to undergo rapid changes. In 1950 workers in agriculture and other primary industries constituted 48.3 per cent of the total work force. This proportion fell to 19.3 per cent in 1970 and 5.8 per cent in 1994. Until the first oil crisis employment continued to increase in secondary industries, particularly service industries, have been the major source of new employment. While the percentage of employment in the primary sector should continue to fall, that in the tertiary sector, which was 60.3 per cent in 1994 can be expected to keep climbing.

Of the nation's 64.5 million workers in 1994, 8 million were self-employed, 4 million were working in a family-operated business, and 52.4 million were employed by others. Growth in the number of employees has slowees from its 1991 peak. By sex, 32 million employees were male and 20.3 million were female. Employment statistics for the past two decades show that employment is growing at a higher rate among women than men.

Another change in the labour force has been an increase in workers aged 55 or over. The proportion of the work force in this age bracket grew from 15.1 per cent in 1975 to 21.6 per cent in 1994 and is expected to keep increasing as Japan's population structure continues its aging trend. To accommodate this development, the government has been urging companies to raise their mandatory retirement age.

Japan's wage system has traditionally been based on length of service, but a growing number of firms are beginning to take into account position and ability. Apart from a period of hefty wage hikes immediately after the first oil crisis of 1973, wage increases in Japan have been relatively moderate. In 1995, when the economy was in the midst of a severe slump following the collapse of speculative bubbles, wages in all industries increased by an average of 2 per cent.

Annual Wage Increases
(per cent rise over previous year)

Year	*Nominal wage increase*	*Increase in consumer price*	*Real wage increase*
1986	2.7	0.6	2.1
1987	1.9	0.1	1.8
1988	3.5	0.7	2.8
1989	4.2	2.3	1.9
1990	4.7	3.1	1.6
1991	3.4	3.3	0.1
1992	1.7	1.6	0.1
1993	0.7	1.3	–0.6
1994	2.1	0.7	1.4
1995	2.0	–0.1	2.1

Source : Ministry of Labour, Rodo tokei yoran (Labour Statistics Manual) 1996.

Under the high economic growth policy, however, prices also rose at a rapid pace, registering an annual growth rate of 3 to 7 per cent during the 1960s and the early 1970s. In 1973, the consumer price index showed an 11.7 per cent increase due to the oil crisis which temporarily disturbed the supply-demand parameters. In 1974, in the midst of the worldwide inflation, consumer prices registered an annual increase rate of 24.5 per cent, the highest since 1949. Prices increased sharply mainly in products of small-scale businesses and the primary industries and in the service sector as well as in agricultural marketing, where increased labour productivity has not kept pace with strong market demand and higher costs, including labour.

Consumer Price Indices (1970-100)

Year	*All items*	*Food*	*Housing*	*Fuel and light*	*Clothing*	*Miscellaneous*
1963	69.2	66.1	72.9	96.0	73.1	67.6
1965	76.7	74.7	79.1	96.3	78.6	75.3
1968	88.2	86.5	90.3	97.8	87.7	89.0
1969	92.9	91.7	94.0	98.2	92.0	93.9
1970	100.0	100.0	100.0	100.0	100.0	100.0
1971	106.1	106.0	104.8	103.7	100.0	100.0
1972	110.9	110.1	109.1	105.3	115.0	111.7
1973	123.9	124.4	120.0	111.0	139.7	120.7
1974	154.2	158.9	151.6	142.1	172.3	143.3

Nevertheless, nominal wages rose well above consumer costs, and real wages (actual purchasing power of wages) have also shown a steady increase during this decade. This increase was an average of 4.4 per cent per year between 1955 and 1960, 3.6 per cent during the 1960-65 period, 8.8 per cent from 1965 to 1970 and 9.5 per cent for the 1970-73 period. The increase rate of real wages for 1974 was exceptionally low in spite of the marked gain in nominal wages. Workers' wage increases came about because of several factors, such as (1) annual increases resulting from collective bargaining, (2) increased term-end payments "bonuses" following the past business booms and (3) regular annual wage adjustments regardless of work content, job changes or skill level.

The most important of the above three factors is the first. Since 1955, the annual labour-management collective bargaining sessions basically within each company have come to be termed the "Spring Labour Offensive" or "Spring Struggle" as labour unions' demands for higher wages are staged in February or March each year and the new agreements take effect in April or May of the new fiscal year. Such confrontations have led to large annual wage increases in the past, which have also benefited non-organised workers. Another reason behind the rising wage levels is the growing labour shortage, as noted above. Japanese enterprises, in a bid to attract young workers, have been raising starting wages sharply. This is particularly true with respect to smaller, low-productivity enterprises to the extent that wage differentials, for young workers in particular, disappeared regardless of the size of the enterprise.

In the years after the two oil crises of 1973 and 1979, wholesale and consumer prices in Japan soared 20-30 per cent. Apart from these two periods, however, prices in Japan have been relatively stable. After the collapse of the speculative bubbles in the early 1990s, wholesale prices fell and growth in consumer prices slowed. The consumer price index fell in 1995 for the first time since 1971, when the current statistical methods were adopted.

Inflation Trends by Country, Wholesale Prices

Year	*Italy*	*Canada*	*France*	*UK*	*USA*	*Germany*	*Japan*
1984	10.4	4.6	9.2	5.8	2.4	2.8	0.1
1985	7.3	2.7	4.4	5.3	–0.5	2.5	–0.8
1986	–0.9	0.9	–2.8	4.3	–2.9	–2.5	+4.71
1987	2.6	2.8	0.6	3.8	2.7	–2.5	–3.1
1988	4.8	4.3	4.8	3.6	4.1	1.3	–0.6
1989	6.4	2.0	5.2	4.8	4.9	3.1	2.0
1990	7.4	0.3	–1.0	6.3	3.6	1.7	1.5
1991	5.2	1.0	–1.2	5.4	0.2	2.4	1.0
1992	2.1	0.5	–1.4	3.1	0.6	1.4	–0.9
1993	5.1	3.3	–2.6	3.9	1.5	0.2	–1.5
1994	3.8	5.8	1.1	2.6	1.3	0.6	–1.7
1995	10.3	8.1	6.8	4.1	3.6	1.8	–0.8

Source: Bank of Japan, Kokusai Hikaku tokei (Comparative International Statistics) 1996.

Employment System

Japan's wage-employment practices include a number of rather unique features. One is known as "lifetime employment" whereby young workers who enter a company directly after graduation normally remain there until retirement. Wage increases are granted regularly according to the length of service. While the labour shortage is tending to weaken this system by increasing labour mobility and by narrowing the wage gap between the new and older employees, this traditional practice is likely to continue for many years to come. Throughout his working life, an employee is likely to receive semi-annual "bonuses" or "special cash earnings" in addition to contract salary, overtime and allowances. In 1974, the average total bonus payment for all industries amounted to the equivalent of 4.8 months of regular salary. Another unique feature is the numerous company-sponsored welfare programmes and facilities, the so-called "fringe benefits" which range from retirement allowance and medical insurance to dormitories and housing, child-care, discount stores, as well as medical, educational and recreational facilities. In fiscal year 1974, the ratio of monthly welfare expenditure per employee to total cash payments was 12.2 per cent on an all-industry average.

Japan's social security system now includes almost every type of programme found in the industrialise world. International Comparison of Social Security Benefits and Medical Expenses, 1993

Comparison of Japan's Social Security Benefits and Medical Expenses with other Countries

	Social Security Benefits		*Medical Expenses*
	Per capita (US $)	*Share of GNP (Per cent)*	*Share of GNP (Per cent)*
France	4,087	19.0	8.7
Germany	2,455	11.6	7.4
Italy	3,358	19.7	8.2
Japan	4,115	10.9	6.5
South Korea	130	1.7	3.6
UK	1,047	6.5	6.7
USA	1,955	8.0	11.1

Source : Bank of Japan, Kokusai hikaku tokei (Comparative International Statistics), 1996.

Labour Unions

The Japanese labour movement has made notable advances since the war. In June 1974, there were 67,829 labour unions with a total of 12,325,000 members, representing 33.8 per cent of the nation's labour force.

A feature of Japan's labour movement is that in most cases the unions are organised on a vertical rather than a horizontal basis. In other words, the unions are in general based on a single enterprise, embracing workers of different occupations in that enterprise rather than covering workers of the same occupation in different enterprises on an industry wide basis. The majority of Japan's trade unions are affiliated with national federations or associations, of which the two biggest are Sohyo (General Council of Trade Unions of Japan) and Domei (Japanese Confederation of Labour).

The principal members of Sohyo are the public workers' unions, such as the All-Japan Government and Public Workers' Union, the National Railways Workers' Union and the Japan Teachers' Union. Domei derives its main support from unions in private industry, principally the National Federation of Textile Workers' Unions, the National Federation of Metal Industry Trade Unions, and the Japan Seamen's Union.

The membership of the different national union groups in June 1974 was:

Sohyo (General Council of Trade Unions of Japan)	4,457,500
Domei (Japanese Confederation of Labour)	2,312,500
Shin Sanbetsu (National Federation of Industrial Organization)	71,400
Churitsu Roren (Federation of Independent Unions)	1,401,200
Other Independent national unions	1,654,600

However, the basic unit of labour union organization and activity is the individual enterprise union. The union in each company or plant enters into its own labour contract. Industry-wide federations of unions serve as coordinators and information sources as well as guiding bodies for the individual unions. These federations formulate the standards for labour's demand for wage increases and based upon this each local union makes its own demand to the management. The progress of these separate discussions is carefully watched by the particular federation concerned and its member unions. Whenever necessary, the organisation formulates union tactics and guides their implementation. These can include refusal of overtime work, workshop rallies, one-or-two-hour walkouts and strikes of limited duration. The implementation of such tactics does not indicate that negotiations have become deadlocked, but rather are used to exert pressure and thus strengthen the union's bargaining position.

When a leading company in a strong financial position can be brought to concede a substantial raise in wages, especially if it is an influential concern in business circles, the labour federation will seize upon this example and use it to influence other bargaining in progress. Using such tactics, major unions usually wind up their push for higher wages by the end of April, through the collective bargaining sessions of the "Spring Labour Offensive". Although efforts are made to carry out industry-wide collective bargaining with the help of industry-wide labour federations, final decisions are left to the unions of the individual enterprises. This form of collective bargaining has generally fostered a desire among these enterprise unions to deal realistically with management in a way befitting the actual state of each enterprise and to maintain a cooperative relationship with management in order to ensure the prosperity of the enterprise to which they belong.

The managements also show utmost concern for the welfare of the labour. When a company is in the red normally it first tries to effect economy at various other levels and seeks wage cut only as a last resort. For instance, when the oil crisis hit the Japanese economy in 1974 managements reduced their profit margins and workers voluntarily gave up their traditional "spring bonus".

As of December 1995 about 12.6 million workers in Japan were organized in unions. These unions are usually formed within a company or a company office or plant, a practice known in Japan as the enterprise union system. The percentage of workers belonging to unions peaked at 55.8 per cent in 1949 and has since declined to 23.8 per cent in 1995. The rate has marked a record low for the past 14 years. The reasons include the stagnation of the labour movement per se and diversification in the structure of employment. With more people working as part-time or temporary staff, workers needs and interests have grown apart and are less easily covered by unions. Amid rapid changes in the employment environment, cross-enterprise unions (rather than single enterprise ones) catering for specific groups, such as managers, part-time workers, and women, are beginning to emerge in response to redundancies, transfers, and other consequences of restructuring.

About 8 million of the nation's unionized workers, or two-thirds, belong to unions that are members of Rengo (Japanese Trade Union Confederation), and umbrella labour organisation that comprises most of the unions of the former Domei (Japanese Confederation of Labour), Churitsuk Roren (Federation of Independent Unions of Japan), Shinsanbetsu (National Federation of Industrial Organizations), and Sohyo (General Council of Trade Unions of Japan). Rengo was originally formed as the Japanese Private-Sector Trade Union Confederation in 1987 through the amalgamation of Domei and Churitsu Roren. Shinsanbetsu joined the federation in 1988. In November 1989 Sohyo, which represented mainly workers in the public sector, disbanded, and Rengo was reorganized to include many of the former Sohyo-member unions.

Wage negotiations, which are held throughout the country every spring, determine the level of wage hikes for the year. Both labour and management, acknowledging that it would be better not to raise wages to a level that would accelerate inflation usually hold wage increases to moderate levels. In the spring 1996 labour offensive, the wage hike settlements averaged 2.81 per cent a slight increase over the previous year in reflection of the modest recovery seen in the economy.

Comparison of Japan, Trade Union Membership with other Countries

Year		*Number of employed (1000)*	*Union membership (1000)*	*Share unionized per cent*
1993	UK	21,588	8,700	40.3
1993	Germany	31,751	12,208	38.4
1994	USA	107,989	16,748	15.5
1996	Japan	53,668	12,451	23.2

Source: Ministry of Labour, Rodo tokei yoran (Labour Statistics Manual), 1996.

Industry

With the help of imported technology and raw material and using their own ingenuity the Japanese made tremendous progress virtually in all areas of the industry except in space, aerodynamics, heavy computers and nuclear and reactor technology. These sectors have been left out deliberately and priority is given to basic and consumer industries whose products have ready market both at home and abroad. Ships made in Japanese yards today sail the seven seas. Japanese cameras, transistor radios, watches and sewing machines are in great demand in world markets. Japanese cars, buses, trucks and lorries and railway rolling stocks are helping to meet transportation needs of the five continents. Electrical generators and other heavy electrical machinery made in Japan are helping supply electricity for homes and industries in Asia, North America, Europe, Latin America, Africa and Oceania. Japanese spinning and weaving machinery is being used in the development of the textile industry in many countries of Asia and other parts of the world.

Metal Industry

Japan's crude steel production in 1995 ranked the highest in the world at 101.6 million tons, up 3.4 per cent over the previous year and recovering to more than 100 million tons for the first time in four years. Steel exports rose for the third consecutive year in 1994, standing at 23.7 million tons and a total value of 14.8 billion dollars, and accounted for 3.8 per cent of Japan's total exports by value.

The Japanese steel industry has achieved the highest standards in the world in terms of technology and production, but it now faces growing competition from Brazil, South Korea and other newly industrializing economies. It has been making great efforts to cut costs and shift to higher-value added products and is also branching out into new materials, such as carbon fiber and fine ceramics. The large steel companies have diversified into a wide range of fields, including the electronics and information industries.

The protracted business slump brought on by the collapse of the bubble economy and a sudden increase in imports of low-priced aluminium have dealt a heavy blow to Japan's aluminium refining industry. Domestic production capacity was 710,000 tons in 1984, but since then all but one of the nation's aluminium refining plants have been shut down either permanently or temporarily. Nevertheless the demand in Japan for aluminium products, such as automobile parts, beer cans, and sash, remains high, and in 1994 imports of crude aluminium from such countries as Brazil and Australia reached 2.3 million tons.

Japan's metal resources have become almost totally inadequate for such a large industrial complex. In 1991 Japan ranked third in steel production and it also has the world's third largest aluminium industry. The small size of Japan's deposits of metal ores, coupled with the scale of production for both export and domestic consumption, makes it impossible to reduce the nation's dependence on overseas supplies.

In the steel industry, for example, Japan imported 99.8 per cent of its iron ore requirements in 1989, mainly from Australia and Brazil; it also imports 99.5 per cent of the cooking cooal essential to steel production.

Similarly, though more than 3 million metric tons (3.3 million short tons) of aluminum is produced annually in Japan, production is totally dependent on imported bauxite, mainly from Australia. Japan in 1989 imported 98.4 per cent of the materials used in making copper and 82.2 per cent of those used by the zinc industry. Domestic supplies of lead meet only 10 per cent of the demand. In other minerals, Japan is virtually wholly dependent on foreign sources.

Machinery Industry

Even before the World War II, Japan was not only self-sufficient in shipbuilding, rolling stock and textile machinery, but was exporting these items in considerable volumes. Since the end of the war, the machinery industry set the pace for Japan's economic growth. Taking the year 1965 as 100, the production index in the electrical machinery industry as a whole stood at 360.1 in 1974, while that of home electrical appliances had risen to 334.0. The production index in the automobile industry rose sharply to 468.7 and that of construction machinery to 520.1, while mining machinery production, for instance, decreased to 79.6. Machinery exports in 1974 amounted to $ 27,891 million or 50.2 per cent of total exports.

Machine tools and industrial robots have grown to form the core of Japan's machinery industry. According to the Ministry of International Trade and Industry, 1995 production levels amounted to 699 billion yen and 290 billion yen, respectively. These products are expected to play an increasingly important role as factory automation progresses in all types of manufacturing.

A transformation is also underway in traditional types of tooling and engineering as Japan's industrial structure moves away from heavy-equipment fields like steel and petrochemicals to automobiles, electronics, and other assembly industries, with a concomitant shift to equipment incorporating electronic devices.

Japan accounts for a major share of the world's production of watches, clocks, and cameras. According to MITI, the country produced 436 million timepieces and 11.3 million cameras in 1995. But watchmakers are now running into competition from the developing countries, and camera manufacturers are finding markets around the world increasingly saturated. Disposable cameras with recyclable parts appeared on the market in the late 1980s.

Electrical Machinery

Electrical machinery represents a significant segment of the machinery industry. Its spectacular growth during the past decade has been stimulated by increased demand for heavy electrical machinery from the expanded power industry and the vast heavy industry sector as well as by the remarkable rise in demand for household appliances. Production of alternate current power generators rose from 40,528 units in 1965 to 396,821 units in 1974. Exports of electrical machinery, including electronic products, primarily to North America, Asia and Europe, amounted to $ 6,721 million, or 24.1 per cent of total machinery exports and 15.1 per cent of total exports in 1974.

After 1960s, a period of high economic growth in Japan iron and steel, chemical, machinery, and other heavy industries expanded rapidly. With the resulting rise in individual incomes, electric appliances became common household items and demand for electricity rose accordingly. Japan's first nuclear power plant for commercial use began operating in July 1966 and after the 1973 oil shock there was an upsurge in the development of nuclear power. As of December 1989, 37 nuclear reactors were in operation with a total output of approximately 187.9 billion kilowatt hours. The construction of 17 new reactors is planned as part of the government's programme. In 1989 total generating capacity amounted to 791.2 billion kilowatt hours, of which oil-fired power stations supplied 32.0 per cent; nuclear power plants, 23.1 per cent; liquefied natural gas (LNG), 18.7 per cent; hydroelectric power plants,

11.3 per cent; coal, 14.7 per cent; and alternative energy sources such as geothermal power, .2 per cent.

Electronics

Electronic products are classified roughly into three categories : (1) television sets, videocassette recorders, and other electric appliances, (2) industrial equipment, such as computers and telecommunications devices, and (3) electronic parts, such as large-scale integrated circuits.

Japan leads the world in the production of electric appliances, exporting its VCRs, audio equipment, and other products around the globe. The 1995 production value of VCRs, however, fell sharply to 356 billion Yen (12.7 million units). The 1995 production value of camcorders (portable video camera), fell to 443 billion Yen (8.7 million units).

The largest shares of VCR and camcorder exports go to the United States, which in 1994 accounted for 1.1 billion dollars of VCR exports, or 4.0 million units (27. 0 per cent of the total) in quantity terms, and 1.8 billion dollars of camcorder exports, or 3.7 million units (43.2 per cent).

Industrial equipment has recorded steady expansion year after year, and the pace of growth should pick up further as the information revolution further increases demand for computers and telecommunications equipment. The United States continues to lead in this field, but Japanese manufacturers are making great strides, and Japan is one of the few countries where the majority or newly installed computers was 2.63 trillion Yen in 1995. When peripherals are included, the corresponding figure reaches 5.25 trillion Yen. The annual production value fell in both 1992 and 1993 but increased again in 1994. In 1995 the production value rose 10.1 per cent over the previous year for computers and 2.4 per cent for computers and peripherals.

The production value of personal computers reached 1.25 trillion Yen in 1995, an increase of 46 per cent over the previous year. This rapid increase was the result of a PC boom brought about by the sale in November 1995 of the Japanese version of Microsoft's Windows 95 operating system and by the spread of the Internet.

The market has also expanded for such information equipment as facsimile machines and Japanese-language word processors, which since the mid-1980s have become much smaller and more portable. In 1995 the production values for facsimile machines and Japanese-language word processors were 291 billion Yen (5.6 million units) and 169 billion Yen (1.8 million units) respectively. However, because demand has come full cycle, and also because of the impact of the PC boom the production of Japanese-language word processors is falling off.

The growth of the telecommunications equipment industry has been spectacular, especially for such mobile telecommunications devices as telephones, pagers, and car phones. In 1994 the production of portable telephones reached 5.02 million units, up a whopping 114.5 per cent over the previous year.

In the category of electronic parts, production of semiconductors—integrated circuits in particular—is increasing dramatically. The production value of integrated circuits was 3.9 trillion Yen in 1994. The Japanese industry is especially strong in memory chips. In 1994 exports of integrated circuits reached 29.3 billion dollars, up 132.9 per cent over the previous year. The main export destination was the United States, which accounted for 25.9 per cent of the total, but exports are also increasing to such South-East Asian countries as Singapore (13.9 per cent).

Japan outstripped the United States in the global semiconductor market in 1986 and gained a 13-percentage-point lead in 1988. In 1993 the United States returned to top spot, ahead of Japan for the first time in eight years. The US also held the top spot in 1994 and 1995.

The Semi-conductor Agreement between Japan and the US went into effect in August 1991, at which time both the parties began to monitor foreign producers' sales figures and shares in the Japanese semi-conductor market. These indicators, adopted to facilitate penetration of the Japanese market by foreign enterprises, were to be monitored through July 1996. The US and Japan were conflicting over what to do after that date, with the US calling for the agreement extension and Japan urging its abolition.

The domestic electronics industry is fast expanding its offshore production capacity for three main reasons. The establishment of production facilities in these countries serves to lower imports from Japan and contributes to local employment. The other factor is the increasing strength of the newly industrialized economies of Asia, both of which have forced domestic firms to seek less expensive labour and means of production to remain internationally competitive. A number of production sites have therefore been moved to Asian countries. The overseas production ratio for TVs has been increasing year by year, exceeding 80 per cent in 1995. The overseas production ratio for VCRs topped 50 per cent in 1994 and reached 70 per cent in 1995.

Shipbuilding

Since 1956, Japan has been the world's leading shipbuilding nation. It is also the builder of the world's largest ships, products of a highly advanced technology combined with modern facilities and thoroughly efficient techniques. There are in Japan more than 1,000 shipyards of which 52 are major ones owned and operated by 23 leading shipbuilders who account for 85 per cent of the nations ship construction. The Japanese shipbuilding industry has had a distinct advantage over its counterparts in the rest of the world in that it can handle the complete shipbuilding process from beginning to end in what may be described as pipeline system. Techniques being used include electronic photomarking of steel plates, block-welding, one-side welding of ship plates and the semi-tandem construction system whereby one and a half ships are constructed simultaneously in a single dock, reducing the equipment required by one-third and substantially reducing the building time and costs. Great advances have been made in developing automated and remote-controlled ship facilities, thus reducing manpower needs while increasing efficiency.

In 1960, Japanese yards launched 1,732,000 gross tonnes of bottoms, accounting for 21.5 per cent of the total world tonnage launched. the figure for 1974 was 17.6 million gross tonnes, accounting for 50.86 per cent of the world total. Of this 1974 figure, 15.6 million gross tonnes was meant for export. With the recent demand of super tankers and mammoth multi-purpose ships, such as ore-oil carriers, ore-bulk-oil carriers and container vessels, Japan has constructed many mammoth oil tankers of more than 300,000 dead weight tonnes. In 1975, a shipbuilding company of Japan built the largest vessel afloat, a 379-meter-long, 62-meter-wide oil carrier of 483,377 dead weight tonnes. Japan's shipbuilding industry, which was in a severe slump after the onset of the first oil crisis, cut back production facilities by 35 per cent from 1978 to 1980. Since 1988, however, it has emerged from the doldrums of recession thanks to increased demand worldwide, replacement of old tankers, and a margin of shipbuilding capacity that has enabled Japan to accept orders actively. In 1994 new ship orders reached 11.9 million gross tones accounting for 45.7 per cent of the global shipbuilding market. In 1993 a decline in competitiveness resulting from the rise of South Korea's shipbuilding industry and the appreciation of the yen caused Japan to relinquish its top spot in the global market for the first time, with South Korea taking over. Japan returned to the top spot in 1994.

Rolling Stock

Japan's highly developed network of public and private railways has always ensured a steady demand for rolling stock. Production levels were high in the early decade because of extensive development of the Japanese National Railways (JNR) system and private lines. Later the production shifted from steam locomotives and motor-driven cars to electric locomotives, diesel engines and electric cars. The Shinkansen line of superexpress trains opened in October 1964, embodying the world's finest rolling stock technology. A standard-gauge double track line, it initially covered the 515 kilometer distance between Tokyo and Osaka with no surface crossings, being elevated for its entire length. The line has since been extended to Okayama and further to Hakata, Kyushu, for a total length of 1176.5 kms. The 16-coach train can attain a maximum speed of 250 km/h. for safety in operations, the line uses the ATC (automatic train control) and CTC (central train control) systems, virtually eliminating the need for handbrakes. The industry used such new materials as steel plates of high tensile strength, stainless steel, light metal alloys plastics of every description, including plastic paints. Japanese rolling stock was exported to many countries of the world, especially in Asia, Africa, North America, Latin America and Oceania, as well as the USSR.

Aircraft

Japan's aircraft industry dates back to 1911, and was held in esteem internationally in pre-war days. But the industry was virtually destroyed during the World War II, and aircraft manufacturing was prohibited until 1952, when the Allies Occupation ended. The technological stalemate caused by these blank years later proved to be a major handicap to the post-war development of the aircraft industry in face of the fast technological advances made in this field by other industrially advanced nations. In 1974, Japan produced 211 airplanes and helicopters (228 for 1973), 106 of which were for the Defence Agency, 21 for domestic airlines and 84 for export. Two Japanese commercial aircrafts in particular achieved international recognition: the YS-11 a 60- passenger, short-range turbo-prop transport, and the MU-2, a six-to-nine-passenger, multi-purpose turbo-prop light plane, both incorporating the latest STOL (Short Take-off and Landing) technology. Another popular light plane built was 4-passenger Fuji FA-20 "Aerosubaru" designed for case in operation and maintenance. This plane had a superior rate of climb and acceleration, compared to other aircrafts in the same class. All three of these planes were being exported. Some 40 per cent of YS--11s, over 90 per cent of MU-2s and about 50 per cent of FA-200s found overseas markets, and most of the exported light planes were sold to the United States.

Production of the YS-11 was curtailed in March 1973, after a total production run of 182, though as Japan's first domestically-manufactured commercial aircraft, the YS-11 was a great success, and it achieved international recognition. A new low noise, medium-range jet with a passenger capacity of 200-250 incorporating advanced automatic approach systems, MU-3, an improved version of the MU-2, and 6-8 passenger twin-engine business plane, the FA-30C, were developed in due course of time. Intense research and development efforts also led to the introduction of a new flying boat, the PX-S. Equipped with a wave-controlling device to permit open sea landings even in rough weather and an extra engine for greater take-off and landing power, the PX-S was designed for use in search and rescue operations, transport, ocean reconnaissance and oceanographic studies.

Great hopes are pinned on the future development of aircraft production, a highly technology-intensive industry that produces, much added value while consuming few resources. The industry's 1995 output, however, totalled only 837 billion Yen..

Precision Machinery

The high technical standards and the rapid technological advances achieved by Japanese industries are reflected in the field of precision machinery. Outstanding examples are to be found in the optical goods industry, including cameras, binoculars and electron microscopes, and in the growing production of time pieces, including watches, clocks and precision timers. The optical goods industry produces still cameras, movie cameras and projectors, telescopes, microscopes, optical measuring instruments and optical surveying instruments. The production of optical instruments in Japan dates back to just after the World War I with emphasis on the designing and polishing of lenses and the manufacture of glass. The Japanese camera industry has been a world leader since 1962 in terms of output. It annually produced more than 5 million still cameras and about 1.5 million movie cameras. In 1974, production figures rose to 7.3 million units and 1.6 million units, respectively. Of these totals, more than half were exported. Exports rose steadily from some 2.3 million units in 1965 to 3.9 million units in 1970 and further to 6.1 million units (still cameras 4.8 million, movie cameras 1.3 million) in 1974. The industry developed many new optical instruments for use in medical research. These include the phase-contrast microscope, the ultraviolet and the infrared microscope, the gastro-camera, the fibre-optics gastroscope and the tele-endoscope.

Japanese binoculars and monoculars, noted for high quality lenses and precision instruments became major export products of the optical goods industry. A total of 4.6 million units were exported in 1974. Major export markets were such advanced countries as the United States, the Federal Republic of Germany and the United Kingdom. Exports of watches and clocks expanded from $ 12.9 million in 1970 to $ 43.3 million in 1974. The high quality and precision workmanship of Japanese timepieces won worldwide fame and recognition when the International Olympic Committee selected Japanese products as the official timers for the 1964 Olympic Games. Further recognition came when a Japanese miniature crystal chronometer won six of the top seven prizes in the annual chronometer competition at the Neuchatel Astronomical Observatory in Switzerland in 1964. Since then, Japan has been a consistent prize winner whenever a Japanese watch manufacturer participated in this annual competition.

Chemical Industry

The chemical industry represents one of the most important fields of industrial development in Japan today. The industry expanded tremendously during the 1960s and Japan now ranks among the world's major producers of various basic chemical raw materials. This rapid growth of the industry has achieved despite a lack of such essential raw materials as petroleum, salt, potassium salt, phosphate ore, and oils and fats, which had to be imported. Along with this expansion, the structure of the industry underwent a significant change with the development of the petrochemical industry and the further shift in production from chemical fertilisers and industrial soda chemicals to synthetic organic chemicals such as synthetic resins and plastics. With the wider use of petrochemical raw materials in industry, the petrochemical industry, started in the 1950s expanded over the next 20 years to become a world leader alongside the American industry, and the production of ethylene, the basic material for the industry, reached 5.1 million tonnes, or one-third of the world total. Total petrochemical industrial production in 1974 was valued at $ 8,200 million, compared with some $ 2,500 million five years earlier, and represented more than one-third of the value of all chemical production.

Japan had a total of 12 petrochemical complexes in operation, all located along coastlines. These complexes were developed in close co-ordination with the oil refining industry located on coastal regions convenient to both land and sea transportation routes and near major consumption centres. Production of many chemical products expanded rapidly until 1973, but in 1974, because of a sharp decline in demand, commodities in stock increased and production became rather stagnant. During the decade of 1964 to 1974, production of polyvinyl chloride resin increased 3.1 times, polyethylene, 6.6 times, and synthetic rubber, 7.0 times. The production of caustic soda increased 2.5 times over the past decade and that of photographic sensitized film, 3.5 times.

The Japanese chemical industry fell into a structural recession in the wake of the first oil crisis as a result both of the overall economic slowdown in growth and the decrease in demand resulting from the shift in industrial structure. The petrochemical industry, which uses expensive naphtha as its primary raw material, found itself at a competitive disadvantage with industries in the US, the Middle East, and elsewhere that use cheaper ethane. The petrochemical and fertilizer industries were rationalized from 1983 to 1988 under the framework of a law for industrial reorganization, and production facilities were dismantled.

The 1995 domestic production of ethylene, a precursor in the production of many petrochemicals, was 6.94 million tons, up 13.4 per cent over the previous year and the highest amount on record. Japan ranks second in the world, behind the United States, in the production of plastics, its main petrochemical product; the figure for 1994 was 13 million tons. Japan also ranks second in the world, behind the United States, in terms of its consumption of agricultural chemicals, accounting for 10 per cent of world demand. Companies in the industry are now devoting efforts to developing fine chemicals, an area where biotechnology and new materials are taking the lead.

Pharmaceuticals, a major subdivision of the fine chemicals industry, has traditionally been dependent on the introduction of technology from abroad. In recent years however, large domestic pharmaceutical companies had developed their own technologies, some of which have been exported overseas. Domestic progress has also been seen in the field of biotechnology, with compounds like interferon and growth hormones now commercially available.

Textile Industry

Japan is still one of the leading textile producing nations of the world, even though it has to import all the raw cotton and wool required by the industry, the cotton coming mostly from the United States and the wool from Australia. At the same time, the textile industry registered a declining role in the economy with the emphasis shifting from a light to a heavy industrial base, and because of the rapid growth of the textile industry in developing countries in later years. Before the war, textile accounted for more than half of Japan's total exports. By 1974, this had declined to 7.3 per cent and was replaced by synthetic textiles which grew in importance for the industry, next to the United States, Japan leads the world in synthetic fibre output, accounting for 15.8 per cent of the total world production in 1974. On the other hand, cotton textiles and silk have suffered a decline in relation to the textile industry as a whole.

The textile industry has a long tradition. At present however, both the spinning and synthetic fiber industries are in serious recession. Excess production facilities in the synthetic fiber industry were scrapped between 1983 and 1988 under a stabilization programme implemented in accordance with a five year structural improvement law. Because of its labour-intensive nature, the textile industry is shifting from Japan to other

Asian countries. The domestic production volume of synthetic fibers was 1.8 million tons in 1995, up 1.7 per cent from the previous year. But imports are increasing year by year; the growth rate reached about 60 per cent in four years after 1990. Companies in both the spinning and synthetic fiber industries are branching out into the fields of new materials and electronics.

Hope for the future lies with the apparel industry, which handles the products of the entire textile industry. To counter rapidly increasing imports from developing countries and a recent jump in high-class apparel from Italy and other European countries, the Japanese apparel industry is upgrading and diversifying its products. MIRI has accorded a central role to apparel in its plans to revitalize industries related to daily life. It aims for Tokyo to take its place alongside Milan, New York, and Paris in the world of fashion and to have the industry produce materials of high added value. This plan has been realized to a certain extent. However, conditions in the Japanese apparel market have changed dramatically since the collapse of the bubble economy.

Recession and Recovery

The Japanese economy prospered during the decade starting from 1955, with high-tempo growth taking place against a background of technological innovation. It was during this period that three waves of expansion, each unprecedented in the nation's economic history, occurred. In sharp contrast with this "golden age", the next decade opened with a severe recession which is remembered as the "1965 recession" and for the policies of the then Finance Minister Takeo Fukuda which sought to turn the depressed economy around. It was considered the worst recession up to that time in the post-war era, with a gap between supply and demand—the pressure of excess production capacity—estimated at 3,000,000 million yen. In character, it was a recession of off-cycle fluctuation in plant and equipment investment, and to a considerable extent it was a recession of credit anxiety.

The first order of business for the newly-installed Cabinet led by Prime Minister Eisaku Sato was to prevent the recession from gaining momentum. Ever since the Public Finance Law of 1947 and the "Dodge line", the philosophy of a balanced budget had been upheld by the

Finance Ministry as a rule that should never be bent. However, in view of the severity of the recession, policy-makers felt that the important thing was not short-term financial balance but long-term equilibrium in the Japanese economy and this resulted in a radical switch of policy in favour of deficit financing. In the fiscal year 1965, Government bonds totalling 259,000 million yen were issued under the authority of a special law to deal with the budgetary deficit that developed in the course of the year. In the fiscal year 1966, 730,000 million yen in revenue from the bonds issues was incorporated in the original budget. For the first time in the post-war period, fiscal policy was resorted to as the prime component of economic administration. The programme formulated by Finance Minister Fukuda to counter the recession worked swiftly both in terms of actual economic activity and economic psychology, with business hitting the bottom in the latter half of fiscal 1965 and immediately turning upward by the first half of fiscal 1966. After the 1965 recession, the Japanese economy moved into the longest boom phase in the country's history, spanning about 60 months until August, 1970. One important factor was that the country's balance of payments, which basically swung toward surplus from 1967, ceased to work as a cyclical disturbance to the mechanisms of high-tempo growth. The boom phase, however, came to a grinding halt in 1970, the year of Expo'70 in Osaka, ushering in a phase of turbulence, which has continued to date.

The international currency crisis and global inflation of the early 1970s affected the Japanese economy adversely. Turmoil in the currency scene dates back to November 1967 when the British pound was devalued by 14.3 per cent. This precipitated massive speculation in gold and caused the crisis of the U.S. dollar. These first cracks in the international monetary system were greeted by the press both at home and abroad as events virtually signalling the end of the world, and this uneasiness was further amplified by the shakiness of the dollar, another key currency stemming from the weakening international competitiveness of the United States. The international currency system regained its poise thanks to the revaluation of the German mark and American steps to defend the dollar. In 1969, Japan took to monetary tightening in an attempt to curb price increases - the first tightening at a time of a balance-of-payments surplus in the post-war period. Mr. Tatsuro Uchino, Councillor, Economic Planning Agency of Japan says that at that time he had privately felt that the revaluation of the yen was inevitable, and a memorandum was prepared by Daiso Hayashi, who then was a ranking official of the Ministry of Finance, seemed to suggest that a study of revaluation was already underway. Perhaps due to high-level political considerations the yen was not revalued at that time, but instead a Cabinet level meeting on international economic matters decided to step up import liberalisation for commodities still under control.

In August 1971, the U.S. Government undertook a series of sweeping emergency economic measures, including the suspension of the convertibility of the dollar into gold, imposition of an import surcharge and a freeze on wages and prices. The announcement was accompanied by a call for the realignment of the parities between major currencies. After switching to floating exchange rates, major currency nations in December that year worked out an international accord on a multilateral realignment of currencies, under which the Japanese yen was revalued by 16.88 per cent, bringing the new rate to 308 yen against the U.S. Dollar. This Smithsonian arrangement was short-lived, however, with major nations returning to floating rates in February 1973. Massive overflow of dollars from the United States over the years not only depreciated the value of the dollar but also tended to cause global inflation (insofar as the currency remained an instrument of international settlement). What was additionally unfortunate was that the worldwide poor grain crops in 1972 pushed up food prices on the international markets to record levels. Moreover, economies around the world expanded sharply in a synchronous manner, resulting in a sudden tightening of the supply of commodities and materials. When major nations adopted-tight money policies in an attempt to control inflation, the fourth Middle East war broke out, resulting in the oil crisis which sent the price of crude oil soaring four-fold within the span of only one year. This precipitated a storm of inflation which engulfed the world. In the midst of this global inflation, Japanese authorities were driven to take a series of steps to fight off a virulent spiral of prices. In May 1973, a Price Bureau was created in the Economic Planning Agency, (the first appearance of such an organ in nearly 21 years since the Price Bureau of the Economic Stabilisation Board), and in July the so-called Law for the Prevention of Cornering and Hoarding was enacted, followed by the hasty enactment towards the end of the year of two so-called "oil laws" — the Law for Oil Supply-Demand Adjustment and the Emergency Measures Law for the Stabilisation of the National Livelihood. In tackling the difficulties in inflation, Japan depended on an orthodox demand-curbing policy. It was argued by Japanese economists that inflation of this kind could only be stemmed by curbing monetary purchasing power as a whole, holding down fiscal expenditures by the Government, consumption expenditures by households and investments by corporations. A slowdown of inflation was soon evident, and it appeared that Japan's free market mechanism had proved to be more resilient and flexible in dealing with inflation than most people anticipated.

Slump of 1998

However in the late 90s a new economic slumps appeared in Japan's economy. For Prime Minister Ryutaro Hashimoto, a proud man, it was an agonising experience when he had to resign on July 13, 1998 after Liberal Democratic Party lost elections to the upper House of Japan's parliament. He had to take this drastic step in view of growing resentment in the country as a consequence of economic recession.

One of Japan's leading industrialists, Sony Chairman Norio Ohga, said the economy was "on the verge of collapsing" and compared Hashimoto to Herbert Hoover, the president who led the United States into the Great Depression. However, it was expected that Japan would tide over the crises through massive public-works spending and tax cuts.

This development has serious implications for Asia, particularly after the financial crisis in Indonesia and Malaysia. Japan's imports from Asia are down, its companies are pulling out of Asian investments, and the Japanese currency is weak.

In the first six months of 1998, the signs of trouble brewing in Japan had spread dramatically. The Bank of Japan's latest quarterly survey of business sentiment, released on April 2, 1998 showed a sharp increase in pessimism among companies. Household spending was down 4.5 per cent in February from the same month a year earlier, and car sales dropped 15 per cent in the year ended on March 31. Unemployment rose in February to 3.6 per cent the highest level since Japan began keeping statistics in 1953.

The Yen has been falling in 1998, to around 135 to the dollar and some analysts are predicting a further weakening to the 145-150 level or worse as investors seek the relative safety and high yield of dollar denominated assets. Such a drop, says William Kaye of the Asian Hedge Fund in Hong Kong would have a devastating impact on Korea, which competes against Japan in a number of industries, including shipping and electronics.

This all means that Japan now faces a classic deflationary spiral, triggered by a lack of consumer demand. Inventory is building up, prompting companies to cut prices—and production. That hurts employment, which in Japan usually means hiring fewer temporary workers and reducing overtime hours. The resulting uncertainty further damages consumer confidence reducing demand even further and restarting the whole cycle. "You have chronic over-supply in the economy, and that's what causes deflation", says Masaharu Usuki, an economist at the research institute of the Long-Term Credit Bank of Japan.

Overall says Giles Ockenden, a strategist at Jardine Fleming in Tokyo, the risks of the whole system having a collapse are much higher than they were six months ago. He says there's a 50 per cent chance that the economy will shrink in 1998. If this happens, if will have a global impact because Japan has emerged not only as a global economic power, but has become a driving force in the world economy.

The Japanese experts, of course, do not see things that way. The standard solution to deflationary traps is stimulating the economy, and that's what Japan is finally beginning to do. A 16 trillion Yen package announced by the ruling Liberal Democratic Party in late March contained few details at first, but it is now expected to include at least 5 trillion Yen in actual government spending. Plans for a tax cut, which officials have hinted will total at least 4 trillion Yen.

Even Yoshio Suzuki, an opposition Member of Parliament who has led criticism of Hashimoto's policy, says he's optimistic that the economy will turn around after two more quarters of recession. Suzuki, a former head of Nomura Securities research institute, predicts to a tax cut in the range of 10 trillion Yen in 1998.

If enough of a stimulus is announced, confidence will revive, says Suzuki. So long as the global economy is stable he adds, I cannot imagine the collapse of the Japanese economy.

Optimists see a precedent in Japan's growth of 2.8 per cent in fiscal 1995 and a further spurt of 3.2 per cent in fiscal 1996 a recovery sparked by public-works spending without any significant structural reforms.

If the economy were to recover this time, Japan theoretically would be in a position to address its structural problems. Already, Japan has begun long-delayed deregulation of protected areas of the economy—the Big Bang in finance being the most notable step—and that might be accelerated.

The bigger worry is that the stimulus package may be of only fleeting efficacy. Many economists fear that nervous consumers will save most of what they receive from tax cuts unless they are more substantial than in the past. And Japan's pump-priming formula is a proven loser for creating lasting growth.

Critics point out that Japan's gross debt as a percentage of GDP is already approaching the levels of Italy and Canada, the two G-7 countries that don't enjoy Moody's top rating.

Asher and Andrew Smithers, a London-based economic consultant, have just published a report that estimates Japan's true total debt at nearly 150 per cent of GDP a level far beyond that of Italy. Asher and Smithers note that the government takes the money deposited in Japan's postal-savings system and lends much of it to questionable borrowers who can't get credit elsewhere. Many of the debts are probably irrecoverable, yet none of these bad loans are included in official estimates.

Not everyone thinks Japan's debt has reached a critical stage. Unlike the US in the late 1980s. Japan has an excess of savings over investment, which means its budget deficit isn't hogging savings to the determent of private businesses that need investment.

All indicators show that a major package of economic reforms has come on the immediate agenda.

Foreign Trade

The United States of America and West Europe played a significant role in Japan's economic progress. If Japan is today a major trading nation and a full-fledged partner in a growing world economy, it is thanks to a great extent the helping hand given to it by the free world. The following tables show the principal commodities which Japan had to import and the degree to which it depended on these imports in relation to total consumption.

Self-sufficiency Ratio of Principal Agricultural Products (Per cent)

Product	*1971*	*1972*	*1973*	*1974*
Rice	92	100	101	102
Wheat	8	5	4	4
Barley	29	18	10	11
Soyabeans	4	4	3	4
Fruits	81	81	83	83
Meat (except whale)	83	86	83	83
Sugar	20	20	20	15

Ratio of Imports to Total Consumption of Principal Industrial Materials (Per cent)

Product	*1971*	*1972*	*1973*	*1974*
Raw Cotton	100.0	100.0	100.0	100.0
Raw Wool	100.0	100.0	100.0	100.0
Iron Ore	99.3	99.5	99.5	99.5
Bauxite	100.0	100.0	100.0	100.0
Copper Ore	94.1	95.1	97.0	80.2
Cooking Coal	58.4	63.7	71.7	85.2
Crude Rubber	100.0	100.0	100.0	100.0
Crude Oil	99.6	99.7	99.7	99.7
Lumber	47.1	51.0	55.7	63.9

Raw materials, fuel and foodstuffs constitute Japan's principal imports. Japan relies on overseas sources for practically all its raw cotton, raw wool, bauxite and rubber and for more than 90 per cent of its iron ore and crude oil. The total value of exports and imports on a customs clearance basis and their ratios in world exports and imports were as follows :

(Unit : $ 1 million)

Year	*Exports*	*Japan's ratio in world exports (per cent)*	*Imports*	*Japan's ratio in world imports (per cent)*
1964	6,673	4.4	7,938	4.9
1965	8,452	5.1	8,169	4.7
1966	9,776	5.4	9,523	4.9
1967	10,442	5.5	11,663	5.8
1968	12,972	6.1	12,987	5.8
1969	15,990	6.6	15,024	5.9
1970	[illegible],318	6.9	18,881	6.4
1971	24,011	7.6	19,712	6.0
1972	28,591	7.6	23,471	6.1
1973	36,930	7.2	38,314	7.3
1974	55,536	7.2	62,110	8.1

Japan's exports increased by an average of 18.8 per cent annually between 1965 and 1974, or at a rate about 1.1 times that of world exports. The share enjoyed by Japan in world exports ranked third, next to the United States and the Federal Republic of Germany. On the other hand, the rate of increase of imports was slightly lower, averaging 17.7 per cent for the same period, again 1.1 times that of world imports. In terms of world imports, Japan ranked fourth after the United States, the Federal Republic of Germany, and the United Kingdom, in that order.

Exports and imports in 1972-74 were :

Exports by Commodities
(Unit : $ 1 million)

	1972	*1973*	*1974*
Foodstuffs	666	841	846
Marine products	449	530	542
Textiles and textile goods	2,926	3,729	4,065
Synthetic fibre/fabrics	814	1,000	1,265
Cotton fabrics	231	195	241
Woollen fabrics	25	23	28
Rayon fabrics	41	42	45
Spun rayon fabrics	34	26	30
Clothing	429	370	329
Pharmaceutical and chemical products	1,784	2,147	4,059
Chemical fertilizer	212	266	494
Plastic materials	536	649	1,152
Non-metallic	479	571	690
Ceramic ware	182	204	228
Metal and metal products	4,871	6,821	13,691
Iron and steel	3,610	5,304	10,758
Metal products	998	1,210	1,789
Machinery	15,377	20,365	27,891
Textile machinery	233	430	632
Sewing machines	191	221	270
Radios	1,033	1,243	1,359
Automobiles	2,965	3,612	5,227
T.V. sets	565	608	719
Ships	2,399	3,819	5,600
Optical instruments	772	970	1,320
Tape Recorders	659	785	738
Plywood	89	74	67
Toys	151	156	139
Others	2,489	2,905	4,294
Total	*28,591*	*36,930*	*55,536*

Imports by Commodities
(Unit : $ 1 million)

	1972	*1973*	*1974*
Foodstuffs	3,607	6,009	8,122
Wheat	361	660	1,211
Corn (foodstuff)	272	552	878
Sugar	445	434	1,157
Textile raw materials	1,348	2,137	1,861
Wool	465	1,065	533
Cotton	620	708	1,047
Metal ore and scrap	2,488	4,033	5,328
Iron Ore	1,275	1,652	2,076
Scrap Iron	109	387	507
Non-ferrous metal ore	6,016	1,884	2,657
Other materials	3,356	6,038	7,189
Raw hides	173	246	186
Soyabeans	474	772	882
Crude rubber	83	184	210
Lumber	1,727	3,411	3,683
Beef tallow	45	91	95
Mineral fuels	5,715	8,327	24,895
Coal	1,078	1,354	2,864
Crude oil	3,727	6,000	18,898
Petroleum products	539	726	2,263
Pharmaceutical and chemical products	1,148	1,865	2,668
Machinery	2,592	3,486	4,748
Metal working machinery	112	118	191
Business machinery	362	476	590
Iron and steel	104	232	400
Non-ferrous metals	922	1,669	2,036
Others	3,217	6,368	7,298
Total	*23,471*	*38,314*	*62,110*

Japan's changing industrial structure at home and new trade patterns and other factors abroad have resulted in a distinct shift both in the substance and the distribution of the country's foreign trade. Before the war, textile raw materials accounted for 32 per cent of total imports, and textiles made up more than half of total exports. In 1974, textile raw materials accounted for only 3 per cent of total imports, while textile exports had fallen to 7.3 per cent of the total export trade. Among raw materials and fuels, there was a sharp rise in the import of petroleum, iron ore and non-ferrous metals, reflecting the growing stature of Japan's heavy industries.

Meanwhile, exports of metal product, machinery and chemicals which before the war amounted to an average of only 16 per cent of total exports, had risen by 1974 to 82.1 per cent ($ 45,641 million), or a level similar to those of other industrially developed countries. Marked progress was made in the latter half of the 1960s in exports of heavy and chemical industrial products, such as iron and steel, ships, automobiles and radio sets. In terms of distribution, the Asian market before the war provided the biggest outlet for Japanese goods. China, India and Indonesia alone accounted for 40 per cent of Japan's total exports. Today, Asia, North America and Western Europe constitute Japan's major markets. In 1974, Asia took 26.8 per cent of Japan's total exports and supplied 22.4 per cent of its imports. North America accounted for 25.9 per cent of Japan's exports and 24.7 per cent of its imports. Japan's exports to Western Europe accounted for 15.1 per cent of total exports, while Western Europe supplied 8.4 per cent of Japan's imports.

Japan's biggest single trading partner today is the United States, which in 1974 took 23.0 per cent of Japan's total exports. Japan in turn is the United States second biggest customer after Canada. When viewed from the area composition of exports, those to developed countries accounted for 47.6 per cent of the total in 1974, those to developing countries 45.4 per cent, and the rest went to the socialist countries. Japan's imports from developed countries, on the other hand, accounted for 41.5 per cent of its total imports in 1974. This was the situation in the 70s. However, the patter of Japanese trade has undergone changes since the 70s.

Japan is the world's third largest trading country in both exports and imports, following the US and Germany. The country's trade balance was negative through the mid-1960s but has generally been positive since. Beginning in 1981 the annual surplus consistently exceeded 10 billion dollars, reaching an unprecedented 92.8 billion dollars in 1986. It then declined until 1990 before bouncing back to reach another record high of 141.5 billion dollars in 1993. In 1995 it slid back for the first time in five years, to 107.1 billion dollars this was also the first time since 1976 that the trade surplus with Asia was higher than the combined surplus with the US and the European Union.

In 1995 exports totalled 442.9 billion dollars and imports 336.1 billion dollars; exports were up 12.0 per cent over 1994, and imports were up 22.3 per cent. In 1993 Japan accounted for 9.5 per cent of the exports and 6.5 per cent of the imports of the member countries of the International Monetary Fund.

Poor in natural resources, Japan maintains a traditional industrial and trading pattern of importing raw materials and energy resources for use in the manufactur of export products. As a consequence, the share of manufactured products among Japan's total imports is low, giving rise to much foreign criticism. The share of such imports stood at 31.0 per cent in 1995. The levels is still low in comparison with other major industrial nations, but it is likely to continue rising.

The following tables confirm this conclusion.

Total Exports and Imports
(Customs Clearance Basis)

	Exports		*Imports*		
	Value (billion)	*Annual growth (per cent)*	*Value (billion)*	*Annual growth (per cent)*	*Balance (billion)*
1985	41,956	4.0	31,085	–3.8	10,871
1986	35,290	–15.9	21,551	–30.7	13,739
1987	33,315	–5.6	21,737	0.9	11,578
1988	33,939	1.9	24,006	10.4	9,933
1989	37,823	11.4	28,979	20.7	8,844
1990	41,457	9.6	33,855	16.8	7,602

1991	42,360	2.2	31,900	–5.8	10,460
1992	43,012	1.5	29,527	–7.5	13,485
1993	40,202	–6.5	26,826	–9.1	13,376
1994	40,498	0.7	28,104	4.8	12,393
1995	41,531	2.6	31,549	12.3	9,982

Sources:Ministry of International Trade and Industry, Tsusho Hakusho (White paper on International Trade), 1996.

Volume of Trade by Country, 1994

	Value (US $ million)		*Share of world total (per cent)*		*Per Capita value (US dollar)*	
	exports	*imports*	*exports*	*imports*	*exports*	*imports*
USA	512,521	689,215	11.7	16.1	1966	2,644
Germany	427,219	381,890	9.8	8.9	5,248	4,691
Japan	397,005	275,235	9.1	6.4	3,177	2,203
France	235,905	230,188	5.4	5.4	4,074	3,976
UK	204,923	227,000	4.7	5.3	3,528	3,908

Source: Bank of Japan, Kokusai hikaku tokei (Comparative International Statistics), 1996.

1

Growth of Automobile Industry and Industrial Structure

One of the factors that facilitated economic boom in Japan was the boost given to the automobile industry by the government. It is an established fact that growth of the automobile industry correlates the growth in many other areas of the economy thus contributing substantially to economic development. According to Mr. Hiroya Uneo and Mr. Hironichi Muto, automobiles not only attracted individuals and enterprises but were also extremely valuable to the national economy for the following reasons:

(1) In an advanced country, the automobile industry has large weightage in production and employment and the automobile sector is expected to raise the income level faster.

In other words, it has a strong advantage in terms of income elasticity. Thus by establishing an automobile industry a country adds new and substantial industrial activity that contributes to its economic growth.

(2) Since the automobile industry is a consumer for many other industries, its development will be accompanied by the expansion of related industries.

(3) As an export trade, the automobile industry has a high foreign exchange earning capacity.

(4) The infusion of automobiles helps to improve transportation capacity in the national economy, facilitates the efficient use of production factors and thus leads to economies of other industries.

Since the end of the World War II, the Japanese automobile industry, having started with the manufacture of trucks, has come a long way. But till 1955 its development was limited in many respects. In that year the

Japanese automobile industry was by far the smallest, being only one-half the size of the American industry and one-fourth that of the British industry, both in terms of value and employment. However, it was one of the high productivity industries, though this productivity was only one-eighth of the U.S. level. It was realised very early in Japan that automobile industry has impact on other industries, inducing the growth of such related sectors as iron and steel, non-ferrous metals, machine tools, tyres, glass and automobile parts. The effect of the automobile industry is most noticeable in the United States.

Percentages of Raw Materials Consumed for Automobile Production

	United States (1935)			*Japan (1955)*	
1.	Steel	24.8	1.	Steel	
	(a) Bar steel	40.1		(a) Ordinary steel	2.4
	(b) Sheet steel	42.5			
	(c) Hoops	57.1			
2.	Malleable cast iron	54.0	2.	Malleable cast iron	23.2
3.	Copper and copper alloys	20.0	3.	Copper	-
4.	Lead	36.8	4.	Lead	-
5.	Aluminium	20.0	5.	Aluminium (die cast)	25.2
6.	Rubber	80.0	6.	Rubber	23.2

The above table shows the percentage of raw materials used in the automobile industry. In the United States before the World War II, the automobile industry consumed one-fourth of the steel, one-fifth of the copper and aluminium and 80 per cent of the rubber. In contrast, in Japan in 1955, these percentages were much lower, namely, 2.4 per cent for ordinary steel, 25.2 per cent for aluminium, and 23.3 per cent for rubber, obviously due to the small size of the automobile industry in Japan at that time.

Popular Car Plan

In 1946, the automobile production in Japan aggregated 1,500 units. Automobiles exported in 1955 were only 0.3 per cent of the total manufactured in Japan. The ratio was way behind West Germany's 8.8 per cent, Italy's 7 per cent, the United States' 4.7 per cent and Sweden's 2.4 per cent. At that time 40 per cent of Japanese export comprised of textiles and apparels. In May, 1955 the Ministry of International Trade and Industry (MITI) announced "General Plan for Fostering Popular Cars". Its objective was, by means of positively fostering the small passenger car industry as a new industry, to expedite the expansion of related industries, expansion of employment and enhancement of the technical level thus preparing the ground for the small passenger car industry to develop as an export industry and raising the national living standard through the popularisation of passenger cars at home."

Protection

This policy declaration showed MITI's intention to develop and protect the automobile industry at home as an important strategic industry. This paved the way for the automobile industry being placed under strong government protection as one of the strategic industries, others being synthetic fibres, petro-chemicals and electronics. It received protection by way of import restrictions, protective tariffs and subsidies. In addition the Japanese government adjusted excise duties, foreign exchange control and special depreciation system to the advantage of domestically made automobiles, including even car bodies, parts and accessories. These measures can be categorised into (1) protective measures to curb the inflow of foreign made automobile and (2) support measures to strengthen the international competitiveness of the automobile industry. The protective measures included the following four :

(1) protective tariff raises;

(2) the excise tax, providing more advantages for Japanese automobiles;

(3) import restriction through the operation of foreign exchange allocation;

(4) control of foreign capital investment.

Automobile Import Tariff Rates (May 31, 1960)

		Fixed rate	*GATT rates*	
Automobile	Passenger Car	40%	35 %	(with wheelbase above 254 cm)
			30 %	(with wheelbase below 254 cm)
	Truck	30 %	27 %	(with wheelbase above 254 cm and loading capacity above 18 tons)
Automobile parts		30 %	30 %	

Excise Tax Rates on Automobiles (April 21, 1959)

	Fixed Rate	*GATT rates*
High-class passenger cars	50 %	(with wheelbase above 305 cm or cylinder capacity above 4,000 cc)
Medium-sized passenger cars	30%	(with wheelbase above 254 cm and below 305 cm or cylinder capacity above 1,500 cc and below 4,000 cc).
Small-passenger cars	15%	(with wheelbase below 254 cm and cylinder capacity below 1,500 cc)

The above two tables show that the tariffs and excise duties gave the most favourable protection to passenger cars made in Japan. The fixed tariff rate on imported passenger cars was 10 per cent higher than the 30 per cent rate on trucks and parts. Moreover the GATT rate of 35 per cent was not applicable to small passenger cars with wheelbase below 254 cm (which covers all Japanese made small cars with cylinder capacity below 1500 cc, the limit inter extending to 1900 cc when the cut-off point was raised to wheelbase over 270 cm. The excise tax rate on small passenger cars was a favourable 15 per cent against 30 to 50 per cent on medium-sized and large passenger cars, which were mostly of foreign make. Another barrier against importing foreign automobiles in the guise of foreign exchange allocation system which was strengthened even more when the overall import restriction policy was adopted during the 1954 recession in order to cope with the threatening inflow of small passenger cars from Europe, which had broken through the 40 per cent tariff barrier in 1952 and 1953. For instance, the amount of foreign exchange allocation for automobile imports had been reduced to $610,000 in 1954 and $ 920,000 in 1955 from $ 13,740,000 in 1953, thus bringing down import of foreign automobiles to 370 and 545 respectively, from 5900. In addition to these protectionist policies, the government also provided the following support measures:

(1) loans at low interest rates from public financial institutions;
(2) government subsidies;
(3) special depreciation;
(4) exemption of import duties on necessary machinery and equipment;

(5) authorisation for essential technology imports.

The Japan Development Bank loans had amounted to a total of Y 1.5 billion or nearly 10 per cent of the total investment of Y 16.26 billion in the manufacturing facilities of medium and small-sized passenger cars during the 1951-55 period. After the automobile parts industry was included in 17 industries to be promoted under the "Law Concerning Provisional Measures for Development of the Machinery Industry", which was enacted in June 1956, fund allocations for the automobile parts industry were authorised through the development banks, financing of primary automobile parts makers and the Small Business Finance Corporation's financing of secondary parts makers. This law was enacted with a five year time limit in order to rationalise production systems, modernise equipment, encourage exports, develop technology and secure raw materials supplies in specially designated industries, which did not include the automobile industry itself. However, the amendments to this law in 1961 and 1966 extended the designation to automobile parts, machine tools for automobiles, internal combustion engines and industrial vehicles. These measures were taken obviously to keep the prices of automobile parts as low as possible.

As regards the government subsidies, the government disbursed a total of 369 million yen of subsidies for the Automobile Technology Association, the Japan Small Automobile Industry Association and other organisations from 1951 to 1959. In regard to special depreciation system, the government authorised a depreciation by one-half in the first year after acquisition of those machines designated for rationalisation by the Special Taxation Measures Laws and an annual 50 per cent extra addition to the authorised depreciation ratio for selected essential machines during the three-year period. Encouraged by these enormous concessions, the automobile industry spent 11.85 million yen or 18.4 per cent of total investments of 64.36 billion yens during 1951-59 for the purchases of machines designated by the law. The exemption of import duties on essential machines and tools was provided as exceptions to the Tariff Law (1954) and the Provisional Tariff Measures Law (1960) for those machines deemed indispensable in automobile production but not manufactured in Japan, including many kinds of machines and machine tools used for automobile manufacturing. As for technology imports, a total of 155 cases were officially authorised, not only for automobile manufacturers but also for automobile parts makers during the period from 1951 to 1968.

These measures and the outbreak of the Korean war in 1950 shot the Japanese automobile industry into a high growth orbit. In 1951, when the war ended, production of four-wheel automobiles had reached 100,000 a year—nearly twice as much as the pre-war boom record. Since then the production kept on expanding to 1 million in 1963, 2 million in 1966, 3 million in 1967 and 5 million in 1970. During the 22 years from 1949, to 1971, Japanese automobile production registered a spectacular increase - as much as 200 times for all cars and 3475 times for passenger cars. In 1971, Japan became the second largest automobile producers in the world, the third in passenger cars next to the United States and West Germany, and the first in bus and truck production. The tremendous increase in automobile production was due mainly to the rapid progress of motorisation at home; expansion of exports added a new dimension only after 1964. The progress of motorisation can be seen in increases in the stock of three-wheel and four-wheel automobiles, which exceeded one million in 1956, 5 million in 1964 and 10 million in 1969. At the end of 1971, the Japanese held 19.86 million four-wheel automobiles (including 10.57 million passenger cars), or 189 (105 passenger cars) per 1000 population, thus almost reaching the European level.

This remarkable development was naturally accompanied by rapid changes in the pattern of demand for automobiles. Production was initially heavy, concentrated on buses, trucks and other commercial vehicles. As much as 70 per cent of total automobile production was in this category. However, this ratio started to decline after 1962, reaching 50 per cent in 1968 and 36 per cent in 1971 against 64 per cent for passenger cars. The passenger cars took the leading role of motorisation in 1961 and recorded a tremendous speed of diffusion in the next decade as can be seen from the high rate of growth in the sector of passenger cars—24.4 per cent in 1956-60, 36.7 per cent in 1961-65 and 30.1 per cent in 1966-71. This high growth was maintained by household demand. Simultaneously, passenger cars for private use increased from 0.9 per cent in 1951 to 50.6 per cent in 1970 as per centage of total sales, while those bought by the transportation industry decreased from 81.4 per cent to 5.8 per cent.

Liberalisation of Car Imports

The protective measures taken by the government greatly helped the automobile industry grow beyond the infant stage. Gradually foreign countries built up their pressure on Japan to liberalise imports and capital investment and MITI also began changing its position. Accordingly, the government liberalised bus and truck imports in April, 1961 and passenger car imports in October, 1965. In June 1967 through the Kennedy Round negotiations Japan announced that it would reduce import duties on large passenger cars (from 35 per cent to 17.5 per cent) small passenger cars (40 per cent to 30 per cent) and buses and trucks (30 per cent to 15 per cent) by 1972. Following the Japan-U.S. automobile negotiations, in August, 1968 the government decided on the following measures:

(1) Japan would annually expand the import quota of automobile engines until its complete removal in early 1972.

(2) Japan would favourably accept application for establishing of joint-venture knock-down assembly companies.

(3) Japan would reduce the tariff rate on large passenger cars to 17.5 per cent beginning in April, 1969.

However, this import liberalisation policy failed to achieve its goals because of monopoly pricing policy being adopted in Japan. The U.S. government and automobile industry further increased pressure on Japan. Finally in October, 1969, Japan announced its full programme as follows:

(1) capital investment in the automobile industry would be liberalised beginning in October, 1971;

(2) the measure and date would also apply to the automobile parts industry and automobile sales services;

(3) in this capital liberalisation these industries would be treated as Category I industries (joint-venture enterprises with foreign share capital below 50 per cent and under specific qualifications for automatic approval).

As a result of the protectionist policy, the Japanese automobile exports grew spectacularly in 10 years from 1971-72. Passenger cars exports increased by 113 times and commercial vehicles exports by 12 times. Their annual average growth rates were 60.6 per cent and 27.7 per cent respectively. The share of exports in total production were 34.9 per cent and 22.9 per cent respectively. The ratio for passenger car exports was somewhat less than some European ratio (62.4 per cent West

Germany, 47.6 per cent France, 37.3 per cent U.K., 36.1 per cent Italy). The increase in Japanese automobiles exports has been not only in terms of quantity but also is being associated with changes in direction of trade towards North America and Europe. Significantly Japanese passenger cars exported to the United States were 654,000 in 1971, which was 50.3 per cent of Japan's total exports of passenger cars, 6.7 per cent of car sales in the United States and 44.6 per cent of U.S. imports of foreign passenger cars.

Domestic Car Sales by Manufacturers (1,000 cars)

	1970	*1971*	*1972*	*1973*
Toyota Motors	1,110	1,169	1,358	1,551
Nissan Motors	928	968	1,153	1,273
Mitsubishi Motors	411	385	375	443
Toyo Kogyo	336	306	338	394
Honda Motors	364	294	276	297
Isusu Motors	123	118	126	149
Fuji Heavy Ltd.	203	155	150	158
Suzuki Motors	268	259	223	235
Daihatsu Kogyo	277	288	227	291
Hino Motors	42	43	51	69
Nissan Diesel Motors	17	16	19	22
Grand Total (Including imported cars)	4,100	4,024	4,346	4,914

By 1975 passenger cars exports rose to 1,827,286 units after expanding at an average annual growth of 33.6 per cent. The share of passenger cars thus rose to about two-thirds of total auto exports. This indicates that Japanese passenger cars have been increasingly accepted in the world market. It is notable fact that a large percentage of cars have gone to highly industrialised countries. Of total exports in 1975, 34.4 per cent or 900,000 vehicles went to the U.S. Exports to the advanced regions, including Canada, West Germany and Oceania in 1975 accounted for 66.6 per cent of Japan's total auto exports. This is a considerable gain over the 47.9 per cent in 1965. In mid-sixties, the main market for Japanese automobiles was Asia and now it has extended to America and Europe. This remarkable progress was brought about by the tremendous improvement both in performance and price of the Japanese automobiles. For instance, there is little difference between compact cars (small car) in the 1000 and 2000 cc class produced by the big three—General Motors, Ford and Chrysler and major Japanese producers. Japanese cars, it is claimed, with some justification, are superior to their American counterparts in the class below 1500 cc cylinder capacity. This great leap in the automobile industry automatically boosted various other connected industries.

Changes in Position of Major Industries in Japan

Industry	*Value* *1955* *(per cent)*	*added* *1969* *(per cent)*	*Persons* *1955* *(per cent)*	*engaged* *1969* *(per cent)*
Automobile and accessories	3.1	6.6	2.3	4.9
Automobile manufacturing	1.7	3.5	0.8	1.4
Textiles	13.6	6.2	19.2	11.2
Chemicals	13.8	10.6	6.6	4.3
Iron and steel	8.1	7.0	5.0	4.7
General machinery	6.3	11.2	6.9	9.7
Electrical machinery	5.3	11.5	4.2	11.1
Total manufacturing	100.0	100.0	100.0	100.0
	(2,099) *	(20,551) *	(5,517)**	(11,412)**

*Value added (in billions of yen).

**The number of persons engaged in production (in thousands)

The above table shows that the automobile industry increased its value added shares in automobiles manufacturing from 1.7 per cent in 1955 to 3.5 per cent in 1969, and its employment share from 0.8 per cent to 1.4 per cent during the same period. In 1967, the automobile industry consumed 9 per cent of ordinary steel following construction industry (48 per cent) and the shipbuilding industry (10 per cent). It was the largest consumer of polished plate, glass and rubber using about 50 per cent of each. On the export front, the automobile industries earnings were simply outstanding, increasing from 0.3 per cent ($ 6,355,000) of total exports in 1955 to 9.9 per cent ($ 2.37 billion) in 1971, following iron and steel (14.7 per cent) and textiles (11.5 per cent).The following ten companies were involved in the production and export of automobiles virtually of all varities.

1. Toyota Motor Co. Ltd. : This was not only the largest automobile manufacturer in Japan but also claimed the biggest sales and profits amongst Japanese corporations. Toyota Motor had over 40 thousand

Automobile Manufacturers' Production and Shares

	1965		*1967*		*1969*		*1971*	
Toyota	477,600	(25.5)	832,100	(26.4)	1,471,200	(31.5)	1,955,000	(33.6)
Hino	51,000	(2.7)	32,700	(1.0)	39,400	(0.8)	48,900	(0.8)
Daihatsu	148,200	(7.9)	255,500	(7.2)	264,300	(5.7)	311,800	(5.4)
Suzuki	42,000	(2.2)	115,600	(3.7)	238,100	(5.1)	267,400	(4.6)
Nissan	436,700	(23.3)	726,100	(23.1)	1,148,700	(24.6)	1,591,500	(27.4)
Nissan Diesel	5,000	(0.3)	11,100	(0.4)	18,200	(0.4)	22,100	(0.4)
Aichi Machinery	33,600	(1.8)	42,600	(1.4)	22,000	(0.5)	-	-
Fuji Heavy Industry	91,500	(4.9)	175,100	(5.5)	187,400	(4.0)	184,400	(3.2)
Isuzu	98,100	(5.2)	132,800	(4.2)	155,200	(3.3)	135,700	(2.3)
Toyo-Kogyo	274,400	(14.6)	388,300	(12.3)	428,200	(9.2)	501,100	(8.6)
Mitsubishi	165,000	(8.8)	317,400	(10.1)	337,300	(7.2)	484,200	(8.3)
Honda	52,500	(2.8)	149,300	(4.7)	364,900	(7.8)	308,600	(5.3)
Total	*1,875,600*		*31,78,600*		*4,674,900*		*5,810,800*	

* Figures in parentheses are shares (%)

prices tended to rise, indicating that the rise in concentration leads to price rigidity or price stability on a higher level.

This shows the price competition in the Japanese and U.S. automobile markets. Common to the two cases is the presence of price leadership with General Motors and either Toyota or Nissan playing the role of the price leaders. However, Japanese and American price decisions differed most conspicuously in that American auto makers were more collusive in raising prices, while the Japanese producers were relatively competitive. Almost all the competitive price reductions in Japan originated in either a price leader's unilateral price markdowns or the announcement of a new model car at the unchanged prices (effective price reductions due to quality improvements). The major exception was Toyo Kogyo's announcement of a price rise for Luce in September 1968 after it was equipped with new safety devices. It took six months for other manufacturers to follow suit; in the meantime, Luce's market share decreased from 4.5 per cent in the first half of 1968 to 3.4 per cent in the latter half of the year. In this respect we must note the following two points:

(1) Insofar as safety device-equipped cars were concerned, all manufacturers' added cost increments to their prices without trying to cover the cost additions by raising productivity.

(2) In September 1968, when Toyota announced price cutbacks on improved Coronna and offered the new model of Mark II on sale, Nissan alone announced price markdowns to compete with Toyota, while others remained unresponsive.

Imported Technology

The automobile manufacturers waged an intense competition for investment in plant and equipment. Although this was primarily in order to meet the rapidly increasing demand for automobiles, it led to higher productivity and remarkable technological improvements. As of the end of 1955, the total plant and equipment at Toyota, Nissan, Toyo Kogyo, Daihatsu, Isuzu and Hino amounted only to 27 billion yen, which was operated by 26,000 employees to produce 135,000 automobiles. As of the end of 1970, these figures increased, respectively, to 1,246 billion yen (46 times), 143,000 employees (5.5 times), and 4.31 million automobiles (32 times). Per capita productivity was thus raised by more than 5 times. According to Labour Ministry's Labour Productivity Survey, direct man-

Changes in the Automobile Industry

They have analysed how Japan's automobile industry rapidly grew till the 80s. However, in the recent years a new trend as unfolded itself in Japan's automobile industry. Japan now has begun to set up automobile manufacturing units in other countries, with its technology. Thus Japan's automobile industry is undergoing rapid changes. In the last decade of the present century.

Japan's automobile industry has continued to lead the world in total output since 1980. Its domestic production in 1995 was 10.2 million vehicles, though this was down 3.4 per cent from 1994. Exports in 1995, totalling 3.79 million vehicles, were down 15 per cent from the previous year. This was the tenth consecutive year of decline and the largest real drop on record, resulting from a 25.3 per cent decrease, to 1.23 million, in vehicles exported to the US. Exports to Asia were 616,000 up 3.6 per cent, while those to the European Union were 792,000 million down 13.0 per cent.

Since 1981 Japan had voluntarily restricted passenger car exports to the US, but it abolished the voluntary restriction in 1994 in view of such factors as fullscale local production by Japanese makers in the US. Honda Motor Co., opened a factory in Ohio in 1982, the first of several that Japanese automakers have since established in the US, Europe and elsewhere. The total annual production of Japanese cars and trucks in the US reached 2.11 million in 1995. Meanwhile, Japanese car exports to the EU have been subject to monitoring since 1992.

Change in Industrial Structure of Japan

Having weathered the period of reconstruction and rehabilitation during the latter half of the 1940s following the devastation of World War II, Japanese industry entered a new stage of rapid growth. The latter half of the 1950s saw the development of an energy revolution in the form of a switch from coal to oil as the primary fuel of industry and the emergence of a steadily growing petrochemical industry. Another major change was the diffusion of electric household appliances throughout Japan. As a result, the emphasis in Japanese industry shifted from light to heavy industries and toward a higher degree of processing.

Before World War II textiles and sundry goods were the mainstays of Japanese exports. These were replaced in the 1960s by transistor radios, ships, and steel. Meanwhile, exports of black-and-white and then colour television sets, tape recorders, and other electric products continued to increase. Products of heavy industries accounted for 70 per cent of total exports in the latter half of the 1960s.

The 1970s were a period of significant readjustment in industry. Environmental pollution caused by various industries became a noticeable problem, the limited supply of natural resources began to be regarded as a major constraint on growth and industries were forced to adapt to the changes brought by the oil crises of 1973-74 and 1979-80, as well as to the technological innovations brought about by the development of microelectronics and the onset of the information revolution. Industry also came to face the long-term socio-economic trends of aging of the population and growth of the service sector.

In the 1980s highly competitive Japanese industrial exports were one cause of the nation's trade surplus. The sources of Japan's competitiveness—its management system and industrial policies—have attracted world wide attention.

To avoid trade friction, corporations began focusing on the domestic market and setting up overseas production facilities. In 1980 the Advisory Group on Economic Structural Adjustment for International Harmony, an ad hoc panel appointed by Prime Minister Yasuhiro Nakasone, issued the so-called Maekawa Report. With an eye to transforming the nation's economic structure, the report called for the expansion of imports and domestic demand. Furthermore, the Japan-US (Structural Impledgiven Initiative) SII talks were begun in September 1989 to reduce the causes of the trade friction between the two nations.

Even after the SII ended in June 1990 however, Japan's trade surplus with the United States continued to swell. To deal with this, a new framework for trade talks, the Japan-US framework for a New Economic Partnership, was launched in September 1993. Negotiations were conducted separately in a number of different areas. Among them, agreement was reached in such areas as government procurement and partly in insurance in October 1994. A settlement was reached in the area of automobiles and auto parts, which had proved especially tricky, in June 1995.

In the wake of the sustained rise in the value of the yen following the 1985 Plaza Accord among finance ministers of the Group of Five industrialized nations, Japanese companies expanded direct investment overseas and proceeded more boldly with their shift of production bases abroad. In particular, the proportion of Asia-bound investment has risen in the 1990s. An international horizontal division of labour has developed, with production of parts, intermediate goods, and finished products taking place in the most suitable location.

Along with this shift in the structure of industry, the pattern of Japan's trade has also changed greatly. The proportion of machinery, mainly production equipment and components, in Japan's total exports had risen to 76 per cent in 1995. With regard to imports, the proportion of raw materials and fuel has dropped, while that of various types of machinery, including electrical machinery and transportation equipment had risen to 26 per cent in 1995. The proportion of manufactures among all imports reached a record high of 59.1 per cent that year.

Against this background, a discussion has arisen concerning the hollowing out of Japanese industry. As companies set up offshore bases, domestic production is replaced by overseas production. And as manufactured imports increase, domestic manufacturing industries languish. Some see this process as leading to a loss of jobs.

Concern about hollowing out have been voiced more strongly as the employment situation has worsened with the current economic slowdown and industrial restructuring. The unemployment rate reached 3.4 per cent in November 1995. For this reason, there are calls for more employment opportunities to be created by spurring private-sector activity through further deregulation, upgrading manufacturing through technological revolution, and promoting productivity gains in the service sector.

Industrial Structure

This shows that the structure of Japan's industry has changed dramatically over the last few decades. While the share of primary industries declined after World War II, that of secondary industries increased in the 1960s, peaked in 1970, and then gradually declined. The share of tertiary industries has increased, particularly in the 1970s.

Gross Domestic Product by Industry (per cent)

	1970	*1980*	*1985*	*1990*	*1994*
Primary industries	5.9	3.6	3.1	2.4	2.0
Secondary industries	43.1	37.8	36.3	36.9	34.0
Manufacturing	34.9	28.2	28.4	27.4	23.5
Mining and construction	8.3	9.5	7.9	9.6	10.5
Tertitary industries	51.0	58.6	60.7	60.7	63.9
Wholesale and retail	13.9	14.8	12.8	12.1	12.2

Source: Economic Planning Agency, Kokumin keizai kesian nenpo (Annual Report on National Accounts), 1996.

Manufacturing

The leading role in Japan's manufacturing sector has passed from heavy industries, which spearheaded high economic growth in the 1960s, to processing and assembling industries. While production in precessing industries jumped by 69 per cent between 1980 and 1994, production in materials industries rose by 47 per cent. In the assembling industries, growth has been particularly pronounced in such hightech fields as electronics and precision equipment, which have become highly competitive in the world market.

Supply and Demand

The energy supply-and-demand structure in Japan has changed considerably since the oil crises. On the demand side, industry has implemented measures to promote energy conservation, as a result of which growth of energy consumption has fallen below the economic growth rate. With the proliferation of house hold electrical appliances and automobiles, however, consumer demand has continued to increase; the consumer share of total energy demand rose from 18.2 per cent in fiscal 1973 to 25.8 per cent in fiscal 1994.

On the supply side, the introduction of alternative sources of energy has meant that the share of oil has decreased year by year, falling from a peack of 77.4 per cent in fiscal 1973 to 57.4 per cent in 1993. Among alternative sources of energy, nuclear power and natural gas have shown particularly rapid growth. Their respective shares of total supply jumped from 0.6 per cent and 1.5 per cent in fiscal 1973 to 11.3 per cent and 10.8 per cent in fiscal 1994.

2

Past, Present and the Future

The question that is often asked is how Japan has been able to perform this miracle and capture world's markets in such a short time. The motivating force behind the resurgence of Japan as a major economic power is psychological—a sense of uncertainty in the Japanese caused by harshness of nature towards this tiny country, manifested in volcanoes, earthquakes and typhoons. Added to this is the problem that nature has not endowed Japan with any mineral resources. It is this complex of insecurity that has always played a dominant role in the lives of the Japanese, often making them strive hard to surpass others even in a mere attempt to survive.

It is this complex that motivated Japanese to absorb with amazing efficiency anything and everything that is alien to them–whether it is technology or music–without losing their own identity. That was why they remained a homogeneous society with only one goal before the entire nation, that is building up the country. It is possibly this complex of insecurity that was responsible in the evolution of a right type of economic strategy which combined efforts of the government, employer and labour that has finally helped the nation to reach the pinnacle of economic glory. Sometimes it is said that cheap labour helped Japan to reach its record heights. But this is not true as the Japanese wages have been very much in line with productivity. There are a number of countries in the world where labour is cheaper than in Japan, yet these countries have not been able to perform any economic miracle. The Japanese wages went up with the growth jump of 16 per cent per year. Another explanation that is offered is that Japan had no military budget. It did create a soft defence force which absorbed about 1 per cent of the Gross National Product. This had slipped down to 0.7 per cent in the mid 70s. Compare it with the American expenditure on military which was 10 per cent of the

Gross National Product. Even in European countries the defence expenditure tends to stand at 4 to 5 per cent of GNP.

It is partly true that saving on military expenditure has been of great help to Japan. But apart from the military expenditure, what is perhaps equally important is the sense of feeling among the Japanese that they do not have to either bother or spend their money for the defence of their country. One significant factor that was largely responsible in creating the necessary climate for Japan to develop in peace is the U.S. presence in South-East Asia. The Americans took over the responsibility of defending the frontiers of this country as also of others like Philippines, South Korea, etc. This umbrella facilitated Japanese to maintain a low posture in power politics. Japanese stayed out of any controversy and concentrated on developing economic relation with a variety of countries of differing political and social systems. Given this protection by the Americans, Japanese exploited with tremendous efficiency the cheap natural resources available immediately after the World War II. That was the time when the prices of raw materials were declining and it was a buyers' market rather than a sellers' market and the Japanese tried to exploit iron deposits all over the world.

They went about getting them at the best prices in the whole world at a time when shipping charges were going down fairly rapidly and transportation from far off parts of the world became a very small part of the total cost. It was a very favourable world which the Japanese found themselves in. Then the Americans provided the Japanese with the necessary technology at bargain prices. This offer was open to others too but only the Japanese had the skill to take fullest advantage of it in shortest possible time. The Japanese got latest technology from the United States (automobiles, electronics etc.), from Great Britain (shipbuilding) and other developed western countries on best possible terms.

In all this, the Government played a very significant role in locating and channelising technology and then providing the necessary inputs for development. And then the Americans opened their vast markets for virtually all the Japanese goods such as automobiles, engineering and electronic items etc. This may be considered the first phase of the incentive given by the U.S. to the Japanese industry to ensure that no restriction was placed on the import of Japanese goods into the country. This went on for quite some time until the ascendancy of Mr. Lindon Johnson as the President of the U.S.A. Mr. Johnson, who hailed from the southern State of Texas—a stronghold of the textile industry—had to give in to the textile lobby pressure to put restrictions on Japanese textile exports to U.S. Consequently, Japanese industrialists were asked not to dump their textile goods in the United States and warned that if they did not behave a quota system would be introduced. However, when the directive did not work, the U.S. imposed a 10 per cent surtax to protect its own textile industry.

A second example of Japan becoming a competitor to its own benefactor was in regard to steel. The landed cost of the Japanese steel in the United States was about $ 1½ less per tone than the steel produced by the biggest U.S. steel corporations. About 80 per cent of the total steel imported from Japan was consumed by the U.S. automobile industry. This helped the U.S. automobile makers to keep down their costs. However, the U.S. steel industry rose against heavy steel imports from Japan and finally Mr. Johnson had to levy a 10 per cent surtax on the landed cost of steel to bring down the narrow the margin of U.S. steel prices and the Japanese steel prices. Nevertheless, the Japanese faced this restriction by forming a consortium of their steel industry and further reduced their steel price.

The Japanese developed a compromise between all the existing economic systems. There was the independent economic order in West Europe and America that was against government's intervention. In the communist system the government itself ran the industry and in the Japanese model a partnership was created between the private capital and the government. The third model, according to many economists, was more successful than the other two models. The Japanese believe in the national economy being developed with the private initiative and drive. The central banking system in Japan saw to it that funds went into types of industries with faster growth chances and larger employment potential.

The Ministry of Internal Trade and Industry (MITI) played a vital role in the development of industry. MITI works in close coordination with the industrial undertakings and feeds them with latest economic, trade and political information. The Japanese employer or the industrialist is different from his counterpart in most developed countries. The Japanese capitalist class has shown a tremendous sense of responsibility towards national welfare and kept national priorities ahead of their personal gains. Their commitment to collective ethos is unparalleled.

They always struck a balance between their profit and communal good. Over a period of time a tradition has been established in Japanese industries that except in extreme cases labour would not be thrown out of employment. Normally, when an industrial undertaking is in the red the first casualty would be profit margin and economy at all levels. Only when all other options to save the unit from collapse, fail workers are called upon to sacrifice part of their wages. When the occasion demanded the workers responded readily as it happened in 1974, when the oil crisis hit the Japanese economy. The workers voluntarily sacrificed their so-called spring bonus.

The Japanese labour force is unique in more than one respect. Nearly 68 per cent of the total labour force in Japan is employed by five large industrial houses. And there is hardly any migration of labour from one company to another. For generations workers and their families work in the same unit. This gives them a sense of attachment and pride in their employer. This also is responsible for high rate of productivity. There are of course strikes for high wages, but these are not accompanied by loss of man-hours as in the case of other countries. Often the protest is reflected by a simple black ribbon and not violence. In return, the labour is paid sumptuously and the management takes care of the welfare of the worker and his family.

The management looks after marriage, education, health, housing, holidaying and death of their workers and their families. The worker is normally paid for 14 to 18 months annually. The extra wage that he earns encourages savings and the Japanese are well known for their capacity to save and at the same time enjoy virtually all the modern luxuries of life. Today Japan has the highest savings rate of 22 per cent. The Japanese industrial worker gets about 6 months wages as bonus. This affluence caused by high rate of productivity produced a very prosperous country. In Japan, everybody has a telephone, a refrigerator and a camera. And their prosperity is symbolised by the three Cs- room coolers, cameras and cars.

In trying to industrialise as fast as possible and also to grab the world markets, the Japanese have undoubtedly compromised on the quality of their goods. They appear to think that no item need to last say more than five years because of the speed of innovation. Once they put a limit on quality, the Japanese have been able to produce mass consumption items at an amazingly low cost and compete with almost all other industrialised western nations like the United States, Great Britain and Germany which believe in greater durability of their commodities.

In order to sustain the economic boom, the Japanese altered their development strategy in tune with changing world economic scenario. As the cost of raw material began escalating in the last few years of the seventies, the Japanese began to invest abroad on a larger scale. According to the Japanese government, as on May 1976, the total overseas investment was of the order of U.S. $ 16 billions. In Asia itself—in countries like South Korea, Thailand, Indonesia, Singapore—the investment was estimated to be $ 3.21 billion. Under a plan, Japan set up industries at the very source of raw materials, the Japanese installed paper and pulp plants in Brazil and Indonesia, aluminium plants in Indonesia and Australia, steel plants in Brazil, India and Australia and paper chemical complexes in West Asia. Simultaneously, the Japanese industry began giving up export of steel and such other items in preference to export of machinery and equipment so as to protect itself from the vagaries of the cost-push economy generated by the oil crisis and reflected in the increase in the prices of virtually all varieties of raw materials. The oil crisis had posed the first ever threat to the Japanese prosperity and growth rate during the period under review.

Among the industries most affected was automobile. The increase in the cost of gasoline had already brought about considerable change not only in production but also in the market of automobiles all over the world and the possibility of Japan, which was at the commanding heights of the automobile markets in the world, losing its pride of place was not unlikely. In 1975, auto exports earned for Japan U.S. $ 6700 million or 12.5 per cent of the nation's total export earnings. The Japanese cars went virtually to all the countries of the world. But the oil crisis affected the balance of payments position of those countries too and most of them began adopting protectionist measures to help their own automobile industry to survive. The sharp rise in oil prices and continuing uncertainty in the supply of oil caused recession in the automobile markets. In Britain, protectionist moves began mounting and are still continuing to restrict import of foreign made cars, because it saw car imports sharply rising and the domestic industry in trouble. Australia, which had provided a good market for Japanese cars, also began to restrict the quantity of car imports from February, 1975 and the U.S. began a dumping probe in imported passenger cars on the ever largest scale in the summer of 1975.

These moves coupled with the efforts on the part of several developing countries of the third world to manufacture their own automobiles was expected to put a brake on the speed at which Japan was able to expand its automobile industry. In the United States itself where Japan had the largest market, the American consumers, preference shifted towards the compact cars made in their own country because they consumed less fuel. Simultaneously, with the oil price hike a new problem confronting the auto makers was car safety and emission control, following greater awareness on the dangers of pollution. This development too caused dent in Japan's auto exports. First of all, the price competitiveness of the Japanese car in the international market has been declining in the recent years as a result of market increase in the production costs due to sharp rise in wages and raw material prices and also the changes in exchange rates. Wage increases in Japan were larger than in any other auto producing country. In 1974 Japan wage increase was as much as 32.9 per cent. From 1965 to 1974 Japan wage level rose 4.1 times compared to 1.7 times in the U.S., 2.3 times in Britain, 2.2 times in West Germany, and 2.6 times in France. As a result Japan's absolute wage level reached almost the same as that of other major auto producing countries. The cumulative effect of all this resulted in price increase in Japanese cars in the U.S. market compared to the indigenous models. In 1971 the price of U.S. sub-compact cars almost equalled that of Japanese compact cars. But lately, the price of the U.S. sub-compact cars compared favourably to that of Japanese popular cars.

Faced with the prospect of decline in auto exports, the automobile industry in Japan made strenuous efforts to maintain and strengthen its competitiveness to retain its hold over the world auto markets. In Asia itself the Japanese faced stiff competition from the ASEAN car project in which U.S. auto makers were involved and the Australian automobile policy aimed at the development of a 4 cylinder engine car. As a result of awareness of problems of pollution, different countries adopted different safety and emission control standards. This meant that Japan had to produce different types of cars for export to different countries and bear additional rise in production costs. Unless safety and emission controls are standardised universally, diversity in the standards in different regions will become a difficult proposition not only for the Japanese car makers but for others also.

Thus the future of the Japanese automobile industry is beset with several question marks, despite the fact that it has the extra advantage of a good image all over the world and a reasonable control on the world auto markets. The future of the Japanese economy will depend largely on the continuation of the "political patronage" being provided by the United States of America. Japan, which has so far been able to steer clear of any international political controversy and concentrate on economic development, might not be able to do so, once the "U.S. umbrella" is withdrawn. The geopolitical situation in which Japan is placed raise doubt over its ability to keep itself from any international power struggle once the U.S. presence in South East Asia is withdrawn.

Apart from this, developments in developing countries could also cause considerable headache for Japan. The growing attempts to achieve self-sufficiency in as many sectors as possible in the third world has already put a strain on the flow of raw materials from the Third World to the developed western countries. Although Japan has exhibited an amazing but understandable flexibility in settling for any type of terms and conditions, it would have to contend with the growing costs of raw materials as also reduced supply. This might affect production as also the export of such consumer items as automobiles by Japan. It is a challenging perspective but the Japanese have always shown an ingenuity that equalled the task.

CONCLUSION

Japan suffered a crushing defeat in World War II. The country lost 44 per cent of the territory that it had claimed prior to 1945, and most domestic industrial facilities were destroyed in air raids. When the war ended, 6 million demobilized soldiers and civilians were repartriated to Japan, which was suffering from an acute food shortage. The economy was bailed out of the gravest crisis it had even known with the help of material and moral support from the US.

The period from 1945 to 1954 was one of hard struggle to achieve reconstruction, stability, and self-reliance, but by 1955 the economy had regained its pre-war level. It then continued to expand with a flood of investment in new technology and equipment. Against the backdrop of a spectacular surge of demand for consumer goods, such as television sets, washing machines, and refrigerators, the economy sustained an average annual growth rate of 9.8 per cent during the period from 1955 to 1964.

In the second half of the 1960s the economy achieved an average annual growth rate of 11.8 per cent. In the first half of the 1970s, however, the economy was buffeted by an international currency crisis triggered by the US economic policy announced in August 1971. A further blow came in the form of the first oil crisis in 1973.

Oil Crises

In 1974, the year immediately following the first oil crisis, the Japanese economy suffered its first negative growth in real GDP in the post-war period, while wholesale and consumer prices surged 27.7 per cent and 23.2 per cent, respectively. The rise in crude oil prices inflated the cost of Japan's imports, plunging the current account balance into a 4.7 billion dollars deficit. Japan was clearly in the grip of an economic crisis, and pessimism prevailed throughout the business world. But the economy bounced back from the 1973 oil cruch fairly quickly.

The Japanese economy's dramatic recovery from the first oil crisis can be attributed to two causes. First, companies succeeded in their efforts to streamline operation so as to lower their break-even points. Streamlining resulted in reducing personnel costs through employment cutbacks, lightening financial burdens through loan repayment, and trimming inventories through optimum inventory control. Though employment in the manufacturing industries fell, increased employment in the tertiary industries offset this loss. Thanks to the tertiary industries role in stabilizing employment, the unemployment rate remained below 3 per cent. Second, increased government spending in fiscal 1977 and 1978 and the low-interest-rate policy that was continued until around the spring of 1979 were effective, so the recovery stimulated by public works investment became self-sustaining.

Following the second oil crisis in 1979, the Japanese economy performed considerably better than other industrial economies, recording real growth of 5.5 per cent in 1979. This performance was possible because increased import prices were not followed by domestically generated inflation. The authorities kept inflationary expectations from arising by keeping the money supply under control, thereby preventing a wage-price sprial from occurring. Economic growth did slow subsequently, to 2.8 per cent in 1980, 3.2 per cent in 1981, 3.1 per cent in 1982, and 2.3 per cent in 1983 but then recovered to 3.9 per cent in 1984 and 4.4 per cent in 1985.

Recent Trends

After the Plaza Accord by the Group of Five industrial nations in September 1985, the value of the yen began to rise rapidly, from 242 yen to the US dollar before the accord to 154 yen to the dollar a year later. Those sectors of the manufacturing industry heavily dependent on exports were especially hard hit by the high yen, and the resulting deflation affected the domestic economy in general. Consequently, the real growth rate in 1986 fell to 2.9 per cent.

In December 1986 the economic picture improved owing to two main factors: heightened personal consumption, spurred by stabilized prices, and increased investment in plant and equipment, made possible by money saved as a result of industrial rationalisation in the wake of the high yen. Real economic growth in 1987, 1988, and 1989 was 4.2 per cent, 6.2 per cent and 4.8 per cent, respectively.

The economy grew by 5.1 per cent in real terms in 1990. After the outbreak of the crisis in the Persian Gulf in August 1990, however, stock prices began falling, and by the following spring economic growth had reached a peak. As a result, real growth in 1991 slowed down to 4.0 per cent.

Growth of Real GDP of Industrial Nations (per cent)

	1990	*1991*	*1992*	*1993*	*1994*
Canada	-0.2	-1.7	0.7	2.2	4.6
France	2.5	0.8	1.2	-1.5	2.9
Germany	5.7	4.5	2.1	-1.2	2.9
Italy	2.1	1.2	0.7	-1.2	2.2
Japan	5.1	4.0	1.1	0.1	0.5
United Kingdom	0.4	-2.2	-0.6	2.3	3.8
United States	1.2	-0.7	2.6	3.1	4.1

Source: For Japan, Economic Planning Agency; for others, Organisation for Economic Cooperation and Development, Dec. 1995.

Corporate capital investment and personal consumption remained sluggish in 1992 and 1993. Real growth for these years slumpted to 1.1 per cent and 0.1 per cent, respectively.

Personal consumption showed signs of picking up at the end of 1993, and the economy seemed to have entered a recover phase. But real growth in GDP remained at 0.5 per cent in 1994 as capital investment was held back by the high yen. In 1995 the pace of recovery remained slow due to such factors as the Great Hanshin Earthquake, another rapid appreciation of the yen, and concerns over the health of the financial sector. The GDP grew 0.9 per cent in that year. In early 1996 the economy did show signs of a recovery at last, although there were doubts whether these would lead to a full-scale recovery.

Statistics are indicators of process taking place in social development in a country. If one goes by a statistical analysis, Japan indeed as emerge as a major economic power in the world in the end of the 20th century, a country which in the beginning of the next century may become a decisive factor in international economic relations. In this sense in the current epoch which is marked by increasingly close interdependence among the states and regions, socio-economic changes that are taking place in Japan have become a key factor in shaping the course of history on our planet. This fact clearly stands out in the analyses given in the first three chapters of the book.

Japan's population in 1990 was 12.36 crores, the seventh largest in the world. Its total land area is 377,818 square kilometres which is about 4 per cent that of the US and slightly more than one and a half times as large as that of Britain. Japan occupies about 0.3 per cent of the earth's land area. This stands as a complete contrast to the place in the international economy, which this small country has already carved out for itself. In 1992 its production of synthetic fibers was 2,589 million m^2 and it ranked third in the world after Belgium and South Korea. In production of synthetic rubber Japan occupied the second position after the US with its production of 1,390 (1000 tons). In production of crude steel in 1993 it ranks second in the world with a total production of 100 million tons. The erstwhile Soviet Union toped the list (140 million tons). China's production of crude steel came after Japan and the US ranked fourth (87 million tons). In production of Television sets in 1992 Japan ranked third with 14.3 million units. China occupied the first position with 28.7 million units, and next with came South Korea. In the production of passenger car in 1992 Japan top the list with 9.4 million units, and next to it came the US with 5.7 million units. These statistics clearly establish that Japan has already become the second biggest industrsilised nation in the world, though there are other countries such as China which are racing to outstrip it.

There is something more to it which confirm this conclusion. Japan in 1995 top the list in Official Development Assistance by it to other countries. It amounted to 14,489 million US dollars. Next to it came France and Germany the development assistance given the US in 1995 was almost 50 per cent of the total assistance given by Japan.

It is significant to mention that in 1995, China toped the list of the countries which received the bilateral official development assistance from Japan. The following table gives the idea about the official development assistance given by Japan to other countries. Again as far as direct investments are concerned the facts are quiet revealing.

Official Development Assistance from Japan 1995

	Amount disbursed (US $ million)	*Share of total (%)*
China	1,380	13.1
Indonesia	892	8.5
Thailand	667	6.3
India	506	4.8
Philippines	416	3.9
Mexico	288	2.7
Sri Lanka	264	2.5
Bangladesh	255	2.4
Egypt	243	2.3
Pakistan	241	2.3

Source : Ministry of Foreign Affairs, Waga Kuni no seifu Kaihatsu enjo (Japan's ODA) 1996.

Direct Investment

Japan's direct investment overseas began to increase in the mid-1960s, stagnated for a while after the oil crises, and rose again at the start of the 1980s to reach an all-time high 67 billion dollars in 1989. Until 1980 Japan's direct investment was concentrated in resources development and labour intensive industries, but since the 1980s it has been directed more toward technology-intensive industries, such as electronics and transport equipment. Much of Japan's current direct investment is centered on manufacturing industries in Europe and the US as well as the shift of the production base to other Asian countries.

Direct Investment Outstanding
(US $ billion)

Investing country	*1975*	*1980*	*1985*	*1990*	*1993*	*1994*
USA	124.4	215.6	229.7	421.5	548.6	612.1
Japan	8.3	19.6	44.0	201.4	259.8	275.6
U.K.	30.8	81.4	116.9	233.6	258.7	286.4
Germany	16.0	37.9	53.3	114.5	184.7	194.1
Netherlands	8.5	39.7	49.3	91.9	126.9	142.3

Source: Japan External Trade Organisation Sekai to Nihon no kaigai chokusetsu toashi (Direct Overseas Investment by All Countries and by Japan) 1996.

If these statistics are any indications, it will not be incorrect to say that Japan indeed has emerge a super economic power.

As a result of this Japan has began to play an important role in the international politics. It is no more a junior partner of the US. As we have examined in the subsequent chapters of this study, its relations with major actors of the world politics, the US in particlular is undergoing a change. Japan indeed has become one of the main centres of economic power in the world.

3

Japanese Model of Economic Development

In the last decade of the 20th century, different models of economic development have attracted the attention of the economists and social scientists, particularly after the collapse of the Soviet model of economic growth. In the previous three chapters, we have analysed the specific features of the Japanese model of economic development and sought to bring into focus its peculiarities. Japanese scholars have always been emphasising that the European model of economic development was evolved in an entirely different historical conditions. This model cannot be transplanted mechanically on the Asian societies. In fact even in some European countries, economists and social scientists have begun to advocate that each country has to evolve its own model of economic development in the context of the globalisation of economy and technological revolution. The recent recession in some of the ASEAN countries, in Indonesia in particular have unleashed a new controversy in the academic circles about the models of economic development in this part of our planet. This aspect has assumed a new dimension because, all said and done, the economic power centre of the world has shifted to the Asia and Pacific region, if all the economic indicators are taken into account. It is, therefore, pertinent to examine the Japanese model of economic development as perceived by some of the top Japanese scholars.

A large number of models have recently emerged to explain Japan's postwar economic success. Although diverse in level of analysis, these models represent, on a theoretical level, different possible approaches. The purpose of this chapter is to organize these models systematically and to summarize and evaluate each model in terms of its contribution to our understanding of the workings of contemporary Japan's political economy.

Broadly speaking, these models may be divided into two groups: the first group emphasises on economic factors and the second on cultural factors. Economic models stress on a set of factors in the objective environment, such as the labour supply, diffusion of technology, or expansion of the world market. Cultural models, on the other hand, focus on factors in the subjective environment including various aspects of traditional Japanese culture such as group orientation or the inclination towards consensus. It seems clear that neither a purely economic model nor a purely cultural model is adequate for analysis of the postwar political economy of Japan or, for that matter, any industrialisation-oriented society, particularly a late developer. Postwar Japan's economic growth indisputably owes much to the favourable objective environment. At the same time, the imprint of Japanese culture on many characteristics of the politico-economic structure is clearly visible. Although much of the cultural determinism in the so-called Nihonjinoron (Japanese national character) literature is too one-sided or inaccurate, cultural influences are important in accounting for the differences between Japan's political economy and those of other industrial societies.

A suggested depiction of the relationship between political economy and the objective and subjective environments should not be ignored. The objective environment consists of the physical environment (nature-to-society relationships) and the international environment (society-to-society relationships). The physical environment includes not only such factors as climate, land, mineral resources and other geographical conditions on and around the Japanese islands, but also such factors as the population or labour force at the beginning of the postwar reconstruction. An initial stock of available technologies is also an essential component of the physical environment. For the Japanese economy after the war, the technological environment meant the array of new technologies accumulated in other nations since the 1930s, particularly during the war. In the present analysis, the international environment is the Pax Americana, including the world wide US defence capability and the IMF/GATT economic system based on the principles of a fixed exchange rate and free trade. The stability of the Pax Americana until the oil crisis was a given condition favourable to Japan.

The subjective environment consists of the cultural environment and national goals. National goals are the broadest possible framework of national policies. Generally speaking, policies are endogenous variables determined within a society's political economy. Most specific postwar policies are explicable in terms of the internal dynamics of Japanese society. The basic policy orientation of postwar Japan was established in the first few years after the war, setting the focus of Japanese society in the following decades. This basic framework included the national consensus of catching up with advanced countries in economic policies. These policy stances constituted the national goals that conditioned the postwar Japanese political economy. There is no need to emphasize here the importance of the cultural environment.

Within the framework of the system economic models focus on one set of factors in the objective environment such as certain physical and technological factors and cultural models focus on a set in the subjective environment.

Much effort has gone into the elaboration of economic models, and cultural models have attracted much popular attention. Unfortunately, these efforts have proceeded separately from each other. What is required is that Japanese model should be examined in totality and seen as a synthesis between objective and subjective factors. This is how modern Japanese scholars have begun to look at the industrial development of their country and its emergence as a super economic power which has not only almost captured the American market but now challenges it in the world market.

The cultural environment is the latent basic pattern in society. The single most important characteristic of the Japanese cultural tradition is a particular type of organizational principle, which may be called the genotype (i.e. originally meant household) or in some cases, the MURA (village variant). This cultural tradition continues to assert in the modern Japanese industrial organizations, which western scholars have not grasped both in its content and form.

These organizational models share the principle that a group decision reached by long-term, multi-issue,often implicit agreements should override a particular person's choice on a specific short-term issue. This model originated in Samurai organization in eastern Japan with its own variations during the eleventh century reflecting the severe conditions besetting this agro-military groups in a frontier region. The MURA assumed its final form in the TOKUGAWA period (1603-1867) as semi-autonomous social units constituting the society's substratum. Obviously, the MURA is a looser and more egalitarian organization than the other model.

Western scholars tend to argue that the interaction between culture and the political economy is consummated at the national level by means of the Japanese government's conscious and consistent policy. Thus they ignore the grass roots reality. According to this perception, the Japanese political economy mimics a single cohesive organization such as a family or a corporation. This is far from reality.

In any society according to some Japanese scholars an average person or household's economic or political behaviour reflects an internalized cultural tradition. The average Japanese, for example, is often said to be hard working, prone to saving, eager to acquire education and skilful in imitation: presumably these traits arise from the cultural tradition. If culture influences economic performance mainly at this level, it should be possible to explain the Japanese economy as a whole by a standard market economy model in which cultural uniqueness is represented by unusually high values for certain structural parameters such as a high savings ratio, the high quality, high educational level of labour, or a high speed of technological diffusion. As another example, the average Japanese is, according to many Western observers, docile, conformist, and obedient to authority. Based on this trait psychology presumption, a standard voting behaviour model would predict. The continued dominance of the LDP till recently confirms this conclusion. However, during 1990s this pattern has changed.

There is yet another factor which should be taken into account. The war isolated Japanese industry from much technological progress and in the end devastated it. For this reason, any analysis of the postwar Japanese politico-economic system should not preclude the possibility that an economy and a polity are linked more closely than standard economic theory assumed.

In order to make critical evaluation of the models explaining the relation between culture and political economy analytically manageable, however, it is most convenient to consider the economy and the polity separately for the time being and to examine the interface of each with culture. This however is not to indicate that the economy and the polity of postwar Japan are not closely linked.

The popular notion asserts that the Japanese cultural tradition is most clearly manifested in the way Japanese society is controlled as a whole. According to this notion Japanese society is monolithic and tightly regulated and thus resembles a single corporation run by a group of clever leaders, who mobilized the postwar Japanese populace for the sake of economic growth. Any closer examination, however, shows this to be a crude and simplistic stereotype. All indications show that both the market mechanism and parliamentary democracy have been at work in postwar Japan, bringing about fierce competition and visible conflicts in many parts of society. The postwar Japanese economic experience has been replete with examples of competitive phenomena, such as the investment race, export competition and competition among banks for depositors. Although continued rule by the conservative party has been a principle feature of the postwar political system, the conservative ascendancy faced serious challenge at least twice: prompted riots in Tokyo and around 1970 when the conservative party lost many major local elections. The same trend was reflected in the ninties. The seeming overall conformity of behaviour in postwar Japan was a fortuitous outcome—under a set of favourable conditions unique to the post-war era —of interaction among various potentially conflicting interests.

However, there is no doubt that the specific features of Japan were beneficial to the rapid growth of the Japanese economy. Had the labour force been less abundant, that is, had there been less disguised employment in agriculture or less educated, economic growth would certainly have been slower. Had households savings been smaller, the growth rate would have been slower. Higher world prices for petroleum or other mineral resources might have slowed the industrial growth. According to some Japanese experts however, the imputed contribution of these factors inputs accounts for less than half of Japan's economic growth. Thus, a difference in the abundance of inputs between Japan and other countries accounts for an even smaller portion of Japan's economic growth. It may be recalled that many other industrial countries could and did import capital as well as immigrant labour. Above all they had markets in their colonies.

The question of relative scarcity of labour too does not explain the situation. To state it differently, a more important question is whether the vast changes in Japanese industrial structure during the rapid growth period can be explained in terms of a relative factor - scarcity. Indeed, there was an ample supply or even an oversupply of labour in the 1950 and early 1960s. At that time, however, Japanese industrial structure was shifting rapidly from the labour-intensive industries, such as textiles, that dominated the prewar era to capital-intensive, labour-savings processing industries, such as steel, synthetic fibers, petrochemicals and oil refining. Three other new industries, automobiles, electric appliances and shipbuilding, were also more capital intensive than the prewar-type textile industry. This structural shift remains, even if we take into account the direct as also the indirect inputs to the industries in question. If such factors as the quality of labour or capital vintage are considered, the picture might be somewhat modified, but no empirical evidence has been given that revise this picture of relative factor scarcity.

Thus, in order to support the relative scarcity argument, we have to assume that capital was relatively more abundant than labour. This assumption, however, seems to contradict the facts. In the 1950s, when the shift towards the heavy and chemical industries occured, the savings rate of Japanese households was still below 20 per cent, comparable to those in other industrial societies. Moreover since the level of income in Japan was very low in the 1950s, even a savings rate above 20 per cent would have yielded only a small amount of savings per worker, roughly one-tenth of the level in 1984. In short, there are no grounds on which to say that Japan in the 1950s and early 1960s was richer in capital vis-a-vis labour, than other industrial nations.

The argument emphasizing the benefit of cheap energy and materials is not persuasive either. This argument could explain why the postwar industrial structure became more energy or material consuming and thus more centered on intermediate products than it would have been had higher energy or material costs prevailed. But it does not explain why the Japanese economy was relatively more inclined to energy-or material-consuming industries than other economies. Low energy costs were common throughout the world, and it must be remembered.

In fact all these factors combined together have led to emergence of Japan as an industrial power.

The postwar Japanese firms faced favourable circumstances in the sense that the dynamic average cost schedule was declining. This cost-curve characteristic arose partly from the worldwide postwar surge of technological innovation, but more importantly it resulted from a set of risk-reducing environmental and institutional factors unique to postwar Japan.

These factors were related to technology, capital, labour, and demand. As latecomers, Japanese industries took advantage of the latest technologies which had already been tested in more advanced economies. With respect to capital, the postwar Japanese financial system succeeded in shifting a substantial part of firms risks to households. Labour was remarkably adaptable to rapidly changing technologies because of high inter-job mobility and on-the-job training within each firm. Finally, the continued dominance of liberal democratic party in the seat of power guaranteed consistent pro-growth policies.

In hindsight, decreasing cost was a global phenomenon in the postwar industrial world, which actively applied, refined and systematized basic technologies born largely during the period 1925-50. Being latecomers, however, Japanese firms had the advantage of being able to detect and utilise, ex-ante, this decreasing cost trend. Moreover, the Japanese government encouraged key industries to take advantage of this latecomer status. Technological innovations could at least partly be expected, especially during the 1950s and 1960s, which were characterised by technological application rather than creation. In this sense, technological progress is one of the expectation variables that could be incorporated into the dynamic cost schedule.

This decreasing cost phenomenon was most evident in industries with large-scale equipment such as steel, automobiles, oil refining, synthetic fibres, petrochemicals, and to a lesser degree, electric appliances and other machinery industries. The cost decreases, however, resulted not merely from the large scale or fixed equipment but also from the late developers advantage in utilising the consistent technological innovations characteristics of these industries in the postwar world.

It is relevant to mention here that in the industrial growth of Japan, mopping of internal resources played a key role. The Japanese financial system as a whole was one big competitive market with perfectly arbitrated submarkets. Compensatory deposit practices were not available to individual depositors, who had to accept the artificially low nominal interest rates of savings deposits and bonds. Japanese households, were, in this sense, unfairly treated vis-a-vis other lenders, mainly the banks. This implies that firms making investments transferred the risks on an enormous scale to households.

Moreover, the artificially low interest rate resulted not from legal enforcement but rather from voluntary interest rate regulation (JISHU KINRI KISEI) under the guidance of the Ministry of Finance (MOF) and the Bank of Japan (BOJ). The Japanese financial system was a typical example of indicative intervention.

But why did Japanese households tolerate such an unfair institutional arrangement? Their eagerness to save probably resulted from a combination of factors, including poor urban housing conditions and the inadequate welfare system (both improved vastly in the 1970s). Many economists argue that the savings rate may be insensitive to the interest rate—particularly if income levels are as low as they were for Japanese households in the 1950s and 1960s. The tax system in postwar Japan was designed to encourage saving. The unexpectedly high-growth of income may have caused an increase in savings because of inertia in consumption and may have also compensated in part for a feeling of discontent with the unfairness that households had to bear.

There is yet another aspect of model of industrial development of Japan. The markets of major industrial products were dominated by the so-called KEIRETSUKA (groupings of large corporations) such as Mitsui group or Mitsubishi group, which had some resemblance to the prewar ZAIBATSU conglomerates. Most large corporations were quasi conglomerates in the sense that each tightly controlled a number of small-scale subcontractors (SHITAUKE or KYORYOKU KIGYO).

Each of the major industrial product markets consisted of a limited number of large corporations of comparable size. Any new entry was subject to Ministry of International Trade and Industry (MITI)'s control, and each firm's investment was at least loosely under MITI's guidance. Even within this framework of entry restriction and investment coordination, the product markets were still very competitive in terms of price, quality and so on-except during the intermittent recessions when MITI-guided recession cartels were introduced.

These facts are meant to describe how postwar industries in the manufacturing sector became the engine of rapid economic growth in

Japan. Declining industries in the manufacturing sector, such as textiles and fertilizers, had a different market structure, as did industries in the non-manufacturing sector.

It is true that the Antimonopoly Law in Japan is more lenient than US antitrust laws. Since the 1953 revision, the Antimonopoly Law statutes (for example, the Medium or Small-Scale Firm Association Law or the Export-Import Transaction Law) have exempted certain types of cartels from antimonopoly jurisdiction.

Last but not least, the Fair Trade Commission in Japan was not powerful enough to curb MITI-guided cartel-like practices. In fact, there were several hundred to more than a thousand legal (recession or rationalisation) cartels, depending on the year. Most of them however, were cartels of small-scale firms in local markets or export cartels (which contributed mostly to restraining the downpouring of exports). Legal cartels involving leading industries were few in number. This is not to say that cartel-like practices were not found in leading industries. In these industries, cartel-like practices under MITI guidance were often introduced during recessions but were discontinued once prosperity returned. From the 1950s to the early 1970s, the prices of major industrial products generally declined. Moreover, no one can deny the existence of competition for market shares. As far as the leading postwar industries are concerned, competitive behaviours during prosperity alternated with cartel-like practices during recessions. Since most of the rapid growth period was an era of prosperity, the primary theme in the leading industries market performance was vigorous competition rather than stagnant collusion.

This explains only a part of the picture during the rapid growth period. A number of Japanese scholars, with bitter memories of prewar Japan, used to warn of the re-emergence of ZAIBATSU-type conglomerates in the form of bank-centred KEIRETSUKA. There is, however, good evidence that each firm's dependence on a particular big city bank weakened from the 1950 to the 1970s. It is also easy to point out many important examples of non-KEIRETSU firms: New Japan Steel, Toyota, Nissan, Honda, Matsushita Electric, Sony and many others. But KEIRETSU in which a network of close transactions and cooperation for risk sharing play some role do exist. However, the KEIRETSU is an organisation across industries (encompassing declining ones); the MITI-guided trade association is an organization within an industry.

The postwar persistence of this balance is an intriguing theoretical problem. There seem to be several reasons for it. First, the system was an effective mechanism for transferring technology from a parent firm to subcontractors and in some cases, even for establishing joint projects for technological development. During the rapid growth period, small-scale firms were not capable of importing and improving new technologies (this situation has radically changed since the mid-1970s). Therefore, this benefit was large enough to induce small-scale manufacturers to affiliate in the Shitauke system. Second, the stability of this balance owed much to the belief of both parent firms and subcontractors in a long-run implicit relationship. In this sense, the Shitauke system is an example of the informal organisation focused interface between the economy and the culture. But although this system was rational for parent firms as well as subcontractors in the rapid growth period, it was not a primary source of economic growth. This system was essentially a way of sharing within an industry the burdens of risk and particularly of technological adventure. The growth potential of the industry as a whole would not particularly be enhanced by changing the pattern of burden sharing within the industry. One piece of direct evidence is that the shitauke system in postwar Japan was by no means limited to the fast-growing, leading industries but also extended to relatively declining industries.

Many empirical studies show that the degree of concentration in Japan was low, or at least not high, compared with that in other major industrial countries and has not exhibited any visible increase according to Japanese economists. More specifically, the leading postwar industries may be said to have consisted of a relatively large number of firms (perhaps ten) of fairly equal size. This mode of competition may be located somewhere between atomistic competition and oligopoly. In order to contrast this situation with the widely used concept of oligopoly.

Theoretically speaking, in order to achieve and catch-up economic development, the best strategy is a proper combination of competition and regulation, that is, market mechanism and government planning because the goal and the path to it are clearly defined by the experiences of more advanced economies, giving a definite guideline for government regulation or planning, some Japanese economists argue. In broader politico-economic terms, however, it is extremely difficult to maintain a proper combination of two conflicting principles, or, more specifically, to preserve the vigour and flexibility of private initiative by keeping governmental regulation to a base minimum. The Japanese catch-up attempt after World War II may be considered a rare example of success in maintaining this proper balance. In terms of regulation, the Japanese economic system during the rapid growth period was based on weak guidance and in terms of competition, it was a system of compartmentalised competition.

Two factors account for the maintenance of this duality. First, the technological paradigm of the twentieth century matured after World War II, setting an unmistakable target for a late developer such as Japan (whereas recent explosive yet uncertain developments in micro-electronics and genetic engineering will be difficult for a late developer to follow). Second, the cultural tradition of implicit, long term, multi-issued agreements provided an organizational mould to combine competition and regulation. In this sense, the rapid postwar economic growth was a result of interaction between culture and the technological and economic structure. Furthermore, crucial to this success was the Pax Americana which provided expanding markets for Japanese industries and tolerated the closed nature of Japanese domestic markets. All these environments, objective as well as subjective, constituted a fortuitous combination for the Japanese economy in the 1950s and 1960s. As of 1986, however, these environments were rapidly changing, and Japan was no longer a late developer.

This study of Japanese model of industrial development will not be complete without taking another factor into account. The coming of the New Middle Class for some time, the modernisation hypothesis seemed to hold true. From the mid-1960s, however, this hypothesis began to lose credibility because of the marked decline of support for the Japan Socialist Party (JSP), including that or urban workers (though support for the LDP did decline as predicted). A new argument, greatly influenced by the line of argument from the end of ideology to those resulting from speculations about the future emerged in the popular writings in the second half of the 1960s.

As mass affluence arrives or at least approaches, the slackening of ideology and the proliferation of diverse opinions and interests will become a central trend. The conservative party (LDP and the ideological opposition parties JSP and JCP) will decline, and the number of independents will significantly increase. New minor parties (such as DSP and CGP) representing the growing diversity in society will emerge. This argument suggests the emergence of the multi-party system rather than convergence toward a two-party system.

The background of this hypothesis was, of course, the phenomenal growth of the Japanese economy during the 1950s and 1960s. Mass affluence seemed to be approaching in the form of an explosive diffusion of consumer durables. However, this hypothesis soon faced a serious challenge. From the late 1960s to the early 1970s mass affluence was unexpectedly accompanied by a flood of pathological symptoms (from the viewpoint of industrialism) such as large scale student riots, massive protests against pollution, visible change in the lifestyle of young people and persistent worldwide stagflation. These symptoms were visible not only in Japan but in virtually all advanced industrial societies. Mass affluence had given rise to criticism of or pursuit of the conventional modern values behind the postwar material prosperity. As a political manifestation of this counter current the New Left movement emerged and was generally expected to revitalize the old left-wing parties such as the JSP and JCP. In fact, JCP support increased, compensating for the decrease in JSP support. Both parties were particularly successful in local elections, including the gubernatorial races in major cities such as Tokyo, Osaka, and Kyoto. However, this revival of the progressive parties was short-lived. Support for the JSP and JCP again started to decline from around 1973. One reason for this setback was that the new and old leftist groups were so far apart in their basic philosophical and historical perspectives: the New Left protested against industrialism as such; the old Left was opposed only to the particular form called capitalism. Another major reason was the effect of the oil crisis and ensuing depression.

Mass affluence, unprecedented in history, thus has had two often mutually counteracting implications. On the one hand, it means a slackening of ideological confrontation based on the class struggle or in political terms, a weakening of classical two-party politics between the conservative and the progressive parties.

On the other hand, it implies a decline of conventional modern values (or, in other words, the values of industrialism), which may under certain conditions trigger a new type of political radicalism voicing a new set of values. In any case, mass affluence has introduced a profoundly new element into the politics of advanced industrial societies and into their sociological and cultural patterns. Basic value orientations appear to be moving away from the conventional modern virtues, such as hard work, fugality, efficiency, sanctity of marriage and family, and so on, that are instrumental in the sense that they are supposedly the means to some intrinsic end or final gratification. Instead, the trend seems to be towards something anti-instrumental or consummatory (in the sense that delayed gratification is no longer meaningful). Similar value trends have been pointed out in other affluent, industrial societies by a number of scholars, including J.H. Goldthorpe, Ronald Inglehart, Daniel Yankelovich and many others. These value changes are gradual, but some sociological symptoms, including an enormous change in marriage patterns especially in (formerly) protestant societies, are already observable. As another example, the class-based social structure is dissolving, and this process is, most visible in Japan.

Essential to the dissolution of the class structure are certain economic conditions: virtually all people (except perhaps some ethnic minorities) in the advanced industrial societies now enjoy living standards well beyond the subsistence level, have access to a certain level of education and information that used to be the monopoly of the few, and are increasingly free from uncertainties in their life cycle thanks to welfare measures. Equally crucial are cultural factors such as lifestyles or values. In a capitalistic class structure, the middle class used to play an axial role; the virtues and lifestyles characteristic of industrial society were preserved and reproduced in the middle class. Under postwar mass affluence, however, the middle class has been losing this distinctiveness (vis-a-vis the working class) in living standards, lifestyle, education and above all, the value orientations that used to be summarized as middle class morality. The previous distinction between the middle class and the working class is blurring, and a new kind of mass is emerging. Since this new mass will occupy a vast central part of the society, it may be called the new middle mass. It should probably not be viewed as a pathological phenomenon growing out of modern society but rather as a crucial component of the still amorphous post-industrial society.

The arrival of the new middle mass will gradually affect every aspect of advanced industrial societies: yet the political aspect will be more sensitive than most other aspects. Two-party politics, for example, will undergo basic changes, although no one can predict what political system will emerge in its place. At least since the 1970s Japanese politics has been experiencing this phase of political restructuring. The new middle mass phenomenon is not so much an environmental factor as defined above as an outcome of the internal dynamic of the postwar Japanese political economy. Any attempt to explain the postwar Japanese political system must account for the effect of this dynamic. The traditional analysis of conservative versus progressive confrontation should be replaced or at least supplemented by an analysis of the new middle mass politics. The decline of support for the two major parties and the concomitant increase in independents ultimately resulted from the emergence of the new middle mass. This is how Japanese model of economic development has begun to influence its political structures.

4

Maximisation of Utilisation of Human Resources

In the previous chapter, we have examined Japanese model of economic development and explained how transformation of economic structures in an Asian society have taken place in the post war period. The key to the success of Japanese model of economic development lies in the maximum utilisation of human resources. There is a consensus among the Japanese economic experts that human resource development and labour management relations have contributed crucially to the performance of the Japanese economy. However, in the recent years the rise of new middle class in Japan has thrown up new challenges and in this sense, Japanese politics is undergoing certain important changes. This is partially reflected in the influence of the Japanese Social Party and perhaps in the stable mass base of the Japanese Communist Party too. Let us look at the problem of utilisation of human resources by the various industrial enterprises in this country. The operation of the industrial relations system and how it has contributed to Japan's economic success raise certain basic questions. Why are Japanese workers keen to promote productivity? Why are they eager to conduct quality circle of duties? And why are Japanese labour unions so cooperative with the managements?

Before one examines the validity of these assertions, it should be kept in mind that this feature of Japan's industrial relations should not be seen in isolation from the fact that Japan's industrial units are highly competitive. It appears that a portion of Japanese blue collar workers have intellectual work skills of the calibre of white collar technicians and engineers. These blue collar workers effectively employ these skills to deal with the frequent unusual operations on the shop floor. These white-collorised skills form a crucial foundation for economic growth and contribute greatly to productivity. This specific feature, which is contrary to the common perception shows that the intellectual level of the Japanese workers is generally higher than that of workers in other industrialised countries. Further these skills form the base for cooperative trade unionism as well as the new middle mass in contemporary Japanese democracy. The crux of the problem is that the workers with this high intellectual skill constitute the foundation of Japan's industrial growth. This also raises another question: Why do people work industriously when their wages are guaranteed regardless of their performance? One explanation of this is that Japanese characteristically behave in a group- oriented way. If their group protects them from risk, they are loyal to their group. Since the most important grouping for contemporary Japanese workers is their firm, once the firm guarantees the employment, it is natural for workers to be loyal and hard working. This creates a sense of involvement in production and creates high morale. It follows that Japanese workers will continue to work hard in the future also because their culture makes them industrious. However, this argument does not explain certain features of Japanese industrial relations. It fails to recognize the variety of experiences with industrial relations both historically and across firms. Not a few of its assumptions are unsupported by reliable statistical data. If cultural variables were as powerful as the culturalists presume, then the features to be explained should be shared by most, if not all, of the work force and should continue over a fairly lengthy period, just as culture is pervasive and continuous.

Although quality-control (QC) circles are said to symbolise the high morale of Japanese workers and their attitudes towards QC circles vary. The larger the firm, the more QC circles prevail. This difference becomes clear when a comparative study is made between large scale and small scale firms. In 1977 nearly two-thirds of the largest firms (more than 5,000 employees) had active QC circles, but only one-sixth of the smaller firms (under 300 employees) had active QC circles. If we had data on firms with fewer than 100 employees, the gap would definitely be greater; only a few QC circles would be working well in small companies. This coincides with information obtained in case studies; most small firms had introduced but not maintained QC circles. In sum, workers attitudes in contemporary Japan vary greatly. We have to explain not only the high percentage of active QC circles in large firms but also their comparative rarity in small firms.

The size of strikes between 1955 and 1980 in terms of working days lost through industrial disputes in selected industrialised countries are revealing. Strikes are undeniably one of the most crucial aspects of industrial relations. It is clear that the number of working days lost in Japan during the latter half of the 1950s was far greater than that in the late 1970s. Also it is clear that the figures for the second half of the 1950s and the first half of the 1960s differ little from or are even greater than those for the United Kingdom and France, but in the second half of the 1970s only West Germany had a lower figures.

This finding strongly contradicts the assumption of the popular view that Japanese industrial relations are exceptionally cooperative and peaceful. It is clear that Japan's strike record did not become peaceful until the first half of the 1970s. If Japanese industrial relations can be called cooperative, then German and Swedish industrial relations would have to be called super peaceful. It is true that time lost due to strikes in Japan has decreased considerably since the mid-1970s, but this trend is of recent origin. It is only in comparison with the United States and Italy that postwar Japanese industrial relations can be termed peaceful.

The assertion that seniority wages are unique to Japan is also unsupported by the most reliable statistical evidence. Since the mid-1970s, high-quality statistics on wages by age have been available for the European Community (EC) countries. Japan has had similar detailed yearly data since 1954. Seniority wages for male white collar workers in EC countries are apparent in the EC statistics. A comparison with Japanese statistics reveals that at EC age-wage profiles differ little from those of male blue-collar workers in large firms and male white-collar workers in all sizes of firms in Japan, both of which have been thought as typically having seniority wages. Consequently, we cannot say that seniority wages are peculiar to Japan. Rather, the Japanese feature, if any, is that some blue-collar workers have an age-wage profile similar to that of white-collar workers.

A similar argument is applicable to permanent employment. Again, the EC statistics supply reliable data on the distribution of workers by length of service. And an EC-Japan comparison reveals that the immobility of male blue-collar workers in large Japanese firms—the symbol of permanent employment—is equal to or even less than, that of male white-collar workers for all sizes of firms in EC countries. Above all, white-collarization of a section of the Japanese blue-collar work force is visible.

It is therefore, of prime importance to analyze the content and basis of this seeming white-collarization of male blue-collar workers in large Japanese firms. Two of the crucial variables affecting wages are undoubtedly the nature of skills and career development.

No definitive approach to the problem of analyzing the content of skill has yet been presented. This does not imply a lack of achievements in the study of skill; a variety of methods have been employed in its analysis. Among them, however, economic methods seem to have achieved the least. They concentrate on costs and returns on investment in human capital and rarely investigate the content of skills. The discipline with the longest tradition in the study of skill is undoubtedly psychology. However, it tends to be an exact science, confining itself to the simplest of jobs or work in an accurately controlled laboratory in order to produce exact academic results. Most jobs on the shop floor in large firms in contemporary Japan, however, are complex. Industrial engineering which employs the method of job analysis, is successful in observing the physical activities of work. For modern industrial work, however, the core of the skill lies not in physical activities, but in mental processes, to which this method of job analysis is not so well-suited. The only way to approach the mental content of skill is to ask many questions of veteran workers. This method has been adopted by some Japanese scholars.

We can categorize the major components of work on the shop floor in large firms as (1) usual operations and (2) unusual operations to deal with troubles or changes. With mass production machinery or in the processing industry usual operations are supposedly repetitive and monotonous, and people are apt to conclude that little skill is necessary. But in any mass production workshop, changes occur more frequently than is generally conceived; variation occurs in the ratio of inferior products to total output, the types of defects in goods, and the extent of defects, a long with variation in products, product mix, and the method of production. The labour mix varies in two ways. One is daily changes because of absences, which cause changes in deployment within the workshop. The other is changes in the weight of experienced workers within the workshop which makes variation in deployment easier and more efficient.

Operators in Japanese workshops are required to locate the smallest problems or defects in goods or parts as soon as possible, to determine the causes, and to eliminate them. Ideally, they anticipate any problems from the smallest indication, so that no actual damage results.

This component of shop floor work is more important in mass production, where speed is crucial; the longer it takes to deal with and eliminate troubles the longer the production line stops and hence the greater the cost. Quick responses are of prime importance; ideally problems are solved while the production line remains in motion.

Some might argue that a careful study of unusual troubles would reveal patterns and that standard ways to deal with them could be described in a manual, so that not much time or skill would be required. According to veteran workers, however, problems are so varied that standardization in the form of a manual is impractical. And even if it were possible to compile a manual analysing problems in terms of many standard patterns, the number of patterns would be too large to ensure quick response.

More important standardization may lessen efficiency. An example is illustrative. In a biochemical plant where the volume of oxygen is crucial to a process, minute adjustments in the flow of oxygen are vital. Practical standardization cannot formalize these minute adjustments, but rather at best simply sets upper and lower limits; only when the figures exceed these limits would the volume of oxygen be adjusted. Highly skilled workers, however, can make minute adjustments between these two limits.

Another characteristic is that in the firms observed, the operator who conducts the usual component of work also performs these responses to unusual situations. Another group of workers such as technicians or even engineers could conceivably make such responses because they require a high level of skill. In such a separated system, one operator would perform the usual work while different workers responded to changes or unusual circumstances. The Japanese system, however, is integrated : the same operator is in-charge of both components of work. This does not imply that Japanese operators deal with all problems. There are naturally many problems that they cannot solve.

There is another aspect to unusual work. The causes of problems may lie in the machinery or in production facilities. Overall maintenance is clearly out of the job sphere of operators, but maintenance on a minor scale is in their hands. To give an example, in one biochemical plant, ten workers, divided into five teams, are in charge of one section. Each two man team conducts usual work (component 1) and the non-maintenance part of unusual work (component 2) in shifts. Three shifts of eight hours are covered by four teams, one of which is resting. The fifth team works in the daytime only, mostly on maintenance, searching for pin holes in pipes and mending as many as possible. The workers contact maintenance men for larger repairs. Another example is the pasting machine workshop of a battery producer. This process involves pasting plates for battery boxes. Since most of the process is automated, the weight of component 2 would seem to be small. Here, however, the work of the operator includes disjointing, cleaning, and reassembling parts of the pasting machines in order to keep them in good condition. Overall disjointing and repairs are done by maintenance men.

What skills are necessary to perform these two components? Although it might seem that no skills are needed to conduct component 1, exact operation at high speed is demanded; for mass production work, the speed with which work is carried out is important. Component 2 involves a series of skill requirements. First, an accumulation of experience with unusual patterns is needed. Because the patterns are unusual, there is no way to know them other than from experience. This does not imply that no other skill is necessary. The causes of problems are either in the structure of products or in the machinery that makes them. In order to reason out the causes and to fix the problems operators need knowledge of the structure, functions, and mechanisms of the machinery and products. Operators share this second requirement with engineers or technicians, whose formal role is to know the mechanism of machines and products and improve them for higher efficiency. Japanese operators can, in this sense, be said to share this crucial element of skill with these white-collar workers. In other words, Japanese blue-collar workers in large firms are partly white-collarized in terms of skill as well as in terms of wages and length of service. Thus there is a very thin line of distinction between white-collared and blue-collared workers. The Japanese blue-collared workers are comparatively better equipped than the workers in other countries.

The nearly 400 training schools in Japan sponsored by local or central government give one year of full-time training to high school graduates and two years to junior high school graduates. The number of trainees amounts to about 30,000 per year. At least for large firms, however, these training schools have played a small role in developing workers skills. Large firms appear to recruit few training school graduates, although no truly reliable statistics are available. This apprenticeship system went into decline around World War I. School education, particularly for the period after World War II, has been heavily inclined to general education. Although there are many vocational high schools, they are unable to recruit bright pupils, and accordingly, the main sources for blue-collar recruits in large firms is the pool of high school graduates of general education courses.

This does not imply that most recruits for blue-collar jobs are new graduates from high school. It is an established myth that Japanese workers enter a firm directly after completing school and rarely move to other firms. Reliable statistics show that for firms with 1,000-4,999 employees, only one-third of male blue-collar recruits are new graduates and that the remainder have some work experience in other firms. It does not follow, however, that the majority of them enter firms as skilled workers. Rather, most recruits lack specific skill qualifications. In other words, the number of employees quitting in their first years with a firm is extremely high. Turnover figures in large firms for male workers in their early twenties have been around 20-25 per cent. Again much of the common perception of Japanese industrial relations is far removed from fact.

Most job training occurs after workers join a firm. Generally there are two types of training-off-the-job training and on-the-job training. Off-the-job training is easier to observe because of its formal structure. In a typical case —in one of the largest plants of a giant heavy electrical machinery firm—the off-the-job training begins with two, completely different entry courses. One is a one-year, full-time course; the other can be as short as one week. The one-year courses are for those recruited directly after they finish their senior high school; the shorter courses are for those who have had some experience in other firms.

The former type of course dates back to around World War I, when large firms typically began to establish their own training schools, recruiting extremely promising young students just completing compulsory education (elementary school at that time). Since social mobility was not high in those days, many promising youths could not proceed to higher education because it was too costly. Consequently, large firms were successful in recruiting promising youths of high aptitude. Companies provided three or four years of full-time technical training as well as further general education somewhat paralleling the secondary education received by the 10-20 per cent remaining in the regular school system. The young recruits were expected to and did become core workers and later foremen on the shop floor. As such, they became a major source of trade union leaders in the 1950s and 1960s. During the 1960s companies gave up this practice because now they were unable to recruit promising youths because of the diffusion of secondary education.

Thus, instead of the three-year course for promising trainees, companies typically maintain only one-year, full-time courses for senior high school graduates. The plant described here acts as a training centre for 40 boys gathered from several plants belonging to this company in the area. Training is divided into three courses; machining, machine assembly and electrical machine assembly. The 975 hours for practice and 710 hours for theory in one year are equivalent to training provided at government training schools and are certified under the Vocational Training Act. This type of formal training for one full year is probably exceptional, although formal systems seem to prevail in only a few large firms. In practice, however, a large part of the one year course tends to be allocated to shop floor practice rather than formal off-the-job training. This means firms do not, in fact, depend much on formal classroom training.

The other course is too short to be important in skill acquisition. A one-week formal course cannot teach trainees any technical skills for work on the shop floor. A short lecture on the products of the plant constitutes the main content of the course. This short course has, contrary to popular perception, drawn most of the new recruits because not many enter the company directly after completing school but after working briefly in other companies.

These are not the only off-the-job training courses in this plant. About every five years, blue-collar workers attend short courses designed especially for them. The courses are connected to the ranking system, which is of a type common in large firms. In such a company, blue-collar workers, including group leaders as well as foreman, are divided into five ranks, master and first, second, third and fourth class. Promotion through these ranks depends partly on achievement in these training courses.

The duration of these courses is short. The course for the fourth class is 32 hours long, for the third class 44 hours and for the first 16 hours, amounting to a total of less than a hundred hours. Even when other voluntary courses in preparation for skill tests are added the total barely exceeds 120 hours. This is extremely short in comparison with the whole occupational career, which extends to about thirty years. Given this short duration, can these courses be effective for acquiring the special skills described above ? There are lengthy courses of 600 hours consisting of one or two days per week over one or two years. However, these are only for supervisors and hence for a small minority, which in turn permits their length.

The national skill test must be noted as a functional equivalent. The national skill test is regulated under the Vocational Training Act and consists of a demonstration of skills and a written test on theory. The national skill test covers 119 occupations, only a small part of all occupations on the shop floor. In other words, the national skill test can test only general skill not the many specific skills needed on the shop floor in large, mass production companies. For example the staff of a large mass production company estimates that only 20 per cent of workers have skills covered by the national skill test. In those cases where the character of work fits the national skill test, the plant encourages its workers to take it by presenting a series of lectures on theory and by making plant facilities freely available to workers preparing for the practical test.

This type of off-the-job training, for recruits or incumbents, is effective not only for acquiring general skills easily transferred to other firms, but also for acquiring specific skills.

Another feature of these short courses is that they are made available to employees of firms supplying parts to the firm offering the course. A comparison of Toyota and Ford demonstrates the greater dependence on parts suppliers by large Japanese firms. Although Toyota produces slightly more cars, it hires far fewer employees: only one-seventh of those employed by Ford. Needless to say, productivity differentials cannot explain such a large gap. The main reason for this difference is the degree of dependence on parts suppliers; large Japanese firms tend to produce a smaller proportion of intermediate products. This feature can explain why large Japanese firms open up their training courses to the workers of parts suppliers. If the workers of parts suppliers could not acquire the skills necessary to make the needed products, or if the quality of the parts deteriorated, the quality of the end product could not be guaranteed. It is common practice for a large firm to circulate among its parts suppliers a list of available training courses. In return, the parts suppliers pay a minimal fee for the courses they participate in; usually these fees barely cover the direct cost. The most popular courses among parts suppliers are said to be on QC-circles activity and computer programming.

This study by Prof. Kazuo Koike, a well known Japanese scholar shows how maximum use of human resources is made in this country through a system of training of workers at every level, which in turn creates a sense of involvement in the productive processes. This perhaps is one of the key factors which has led to rapid industrialisation of the Japan.

Japanese industrial relations have another feature. The most important among them is seniority wages and permanent employment. Seniority wages reflect the nature of skill; skill is developed into a career over a long period within a frame, and accordingly the age-wage profile is positively sloped. This profile is not peculiar to Japan in two senses, it is confined to only a minority of Japanese workers, and it is common to male white-collar workers in the West. This similarity is also explained by the nature of skill, the skills of Japanese blue-collar workers in large firms are partly of an intellectual character being employed in determining the causes of problems and adjusting to minor changes on the shop floor and this intellectual character of skill is shared with white-collar workers in general. Therefore, seniority wages are not a unique Japanese feature; the Japanese feature, if any, is the extension of white-collar wages to a section of blue-collar worker.

With this type of skill, it is natural that both management and workers benefit from long-term employment which has long been thought of as Japan's unique permanent employment. For workers, it is beneficial to stay with one firm because skills can be developed; for management, finding and training substitutes takes time and is costly. And again, this long-term employment is not unique to Japan in two senses: it is confined to large firms and it is also common for male white-collar workers in Europe. A Japanese feature is the extension of the white-collarization of a section of blue-collar workers.

The specific feature of maximisation of human resources in Japan, therefore, can be broadly traced to a system of improving the skills of the workers and bringing a section of them to the level of white-collar workers. This creates a sense of involvement in productive processes. In order to elevate their own skills quickly, workers take an interest in the growth of their firms. If the company declines, promotion will be delayed and skill development slowed. In extreme cases, when the economic condition of the firm deteriorates, the workers may be laid off.

Trade unions adopt a policy of cooperativeness with respect to production because they are democratic and reflect the members desires. The apparent difference between Japanese and Western unions results mostly from a simple fact. Formal trade unions in European countries still consist, by long tradition, mostly of blue-collar workers although the situation is changing and unions now include more white-collar workers. This was common, too, of Japanese unions in the pre-war days. Defeat in the war brought new organization and the inclusion of both blue and white-collar workers in the same workplace union. Formal trade unions in Europe usually do not include white-collar and white-collarized workers in the same organizations as blue-collar workers, and consequently, formal unions are not so cooperative as in Japan. If we compare Japanese unions with Western white-collar workers organizations, more similarities emerge. In other words, a comparison of Japanese unions with workers councils in Europe might be more meaningful because the latter include white-collar workers.

One of the problems of Japanese industrial relations is finding ways of adjusting to contractions in output. Contrary to the popular belief that Japanese system is flexible in adapting to changes, redundancy do happen in Japanese firms. They lay off workers who suffer the greatest costs when unemployed. Workers with the longest service, aged 45 and over, are most vulnerable to redundancy. Consequently, social tension is high even with a small volume of redundancy; more redundancy would make industrial relations as militant as they were in the late 1940s and the 1950s. The upper limit of redundancy or unemployment that can be endured in an industrial society is lower in Japan than in the West. This makes the capacity for adjustment to change smaller because changes, in industrial structure, for example, require a certain amount of unemployment.

The white-collarization of blue-collar workers has great implications for contemporary politics in Japan. Along with white-collar workers, blue-collar workers with intellectual skills form the economic foundation of the new middle mass.

5

Japan's Experiment in Technological Revolution

Recent recession in developed industrial countries has raised a controversy among the economists whether the developing economic crisis can be solved through the technological revolution. In this context Japanese technological revolution needs a close examination.

Since the mid-1970s, the relatively sluggish performance of the leading industrial economies of the world has given rise to a growing sense that the industrial world may be facing yet another crisis. However, this was a short term phenomenon because this trend was reversed through technological revolution. As against this the Soviet Union began to lag behind because it failed to adjust itself to this trend. In India partial attempts were made to come to grips with this new development.

The 1970s and early 1980s had seen a marked decline in the growth rates of both GNP and productivity in developed countries. Any explanation of this decline is bound to be controversial. Nevertheless, it is certain that American expenditure on research and development changed the course of economic growth in the developed countries.

As far as Japan is concerned it gave a top priority to research and development (R&D). Major industrial powers like France and West Germany received only 55 per cent of the number of patents in the mid-1960s whereas the number of patents received by Japanese had almost quadrupled between 1967 and 1984. The Japanese were active in overseas patenting. Their contributions had offset what would have otherwise been much sharper declines in the patents granted in the other major industrialized economies.

If, for instance, patent approvals for Japanese were excluded from US patent totals, the recorded 0.5 per cent increase in total patents granted between 1967 and 1984 would have turned into a 15 per cent decline. This fact speaks for itself. However, this clearly brings out how both in qualitative and quantitative terms Japan evolved its own system of scientific research and development. This has paid rich dividends to it. This among other factors has enabled Japan to virtually become an economic super power. That a small country like Japan in geographical terms should be competing with the US, Great Britain and Germany underlines how a country without major industrial raw materials can become world's major industrial power with technological revolution.

Japan has perhaps some characteristic features of its scientific revolution which stand in a complete contrast to the American road to technological revolution. It has three main components. These are: (i) the role of small companies in technological revolution; (ii) the role of government in R&D funding; and (iii) the character of advanced training for technical personnel.

The fundamental characteristics of Japan's R&D system, particularly as it compares with what is arguably the world's leading R&D system, the United States, are revealing. The fact of matter is that in certain areas Japan is more developed in scientific technology. This conclusion will be of deep interest to developing countries, including India, which is most developed among them.

Although Japan appears to have made great technological progress against the strong currents of worldwide trends, the scope and significance of its technological development is being widely debated both within Japan and outside it. How much of Japan's technological progress continues to rest largely on technology transferred from abroad and how much it relies uniquely on Japan's R&D activities remains an open issue. Does the decline in the growth rate of Japan's total factor productivity rest entirely on diminished technological transfer? Has the productivity of Japanese R&D activities increased markedly at a time when those of other countries have declined sharply? These questions are relevant. However, Japan's technical advance should not be ignored.

The enormous rise in Japan's patent productivity can be attributed, in part, to the sustained and steep increases in R&D investment. From 1965 to 1980, real growth rates in Japan's R&D expenditure rose faster than those of any other major industrial state. Increases in R&D expenditures may be necessary to raise patent productivity, but they hardly constitute a sufficient explanation. However, it has to be admitted that other countries have poured larger amounts into their R&D efforts. For example, in terms of increases in real R&D expenditures, West Germany's slope is virtually indistinguishable from Japan's; yet patent applications in West Germany have fallen over a period of time, and the number of patents actually granted has dropped by half. This suggests that investing more R & D money is no guarantee of greater patent productivity.

Japan's extraordinary performance can be attributed to intangiable factors at the micro-level such as superior company incentives; greater research continuity made possible by lifetime employment; closer contact and better communications among divisions engaged in research, production, and marketing; fierce competition among firms; and greater company prestige derived from patenting. Though it is difficult to quantify the contribution of each one of these factors. What stands out is that it is this system and synthesis of all factor, which has elevated Japan to the status of a highly technologically developed country. Significantly, many Japanese companies, including such giants as Hitachi, Matsushita, Fuji Film, Toshiba and Sony, give their employees special bonuses, both when their inventions result in the filing of a patent application and when the patent application is granted. This may mean that the Japanese apply for, and register, more patents than others because the knowledge they seek to protect tends to be less significant technologically. Larger quantity may reflect lower quality, or at least a greater propensity to seek patents for knowhow that others would consider too mundane or short-lived to bother about, according to some experts.

This interpretation is supported by the low rate of success for patent applications in Japan. Nearly half of the applications made by Japanese to their own patent office are turned down — compared with less than 20 per cent of foreign applications. In the United States, the ratio of approvals to applications for Japanese nationals is about 75 per cent of that of Americans and only 60 per cent of that of other foreigners.

Although an unusual zeal to protect run-of-the-mill products and processes may explain the sharp rise in Japanese patent applications, it does not account for the simultaneous decline elsewhere. One explanation may be that patent protection has never been an important feature of the incentive structure underlying R&D investment in the United States and Western Europe. In certain industries, the pace of technological change may be so rapid as to make the lengthy patent approval process an ineffective device for protecting proprietary rights. Moreover, with greater public access to the proprietary information contained in patent applications, US and European companies may be having the feeling that patents simply cannot be obtained without disclosing vital information that will help competitors.

Of course, the risk of leaking information to competitors is not entirely new. The term trade secret long antedates the Industrial Revolution. What is new is the mounting concern in the United States and Western Europe that the advanced state and current orientation of Japanese R&D place Japan in an advantageous position to derive special benefits from the disclosure of proprietary information. This factor is leading to a new contradiction between Japan and other industrialised countries, between Japan and the United States in particular.

Although the evidence strongly suggests that Japan has made exceptional technological progress over the past two decades, one must be careful in drawing firm conclusions.

Throughout the entire post-war period, Japan has relied heavily on imports of foreign knowhow to upgrade its manufacturing capabilities and step up the tempo of industrial output. Although Japan, like West Germany, still runs a large deficit today, the imbalance is shrinking steadily as the value of exported technology rises. In 1971, the ratio of exports to imports stood at 0.12; by 1983, it had risen to 0.30. This trend seems to have undergone major changes in the last decade of the 20th century. The data on the overall size of new contracts for technology sales and purchases partially confirms this conclusion. According to the data, the ratio of technology exports to imports has changed. Japan's export of technology is registering an upward trend as compared to import of technology.

Significantly in 1984 only about 40 per cent of technology exports went to advanced industrial states; 60 per cent was sold to developing countries. By contrast, over 85 per cent of US technology exports went to advanced industrial states, with less than 15 per cent being transferred to developing countries. This fact is revealing. It shows that Japan is exporting technology to the developing countries. This also shows that

Japan's technology export is in production technology for the heavy manufacturing sectors, especially chemicals, iron and steel, and transportation machinery. These industries are Japan's biggest foreign exchange earners.

Another feature of Japan's technological development is that it has allocated a disproportionate share of its R&D resources to basic research. As long ago as 1967, Japan was devoting 28.2 per cent of all its expenditures to basic research. Moreover the real rate of growth of Japan's R&D expenditure for basic research has almost always exceeded the real growth rate in the United States since that time. In contrast with the US and European practice, Japan treats the salaries of all university and college science teaching personnel as if they were fulltime researchers. This leads to a substantial overstatement of the academic sector's role in Japanese R & D. Nevertheless research in the universities gives a broader base to basic research in Japan unlike the United States and European countries. This means that starting from an extremely small base in 1965 there was an extraordinarily rapid increase in the research role of Japanese universities and colleges and an increased role for basic research within Japan's R&D effort. However, according to some experts, the aggregate Japanese effort in basic research remains modest by US standards.

According to one Japanese scholar, Japan's contribution to basic research and human knowledge is fairly high. He has pointed out that in 1982 Japan ranked third in terms of research papers published in the world's leading scholarly journals, accounting for 7.3 per cent of the world's total, behind the United States (38.2 per cent) and England (7.9 per cent) but ahead the Soviet Union (6.4 per cent) and West Germany (5.7 per cent). Over the past 30 years Japan has increased basic research. In chemistry in 1982, for example, Japan accounted for nearly 12 per cent of all scholarly papers published in the world, placing it third behind the United States (21.9 per cent) and the Soviet Union (15.8 per cent) but well ahead of West Germany (6.4 per cent) and England (5.7 per cent). In the telecommunications field between 1981 and 1984, Japan accounted for nearly 10 per cent of the research papers accepted by the Comite consultantif international telegraphique et telephoniques, ranking second behind the United States. In fields such as chemistry, telecommunication and semiconductors, the Japanese have become major participants.

According to an authoritative survey of Japanese businessmen, Japan has reached a high level in technology in some key areas such as iron and steel production, agricultural chemicals, nuclear energy processing, for example fast breeder reactors, semiconductors, metal oxide semi-conductors and gallium arsenide, mass memory chips, computer peripherals, office automation, robotics, flexible manufacturing systems, certain areas of telecommunications, power transmission cables and digital switching equipment, pharmaceuticals, artificial blood, biotechnology, fermentation and gamma interferon from synthetic genes and industrial lasers.

This shows the area of specialisation by Japanese scientific community. This also shows how Japan has not only made remarkable progress in technological revolution and in certain areas in doing pioneering work. The cumulative impact of this research on the commercial competitiveness of Japanese industry has been substantial. From an economic standpoint therefore, their significance should not be underestimated.

In the early 80s, Japan was found to lag far behind the United States in various military technologies; aerospace, jet aircraft, avionics, computer-aided design and computer-aided manufacturing, security related information processing and so forth. However, Japan has made significant progress in other areas such as certain dual purpose technologies (that is, technologies with both military and civilian applications) where commercial markets are large and the barriers to new entry are not prohibitively high, such as superconductivity components, gallium arsenide, nuclear energy and supercomputers. Although still behind in lasers and artificial intelligence, Japan is thought to be catching up rapidly, owing to the motivation imported by the enormous commercial potential of those technologies.

Aerospace is an example of an industry in which Japan-despite industrial targeting, has encountered difficulties in catching up with the technological front-runners. Unlike the United States and Russia, which were motivated by considerations of national security or international prestige, Japan entered space research in order to take advantage of long-term commercial opportunities in communications and broadcasting and for purposes of scientific observations; more recently, its goals have also come to include the construction of space factories for bioengineering and new materials.

Although small-scale Japanese firms account for a much higher proportion of R&D expenditure than do their US counterparts, the level of research intensity is lower. In 1981, R&D expenditures of small firms with under 1,000 employees in the United States were 1.6 per cent of their total sales. For Japanese firms of this size, R&D expenditures came to only 1.32 per cent of sales. The larger R&D expenditures of small firms in Japan can be explained by their larger overall presence in the Japanese economy. Indeed the long-term decline of R&D expenditures by small firms in the United States (from 11 per cent of R&D in 1957 to 4.1 per cent in 1985) is only marginally affected by changes in the research intensities for large versus small firms; the main explanation is the smaller number of firms that employ less than 1,000 workers in the US economy. Because the aggregate number of small and medium size firms in Japan has not shrunk as much as it has in the United States. The R&D expenditures of small Japanese firms have declined only modestly over the past 15 years, according to Japanese scholars.

Japan's R&D system also differs markedly from that of the United States in the role played by the government. Contrary to common misperception, the Japanese government spends much less to underwrite industrial R&D than the US or European governments. The US government funded 32 per cent of all business R&D expenditures in 1982 whereas the Japanese government supplied no more than 1.7 per cent in the same period.

Some Japanese think that they are at a disadvantage in competing with the United States in high-technology industries because their government underwrites so little of the business sector's R&D in comparison to the US government. The US government underwrites a substantial proportion of R&D. It compensates for market failures or even unemployment. When Japanese firms faced the same market failures, they are forced to face them without government support. Significant government funding of R&D enhances international competitiveness in the USA. Much of the US government's R&D expenditures are related to the provision of public goods. Indeed in 1980, 44 per cent of all government R&D (equivalent to 0.5 per cent of GNP) went to war improvements in missiles and aircraft. Since 1980, government support of missile and aircraft R&D has risen to 0.75 per cent of GNP. The US pattern contrasts sharply to that of Japan, where about 40 per cent of government support of R&D (equivalent to 0.22 per cent of GNP) is directed toward the promotion of agriculture and industry. Roughly two-thirds of this support in Japan is directed to the needs of agriculture and has relatively little to do with enhancing the productivity of the Japanese economy. This shows how Japan's technical development has certain limitations unlike the USA.

The results indicate the defence procurement heavily influences the allocation of US government R&D. On the other hand, defence procurement scarcely affects the R&D spending priorities of the Japanese government. The US government supports R&D in those industries in which it is a major customer. The Japanese government responds more positively to technological opportunities in its allocation of R&D expenditures to other sectors. The Japanese government for instance gave special attention in its R&D funding to industries that are electrically or mechanically based.

This analysis shows that in the area of technological development, Japan has evolved its own model, which is different from that of the United States in many respects. Japan may not have become a pace-setter in certain areas of technological revolution such as space, it stands in the front rank in development of technology. But there is something more to it. Japan has evolved a unique system of technological development in which the new technologies are transmitted to industrial production on a qualitatively new scale. This perhaps is the main asset of Japan.

6

Japan's Role in International Financial System

In the previous chapters, we have examined specific features of Japan's economic development and how it has become a super economic power. It will be relevant now to study its role in the new pattern of international relations.

Statistics are indicators of process taking place in social development. If one goes by statistics, Asia-Pacific is indeed emerging as a region of the future, a region which in the beginning of the next century may become a decisive factor in international relations. In this sense in the current epoch, which is marked by increasingly close interdependence among states and regions, social changes that are taking place in this region have become a key factor in shaping the course of history on our planet towards the end of the present century.

Sometime early in the 21st century, on a Friday afternoon after the closure of stock market, the US Department of Commerce will announce the latest trade statistics. For the 100th month in a row Japan, South Korea and China will all have sold out more goods to the United States than they have bought from it. To stop a run on the dollar and retain Asian capital needed to finance America's 500 billion dollars deficit, the Federal Reserve Board will announce yet another hike in interest rates. Some American leaders will blame the FRB for caving into pressures of the Bank of Japan. All that Japan's financiers are interested in, they will charge, is the profit margins of institutions like Nippon Life- which hold so much American debt that they virtually own the US government. These pessimistic forecasts were made in the late eighties in the American mass media. Whatever may be the element of truth in these estimates, one thing is certain that Japan has become a major player in the international economy, in the financial area in particular.

Not long ago, the idea that the world could look like this in the next century seemed unthinkable. Americans, protected for two centuries by vast oceans, enriched by natural resources and a risk-taking spirit, have never taken easily to changes beyond their control. Vietnam drove home the bitter lesson that the United States was no longer a hegemonic power, and the oil shocks of the 1970s showed its resources were not sufficient enough to insulate it from economic calamities. But after the disintegration of the Soviet Union, Americans yearned to turn back the clock—and for a time, American ruling elite succeeded in making the country believe that it had. The economy expanded, the stock market soared, the United States won a minor skirmish on the island of Grenada.

That moment of confidence and security didn't last long. As the 20th century draws to a close, the world is in the midst of a profound geopolitical shift. Moving to the fore today is a nation that just under 51 years ago was extricated from the wreckage of war by its conqueror. Now Japan is arguably the world's most powerful economic factor, ready to assume leadership in an era of rising Asian power—a period that experts have already dubbed as the 'Pacific Century'. If things continue as they are now, predicts Richard Rosercrance, Professor of International Affairs at Cornell University, it won's be much beyond 2010 before Japan becomes the leading power in world politics. Reinforcing the Asia-Pacific's rising economic influence are the so-called fourtigers—the newly industrialised countries (NIC's) of South Korea, Taiwan, Singapore and Hong Kong; notwithstanding the recent economic problems; some of these countries are now facing. And stirring ever more energetically after decades of economic idleness is China, a once and perhaps future superpower. With Asia coming on so strong, says William Overholt, a Bankers Trust economist in Hong Kong, the United States in the next hundred years could become a giant Australia.

While the Asia-Pacific region is rapidly expanding its global economic influence, the United States has gradually shifted its global interests from Western Europe to the East. The readjustment of US economic strategy will have far-reaching influences.

It is in this background that Japan's role in the international monetary system should be examined. The international monetary regime, the set of rules that governs the monetary mechanism of international trade and investment, is one of the foundations of the world economy. The development of every national economy is conditioned by the way the international monetary regime is arranged and every major economy has contributed, though with different degrees of importance, to its evolution. The Japanese economy is no exception. One should review the postwar development of the international monetary regime and Japan's growing involvement in it to understand Japan's weight in the world economy.

The United States played the dominant role in the postwar evolution of the international monetary regime. In the Bretton Woods system, particularly in its practice, the United States was such an important leader that, before Nixon's New Economic Policy in 1971, the Bretton Woods system was called the dollar standard. However weak it was, the link between the value of currencies and gold remained a link between the dollar and gold. The dollar was the major if not the only, vehicle currency. This US leadership role declined after the breakdown in 1971-73 of the Bretton Woods regime, that is, the old IMF regime. European countries have come to play an increasingly important role, and in the past two decades Japan has played a relatively significant role. The United States, however, continues to be the dominant factor in the sense that changes in rules cannot occur without its cooperation. The best example of this is the intervention after September, 1985 of the Group Five (the United States, Great Britain, West Germany, France and Japan), which was organized under the leadership of the United States and reflected a major shift from the earlier policy of non-intervention in currency markets. The United States has been an important actor over the past several years in the international monetary system. The dollar was overvalued for several years. The United States still has a special position in the world economy because of its dominant role, because of its huge size and because, unlike every other country, foreigners were and are still willing to hold large amounts of their wealth in dollar-denominated financial claims, even though they assume substantial foreign exchange risks in the process.

Japan was a negligible player till recently and passive accepter of the international monetary system. Japan has now emerged as a country with some destabilizing impact on the system and even as a catalyst for change. In the 1980s Japan has become one of the major actors in the system, given its immense financial involvement in the rest of the world and burgeoning current-account surpluses and concomitant net capital outflows. Between dollar and yen a new equation has developed. Stability of dollar is influenced by yen.

The significance of this shift has to be seen in the context of the fact after the wartime destruction, the Japanese economy occupied only a tiny place in the world. It was generally conceived of as an economy closely associated with, and often subordinate to, the US economy. The favourite phrase was—when the United States sneezes, Japan catches pneumonia. Japan was completely under US hegemony in the economic as well as the political sense. This conclusion is based on the assessment of Japanese scholars.

During the period of rapid economic growth in the 1960s the relative importance of the Japanese economy increased substantially. However, Japan's sudden and large balance of payments current-account surplus and the reluctance of the Japanese government to revalue the yen were among the main factors that triggered Nixon's drastic adoption of the New Economic Policy. Because of its increased role in the world economy, Japan functioned as a pivotal element in this critical change in the international monetary system.

In the 1980s, particularly, after Japan became a major industrial power, its influence on international monetary system increased as a member of Group of five.

An implicit principle of the dollar-standard system was that the United States would maintain domestic price stability, which would result in international price stability. In other words, the implicit quid pro quo for an increase in the US dollars held by foreigners was a US commitment to price stability. Robert Mundell advocated the following assignment of policies under the dollar standard: the United States adjusts its money supply so as to stabilize the international price level, and Europe and Japan (the rest of the world) adjust their money supplies to maintain balance-of-payment equilibrium. This application of his celebrated principle of policy instruments works well so long as these rules are observed.

In fact it was West Germany, which began to challenge American domination over the international monetary system as early as in the 60s. There was strong pressure on Germany to expand its domestic macro-economic policy, but the Germans resisted. This German problem spread to other countries in the late 1960s as the United States financed the Vietnam war through inflationary means and as Japan's current-account surpluses grew substantially. Moreover, de Gaulle and France were unwilling to finance the United States by holding dollars since France, too, had started to run current account surplus and came to insist increasingly that it be allowed to convert dollars into gold. The United States exercised moral pressure on other countries, particularly on Japan and to some degree on Germany. But it did not work. To some extent, it reflected an unwillingness to go along with US macro-economic policy, not only for reasons of price stability but for political reasons over the United States' use of its assets for war against Vietnam.

In fact, two of the major reasons why the Bretton Woods regime collapsed are that the rest of the world did not play the game symmetricaly with respect to booms and recessions and that the United States, particularly after its involvement in Vietnam, came to be concerned not so much with world price stability as with its own national policy objectives.

At the beginning of the 1970s, the adherence of the Japanese government to the fixed parity of 1 dollar to 360 yen was too extreme. The mere discussion of flexible exchange rates was virtually a taboo in the mass media. Whereas most countries that had been under the fixed exchange rates immediately closed their foreign exchange markets on President Nixon's announcement and shifted to floating exchange rates a week or so later, Japan alone kept its foreign exchange market open. As a result, the Bank of Japan bought about 4 billion dollars at the overpriced exchange rate of 360 yen incurring a huge loss for Japanese tax payers. Finally, the monetary authorities gave in, and the yen was allowed to float and appreciate. However, this unequal relation between dollar and yen created mass discontent. Thus step by step Japan began to assert its economic independence.

The resurgence of financial crises in Europe and the increased demand for the yen made it necessary for Japanese monetary authorities to join in adopting flexible exchange rates in February, 1973. Japan adopted the flexible exchange rate system at a time when all the other major countries were adopting the same course of action.

The adoption of flexible exchange rates was not the result of a coordinated, planned, and deliberate decision of the participating countries. Rather, it was a necessary escape from an impasse and a measure against an emergency. Only, in 1976 in Jamaica did the IMF interim committee agree on the basic rules of the international monetary system and allow adoption of flexible exchange rates. The flexible exchange rate system itself does not, at least prima facie, call for any cooperation between governments. The direct link among price levels in the participating countries that had existed under the adjustable-peg system was ended by the adoptions of flexible exchange rates.

However, when the dollar hit a record low in 1978, Japan's international reserves reached a historical high. After an announcement of joint action by the Japanese and US monetary authorities, the exchange rate changed direction. This movement towards lower values for the yen was reinforced by the second oil crisis. The pattern of buying the dollar at a trough and selling it at a peak generally continued until 1983.

It also should be emphasized that an important turning point in the yen-dollar exchange rate was induced by the announcement of joint actions by central bankers. By October, 1978, for example, the value of the dollar had fallen to 176 yen, less than half of the 360 yen rate that had prevailed for more than 20 years before the collapse of the Bretton Woods regime. It shows clearly that the dollar was overvalued and the yen was undervalued.

During 1982-86, however, Japan's overall current-account surplus, the United States overall current-account deficit, and Japan's bilateral current-account surplus with the United States began to grow to huge levels. By 1985, the United States was no longer willing to accept its intolerably large and rapidly growing trade and current account deficits and not surprisingly, it associated much of its trade problems with Japan's burgeoning success.

Japan's current-account surplus was a consequence of the tendency for private saving to outstrip private investment demand while government budget deficits, so large in the latter half of the 1970s, were being reduced. With low interest rates at home, Japanese were eager to accumulate net wealth abroad. In the United States, the major change in the domestic macro-economic balance lay in the rapidly increasing federal budget deficit far beyond the capacity of domestic savings to finance if it were also to finance domestic private investment. Monetary policy achieved price stability in part by maintaining relatively high interest rates, especially in real terms; those interest rates attracted foreign capital to finance, indirectly at least, up to one-half the federal budget deficit, with a concomitant inflow of imports of goods and services in excess of exports.

Then came the fascinating experiment of the Group of Five. The finance ministers of the five countries announced their intent to intervene in the foreign exchange market. As a result, the value of the dollar dropped by 37 per cent from 243 yen in September 1985 to 153 yen in September 1986.

Despite its imperfections, the present system of flexible exchange rates does provide an international monetary framework that satisfies minimum standards. The present system allows sufficient freedom to monetary authorities to pursue their own policies almost independently of the activities of the monetary authorities of other countries. However there are some positive or negative spillover effects even under the freely floating regime. The intensity of inter-dependence is indirect and of a second order compared with the intensity of inter-dependence in the fixed exchange rate system, in which national price levels are directly linked. Nevertheless, this inter-dependence varies from country to country, depending upon the strength of their currency and other economic factors. After the adoption of flexible exchange rates, the world economy came under the strong attacks of real disturbances, notably the two oil crises. Nonetheless, the present flexible exchange-rate system survived these disturbances without the financial panics experienced under the adjustable-peg system and without the imposition of exchange controls.

The flexibility of exchange rates by itself does not provide any automatic mechanism to stabilise monetary system as was reflected in recent developments in some ASEAN countries, Indonesia in particular. Most of the earlier advocates of flexible exchange rates seemed to think that flexible exchange rates would balance current accounts; presumably, theoretically they assumed a world in which capital flows were not particularly large. In contrast, in the present world where capital mobility is nearly perfect, the flexibility of exchange rates does not equilibrate current accounts. Whereas goods markets are sluggish in adjusting, the foreign exchange market is a volatile market where the excess demand for outstanding stocks of foreign denominated financial assets clears instantaneously. Moreover, goods markets are usually constrained by the past course of prices, but foreign exchange rates jump around in response to expectations of future exchange rates and underlying macro-economic variables.

Japan's current-account surplus and the United States current-account deficit should be examined in global terms and not just in terms of the bilateral imbalance, because the efficient allocation of resources should be achieved globally rather than bilaterally and should be reflected in the global balance of payments position of each country. Moreover, it is not simply the difference in savings rates between two countries but the differences in rates of return on new investments that make it attractive to invest in one country or the other. Further complicating the case of the United States has been the American administration's commitment to increasing total budget expenditures substantially, mainly for military purposes and a concomitant increase in tax revenues.

Japanese financial experts are of the opinion that there have been times, for example, 1982 or early 1985, when many people considered the yen-dollar exchange rate to be misaligned. During these periods, however, the yen remained relatively weak and the dollar strong. Market participants were aware of possible misalignments, but the market exchange rate did not change.

Another factor of importance is the ongoing and large difference in long-term interest rates between the United States and other countries, notably Japan. Added to that was the liberalization in Japan of portfolio restrictions on life insurance companies and pension funds to allow long-term investments in foreign assets. In early 1985, a portfolio manager for a Japanese life insurance company stated that his company focused on the long-run yield over 20 years to balance its requirements for payout periods, and that he regarded it as extremely unlikely that the yen would appreciate 5 per cent a year on average over 20 years, which was the difference in interest rate returns on long-term financial assets in Japan and the United States. His was apparently a good long-run investment strategy. However, it turned out to be a poor short-run investment strategy since the yen appreciated so much after Japanese insurance companies started purchasing dollar financial assets. These losses were fortuitously offset in part by higher bond prices as US interest rates declined. Nonetheless, it does suggest that if the substantial interest rate gap for long-term assets persists, Japanese long-term financial institutions will continue to enter the market and demand dollars.

The exchange rate system cannot be evaluated in isolation from its impact on other systemic components of the international economic system. The large US trade and current-account deficits in the 1980s had profoundly adverse implications not only for the US economy and for US-Japan economic relations but for the international economic system as a whole. The two major systemic effects are—the increase in protectionist sentiments and policies in the United States and the shift in the United States position from the world's largest creditor nation to its largest debtor. During the same period, Japan emerged as the largest creditor nation in the world, most of its foreign assets were held in US bonds and short-term financial instruments, but investment in equities, direct investments, including investment in real estates, and other dollar-denominated claims were also increasing. Although Japan began to be a creditor nation in the early 1970s, the tendency was masked by the two oil crises. Its emergence as a creditor nation in the 1980s was amplified and accelerated by the US deficits. That is the reason that American financial experts till recently were disturbed over this trend as has been indicated in the first part of this chapter.

The increase in United States protectionist sentiment and actions in the 1980s and 1990s stem from many causes. Surely the immense trade deficits contributed substantially to perceptions—correct or not—in the United States, particularly in Congress, that the US economy was being seriously hurt and that the foreign trading system somehow did not treat US participants fairly. In fact, the growing trade deficits of the 1980s and 1990s were primarily the consequence of domestic economic policies, and the expansion of the federal budget, after 1981, on military. In retrospect, it was a profound policy error. One great danger is that the United States will shift to a substantially more protectionist position in the future. That would have significant adverse effects on the international trading system.

The longer-run implications of the United States becoming a huge debtor nation, say, of 600-1,000 billion dollars in the 1990s and of Japan's becoming a major creditor nation, say, of 450-600 billion dollars in the same period of a new economic relationship between the USA and Japan. It is unclear how long and in what amounts these respective foreign debts (current account deficits) and assets (current-account surpluses) will accumulate. What is clear is that even if these imbalances are eliminated completely, the adjustment process will take time, and at the minimum the respective debtor and creditor positions will be absolutely very large.

It is likely that a great preponderance of Japanese claims will be in dollars, and on the United States. This factor financial experts of other countries including India cannot and shouldn't ignore.

The interest, dividend and profit income to be paid by the United States and received by Japan will become substantial and will affect the structural composition of merchandise and service trade in each country. Manufactured goods production in Japan will slow down with potentially significant effects on the structure of domestic production in each country. How much, will depend on the cumulative size of the net debt or assets, foreign investment income flows, and the degree to which current-account imbalances persist.

The continuing net outflow of Japanese capital and the accumulation of such a large net foreign asset position will mean that both the Japanese government and Japanese private financial institutions will become a dominant player in world financial markets, a rapid quantitative and qualitative expansion of trends began in the early 1980s. The yen becoming an increasingly important reserve and transaction currency. This implies that international monetary system has already begun to change. Such a large US-Japan debtor-creditor position will inevitably make the bilateral relationship more complex and its management more complicated. This in turn has changed both political and economic relations between the USA and Japan. From being a junior partner of Washington only two to three decades ago, Tokyo has already begun to challenge the American hegemony.

But there is another aspect of this development. If Japan withdraws capital from the USA and increases its investment to other countries, it will lead to new contradictions between the two countries. Again, actions by the United States that might reduce the value of Japanese assets by inflation, freezing, or other acts—would also reduce much of US credibility international market. Even the threat to take such actions would sharply reduce confidence. At any rate, this new debtor-creditor relationship almost certainly will become an important new element in the interrelationships among bilateral issues of trade, finance, investment, exchange rates, macro-economic policies and perhaps even defense. Although the United States may, in time, eliminate its deficit it can be anticipated that Japan may continue to have surplus in the foreseeable future.

Where will Japan stand then? Japan's economy now occupies a substantial share of the world economy—about one-tenth. Its trade structure and wage and price determination mechanisms are quite different from those of the United States and Western Europe as well as from those in developing countries. It seems therefore that the optimum currency area for Japan is Japan itself. In addition there seem to be many factors in Japan that obstruct the achievement of international reforms in the direction of stable and quasi-fixed exchange rate regimes. The only likely exception would be if protective pressures from outside Japan become more stringent. This catastrophic situation might make a drastic reform possible, even though exchange rate reform by itself will not solve balance-of-payments problems unless accompanied by appropriate changes in macro-economic fiscai and monetary management. Thus a realistic role in the monetary regime for the foreseeable future is for Japan to continue to be passive and to practice a managed float. From whatever angle you look at the situation, it becomes clear that in the present period of globalisation of economy and inter-dependence, Japan and therefore yen have come to occupy a key position. Yen is no more in the periphery of international monetary system. It has already moved to the centre. It has now become a challenger to dollar.

7

US-Japanese Relations

US-Japanese relations have begun to change rapidly for three main reasons, namely, rise of Japan as a supereconomic power, disintegration of the Soviet Union and weakening of hegemony of the United States, both in economic and political terms, according to various Japanese scholars. For obvious reasons, Japanese scholars have begun to devote maximum attention on US-Japanese relations in the new era. However, it will be naive to conclude that these relations are not a significant factor in the international economy and politics.

Prognosis for stability and cooperation in the international political economy depend heavily on assessments of changes in the relative power of the United States, Japan, and other major powers. Has US hegemony declined greatly over recent years? Much of the recent literature on hegemonic stability has been devoted to explaining the effects of a decline in US hegemony on the international system since the highpoint of US dominance immediately after 1945.

The research work carried out by Japanese scholars shows them to agree that American hegemony has declined, though there are differences over the degree of the decreasing American influence.

Even as the United States commemorates the fiftieth anniversary of the Pearl Harbour attack by Japan and ultimate victory by America, tension seem to be replacing the last forty-five years of close cooperation and friendship. The US-Japan alliance, which was established after dictating a Constitution by the American occupying forces and carefully grooming to counter the Communist threat, particularly after the Chinese revolution in 1949, is apparently developing cracks after the Communist threat has receded. Obviously, the economic issues are coming to the forefront overshadowing the political issues.

The perception of a significant decline in US power over the past two decades is widespread, indeed virtually universal. Nearly every scholar of Japan barring some marxist economists recognize that the United States retains great power in the economic sphere; at least a greater power than any other state. These same writers typically carefully note a continuing degree of US pre-eminence. The decline is relative only, to the past US power or perhaps to the amount necessary for a hegemony to maintain essential elements of the world economic order. However, the United States has not declined to a position of secondary importance. What is important is that both Japanese and other scholars recognize this decline.

The standards used to measure the decline are seldom clear. Part of the difficulty stems from the lack of agreement on how much power is necessary to produce a hegemony, according to Japanese scholars. That is why some Japanese scholars have divergent views on this question.

However, one thing is certain that the United States' power, as measured by various power based indicators, surely has declined. Loss of strategic nuclear predominance; decline in conventional military capabilities (relative Russia), especially for interventional and in military capability generally, diminished economic size (relative GNP), productivity, competitiveness in foreign markets, value of the dollar on foreign exchange markets and terms of trade with some commodity producers, principally oil until recently, the loss of a reliable majority in the UN and the loss of assured scientific pre-eminence in the knowledge industries at the cutting edge, all these factors have diminished the dominant role of the USA.

The United States' economic and industrial predominance in the world looks slightly less impressive if one considers its share of world GNP rather than its share of world manufacturing production. All of these as well as other power based measures would show a clear decline in US predominance over the past fifty years. However, this decline has not been uniform during the cold war, its scale was different. In the post-cold war period, there was an upward trend, after the demise of the Soviet Union. In the late 90s, again a downward trend has begun, though as yet muted.

There are three main indicators which determine as to who dominate the centre of the world economy, namely the Gross National Product

(GNP), the military expenditure and the manufacturing product. After the disintegration of the Soviet Union, two other power centres—the Eurcpean Union and Japan have come to the forefront. China is a superpower in the making. Russia has begun to reassert itself. India has the potential of becoming a major power. Thus in the emerging multipolar world, the concept of a hegemonic power or a leading power will undergo changes. Let us look at this concept from another angle.

The United Kingdom was never, even at its peak in the nineteenth century, the dominant power as measured by either GNP or military expenditures. The wealth provided by its industrial strength was always overwhelmed in GNP terms by the demographic base of its sometimes less wealthy but more populous chief competitors; its military expenditures were always markedly below those of one or more of its continental rivals. Only in manufacturing production, and for that matter only rather briefly, did it lead the world. (For purposes of this analysis, however, we probably should discount the surprising manufacturing capacities of China and India since they were hardly great powers in the world system.) These data should encourage only a cautious interpretation of Britain's hegemonic status during this era. Britain's commercial power (which would be reflected in trade or financial indicators) was not evident in other important power base indicators. Second, despite slippage since filling the immediate post-World War II void, the United States retains, on all these indicators, a degree of dominance not reached by the United Kingdom at any point of time and comparing well with the US position in 1938. (US military expenditures for 1950, not yet reflecting the Korean war, are artificially low for the cold war period.) The basis of US hegemony may have declined, but it has hardly vanished, according Japanese scholars.

Though the concept of hegemony is being given conflicting interpretions and different factors are attributed for a nation-state to provide hegemony, one cannot deny the fact that in the post-war period, the United States played this role, till its hegemony began to be challenged by the Soviet Union and that too in the military sense alone. After the disintegration of the Soviet Union for nearly one decade, the US again began to play the role of a hegemonic power. In the last years of the present century the hegemonic role of the USA began to shrink economically, militarilly, and politically. Japan's emergence as a economic power should be seen in this context.

It is widely acknowledged that the United States occupied a position of hegemony in the international system immediately after World War II, because its enemies were defeated and its allies exhausted. The productive base of the US economy alone escaped wartime devastation; indeed it was enormously expanded by the war effort. The United States was the world's foremost military power, and it alone had the nuclear weapons. It should be kept in mind that after the World War II, the United States influenced almost 80 per cent of the world, both politically and economically.

Since 1945, there have been no wars between the developed capitalist industrial states. This can be attributed to the spread of advanced industrial capitalism and spread of representative democracy in the world. The two potential explanatory variables are so closely correlated.

It is also relevant to mention that decolonization as an ideology was attractive to Americans; it cost them almost nothing and created enormous economic opportunities. The only American colony was the Philippines. With its then dominant technology and industrial organization, the United States was in position to move into these hitherto closed markets.

Decolonization meant acceleration of the introduction of advanced capitalism into the Third World—and the United States was the most efficient capitalist. The post-war international trade and finance regimes brought world-wide prosperity, not least to the United States.

However, before the demise of the Soviet Union, US predominance vis-a-vis the Soviet Union had gone. US nuclear predominance over all other states remains and is perhaps stronger than ever before. There is little sign that it will erode in the future. Europe seems unable to put together a substantial deterrent of its own. In a nuclear world, US military hegemony over its allies may never end. And that kind of hegemony provides the United States with an advantage for maintaining a degree of hegemony in other areas.

In the economic realm, the structure of a relatively open world economy remains substantially intact. It was in this international environment that Japan surged forward in industrial development.

In the academic circles of Japan in the end of the present Century a serious debate in going on about US-Japan relations in a new era, there are conflicting perceptions about it.

Japan's emergence as an economic superpower, and the accompanying change in the American perception of Japan from that of an economic competitor to an economic challenger of US pre-eminence, has caused the focus of the relationship in the United States to narrow. While Japanese financing of the US federal deficit has been welcomed as a way to prevent the drying-up of private capital markets, public reaction to direct investment in areas such as real estate has been much less receptive, and its role in aggravating many of the broader aspects of the relationship cannot be discounted. Instability on Japan's domestic political stage has served to heighten awareness of issues in the bilateral relationship. However, this unsteadiness has hampered the formulation of policy in Japan and significantly affected US perceptions of Japan's capacity to assist in solving problems facing the relationship. While events in Eastern Europe, the Russia, and China have temporarily shifted the focus away from US-Japan relations, the implications of these events will have a profound effect on the bilateral relationship.

The ongoing debate in Japan has significant implications not only for US-Japan relations, but for economic development and strategic cooperation in several regions of the world. The outcome of the debate seems to revolve around one main point. Given that economic considerations have come to play at least as important a role in the relationship as strategic and military aspects, are Japan's economic objectives mutually compatible or mutually exclusive? The future of the strategic relationship rests on this question. If Japan is in a state of economic warfare, it is hardly conceivable that it can achieve meaningful cooperation on the strategic front at the same time, Japanese scholars argue.

Serious cracks in the foundation of the relationship began to appear early in the present decade as the trade imbalance between the two countries grew. These cracks were further enlarged by the failure of the US trade deficit with Japan to decline following the Plaza agreement, as did the deficit with the EC as a whole. Looking at specific countries in the EC however, we see that the US deficit with Germany, Europe's manufacturing power-house, was virtually unchanged. The fact that Japan's trade surplus with the EC diminished, and that Japan's imports of manufactured goods surged ahead in the latter half of the decade went virtually unnoticed in the United States. This is perhaps due to the fact that Japan's imports of American manufactured goods, while increasing in terms of volume, declined in terms of Japanese market share during the period and were replaced by goods from the EC and the other countries. A factor which seems to have captured more public attention was

America's shift from being the world's largest creditor to become the world's largest debtor—a shift that prompted Senator Daniel Moynihan to note that this decade may well be remembered as the period when the United States borrowed a trillion dollars from Japan. The US government's limited effectiveness in dealing with the federal budget deficit, a major cause of the country's shift to debtor status, was partially masked by shifting emphasis to the trade deficit.

Concern in America over whether the country could protect its strategic interests in light of waning economic strength brought under consideration not only policy options for revitalizing the economy but the wisdom of some of Japan's current strategic commitments. The finding of several studies in Japan that the country's defensive capabilities were being weakened by declining dominance in key strategic industries and increasing dependence on foreign produced components, specifically on Japanese electronics, enhanced the significance of these considerations. The furore in Congress over the sale of milling technology by Japanese and Norwegian companies to the erstwhile Soviets, compounded by bickering over the FSX agreement, has caused doubts on both sides of the Pacific.

American companies, which had traditionally been competitive in the global market-place and on the leading edge of technological innovation, reeled from the effects of the deep recession of the early 1980s and the ensuing period of high-cost capital and the overvalued dollar. Moreover, pressure of certain circles in the United States kept constant pressure on immediate returns ahead of long-term investment strategies in the minds of many business planners. Conversely, Japanese firms, unburdened by the need to produce consistent quarterly returns and increasingly awash with cash, surged ahead in many of the most promising future industries. Major advances in Japanese technology also began to challenge the notion that most Americans held of the United States as the world's unquestioned technological leader.

The role that Japanese direct investment in the United States, has played in shaping public opinion about the relationship may in fact be more important than any other issue that has been raised so far. Moreover, the issue appears couched in far more alarmist tones, than, say, the large scale Japanese financing of the US federal deficit.

Although, and no doubt partly because, every Japanese administration since Prime Minister Yoshida had used gaiatsu—foreign pressure— to force the resolution of difficult domestic issues, popular resentment of unrelenting foreign pressure, especially from the United States, became increasingly strong. At the same time it became apparent to more and more policy makers in America that the only way to gain concessions from Japan was to apply unswerving pressure.

The Japanese also began to question openly whether the real cause of most of America's economic difficulties did not indeed rest with American policies, and were not thus the responsibility of the United States itself to remedy. A growing sense of pride for Japanese accomplishments did not harmonize well with increasingly virulent criticism from America. The unwillingness of the Japanese to accept full blame for the economic imbalances that exist between the two nations is seen as but another sign of stubbornness by some American observers.

Developments outside the bilateral relationship have had a direct impact on both nations, perceptions of threats and opportunities for the decade ahead. What began as a decade of cold-warriors and large defence build-ups against the threat of the Evil Empire has seen the ratification of the first major arms reduction treaty, the opening of the Berlin wall, and the assertion of the right to self government by the nations of Eastern Europe. The march of the EC towards its goal of market unification in 1992 is continuing unabated, which raises concerns over increased economic competition and the development of closed trading blocks. Moreover, the emergence of the Newly Industrialised Countries of Asia with their emphasis on export trade, has further underscored the growing importance that economic vitality will act as the measure of national strength in the decade to follow.

The chronology of events mentioned above is a limited sampling of the factors that have played a role in shaping the current debate over the future of US-Japan relations. From this debate there have emerged several rather distinct factions within the United States, each holding significantly different views of how the relationship should be pursued. There are, of course, differences within each of the factions and no one member may subscribe to all of the ideas that the faction espouses. The ultimate outcome of the debate yet to be resolved, will set the course of future US-Japan relations for better or for the worse.

An active debate over the future of the relationship between the world's two greatest economic powers is healthy, but the trench warfare arising from the current debate is not. Character assassination has become a standard strategy for overcoming the enemy, especially when his arguments are logically sound and supported by an arsenal of evidence. It is important to remember that much of the debate in both the countries, especially the one going on in America is designed mainly for domestic consumption. Many Americans are, in a sense, using Japan as a tool to evaluate and criticize domestic policies. Ironically, all but the most sensational points of the debate seem to garner more attention in Japan than in the America, and are interpreted there as Japan bashing. Although there are no doubt elements of bashing entering into the debate, this does not appear to be the main intent. It is actually an indigenous form of gaiatsu—a unique American form of self imposed foreign pressure aimed at addressing weak points in American policy rather than the unfair points of Japanese. If the debate over the future of the relationship becomes hostage to political grand standing, as the current tenor of the arguments on both sides of the Pacific portrays, both countries will suffer considerably from its inevitable fallout. This is how some Japanese scholars such as Prof. Brent Boultinghouse look at the problem.

In Japan, the tone of the debate is also becoming sharper. This reflects not only the turmoil on the political front, but also changing opinions about the traditional bilateral relationship and the effects of Japan's accession to economic superpower status. Japan's emergence as a technological powerhouse and the rapid expansion of the domestic market combined with the growing realization that America faces many serious economic difficulties domestically have led many to believe that the country is not as dependent on the United States as was once the case. The furore occasioned by Mr. Shintaro Ishihara's remarks to the effect that Japan should consider using technological blackmail against the United States was justifiable to most Americans. The more important point that many in Japan have also tired of the paternalistic nature of the traditional relationship, received much less notice .

Both countries are, in fact, undergoing a crisis in their perceptions of inter-dependence. For Japan, the time of junior partnership is over. For some Japanese this is a welcome change, but at the same time many are happy with the current role of Japan in the bilateral relationship and hold little desire to change Japan's responsibilities. For America, the era of forming policy unilaterally has also passed. Likewise, many Americans are unhappy with this changing role. Some in America seem to be taking a giant leap from policy independence to policy dependence, completely missing the fact that the global economy has in fact simply reached a level of interdependence in which all players are more or less interdependent. American economic well-being is more closely linked to the health of the global economy than at any other time in post-war era. This will require policy coordination on a scale heretofore unseen.

US-Japan relations have reached a watershed, a point from which their future course may shift from the alliance that has lasted since the end of the Pacific War. In America, there has been a recent polarization of Japan specialists, journalists, congressmen and government officials into two groups—one protective of and the other antagonistic towards Japan. Those engaging in lobbying on behalf of Japan in Washington become the object of ridicule for selling America out to Japan by a group that has been described as new McCarthyites. Japanese views of the relationship are in an unsettled state, a situation that is complicated by the recent decline in political leadership and the ensuing difficulties in forming a consensus among the Japanese, according to Prof. Reizo Utagawa.

In recent years, Japanese perspectives on America do not fall nicely into distinct favourable and unfavourable groups. In the 1960 debate over the extension of the US-Japan mutual security treaty, lines were clearly drawn between yes and no factions. However, the last forty years have witnessed Japan's emergence as an economic superpower causing increased friction in US-Japan economic relations, as well as a dramatic reduction in East-West tensions which has ended the traditional bipolar global structure. These events have greatly complicated Japanese perspectives on US-Japan relations. A pattern of saying 'yes' to the US on some issues, but saying 'no' on others has emerged as has a pattern of agreeing that the overall relationship is extremely important and at the same time refusing to cooperate on specific issues, reflecting a disintegration of consensus.

It is in this context that the relations between the two economic superpowers, the United States and Japan, assume greater significance. Together, the two nations account for roughly one-third of the global gross national product (GNP) and their capital markets provide over two-third of the total world stock market capitalisation. Their bilateral trade and financial flows are the largest and most intense transoceanic flows ever, and management of resulting imbalances that render the United

States the world's largest debtor and Japan simultaneously the most substantial global creditor have consequences far beyond the borders of these two economic super powers.

Hit by the worst ever recession since the Great Depression in the early thirties and unable to bring the twin deficits of current account and trade under control, the conservative elements in the US seem to be finding a responsive chord from the middle class Americans centered around the theme of 'America First'. This calls for a more inward looking America and taking stern action against those countries that act against American interests. From President Bush to the present administration of President Bill Clinton, the American policy is under growing pressure of the middle class which is more concerned about recession and unemployment.

The readily available target is Japan which is held responsible for the American recession. It is perplexing to accuse the Japanese for unemployment in the US because the American manufacturing industry is losing out in the competition with the Japanese. There have been broad structural changes in the patterns of employment generation at the global level which are more pronounced in the developed countries. For instance, though manufacturing is still the most dynamic force in the economic activity more and more jobs are becoming available in the services sector than in industry or manufacturing.

Though in Japan the role and contribution of the service sector is gradually increasing, it is not as much as that in the United States. Japan's advantage vis-a-vis the United States lies in the relocation of labour-intensive industries to the North-East and South-East Asian countries in a systematic manner starting from the early seventies. It is a continuous process.

Japanese scholars have pointed out that opinion polls in the USA clearly show a steady and marked increase in the number of people who considered Japan as the long term threat—more-threatening than the erstwhile Soviet Union—much before the demise of the Communist regimes in Eastern Europe and the Soviet Union. The following points, for instance, were cited as demonstrating Japan's growing clout as a financial power: (i) The United States government relies on Japanese investors to finance upto 30 per cent of its deficit; (ii) All of the world's 10 largest banks ranked by deposits are Japanese; (iii) The market capitalisation of all the shares on the Tokyo Stock Exchange surpassed the market capitalisation of all the shares on the New York Stock Exchange in early 1987; (iv) Japanese banks control nearly 10 per cent of US retail banking assets: (v) Japanese investors have bought about 18 billion dollars worth of prime US real estate between 1985 and 1988. These facts are mind-boggling.

According to some estimates, if the Japanese economy grows with same present vigour, by the year 2020 it might even overtake the US to become world's largest economy. Given Japan's strides in emerging technologies, it may not be very difficult to translate its economic might into military prowess in a short times.

By the end of the last decade, Japan's aggregate stake in the US economy reached about US dollar 300 billion. Japan's willingness to finance American deficits by its savings is mostly because of political reasons rather than to keep the critical market of the United States, for the contribution of trade to Japan's GNP is at around 15 per cent, slightly less than that of the United States and far less than that of either Germany or Britain. Japan has also been supplying nearly one-fourth of all funds flowing into the developing countries, the chunk of the share being cornered by the American strategic allies.

From whatever angle you look at the US-Japan relations at the end of the 20th century, one conclusion is that from being a junior partner of the United States, Japan has already become an equal partner and with passage of time, it looks set to overtake the United States in the pace of economic development. This trend has a far-reaching significance in a period of globalisation of economy and technological revolution and that too in a period when the global centre of gravity has already shifted to the Asia-Pacific region. The dominant thinking among the Japanese scholars is that US-Japan relations have already undergone a fundamental change. These relations cannot be objectively assessed with old parameters. Some of the Japanese experts think that the causes for deterioration of the relations between the two countries can be found in the deepening inter-dependence and globalisation of the economy. Inter-dependence between the two nations, one which till recently was the dominant economic power and its weightage in the world economy increased after the disintegration of the Soviet Union and the other, that is Japan, which is on the threshold of becoming an economic superpower, if it has not already crossed that limit, will be of far reaching importance. The old theory of hegemony has become outdated. The American ruling elite, however, has yet to shed its old moorings. Multipolarity in economic relations based on balance of interests perhaps may born out of this US-Japan friction or clash of economic interests.

Japan in the 1990s has been taking an independent stand on vital economic issues. To take one example, Japan has pushed a sluggish domestic economy to a soaring current account surplus in Japanese trade with the United States in 1997-98. This has led to a renewed trade war between the two countries.

Tokyo's current account surplus rose by over 77 per cent in August 1997, from a year earlier. Japanese Government officials, however, said that domestic demand was expected to revive in the coming period thereby cutting down reliance on exports.

The surplus in merchandise trade alone rose by 68 per cent to 912.6 billion yen (7.60 billion dollars) in August 1997, according to a Japanese economists. The surplus is expanding due to an increase in Japan's consumption tax, and brisk economies abroad. However, economists have warned the consistently soaring trade account surplus could provoke the United States to put pressure on Tokyo to take additional financial measures to stimulate domestic demand while curbing reliance on exports to hold up the sluggish economy.

In August, 1997, Japan's exports rose 13.8 per cent from a year earlier with cars and semiconductor exports leading the way. Imports, however, rose only by 3.4 per cent. Japan has ruled out an increase of fiscal spending to boost domestic demand saying a new spending package would run counter to the government's efforts to cut down the nation's fiscal deficit.

The USA is putting pressure on Japan to boost its internal consumption and open up imports to restrict the soaring current account surplus.

Japanese analysts in Tokyo were of the view that the current account surplus would continue as long as Japan's home economy remained sluggish and the yen stayed weaker against the dollar, pushing up exports. This shows how new frictions are developing between the US and Japan.

8

Character of Japanese Middle Class

Japan's emergence as a super economic power in the end of the 20th century is now admitted even by the top economists of the United States. However, what needs an objective study is: how Japan has emerged as a super economic power and why China too is fast moving in the same direction? It will be unscientific to draw a mechanical parallel between the experiment of industrialisation in these two countries. However, it will be equally wrong to make a concrete study of these developments, keeping in mind the specific features of this experiment both in Japan and China.

Nevertheless, it is pertinent to mention here that both in Japan and China, a conscious and deliberate policy has been followed to stop the brain drain. Japan has evolved a system in which Japanese scholars, scientists and technocrats prefer to work in their own country, rather than settling abroad. Those who go abroad, to the United States in particular, after improving their skills and gaining knowledge generally come back home. Till recently, migration of Chinese technocrats and small scale industrialists were a common feature. These trends now have been reversed in China. As a matter of fact investments of Chinese settled abroad to mainland China is one of the biggest factors which has led to a high rate of foreign investments in the country. This stands in a complete contrast to India. Despite euphoria about economic reforms by the Indian political elite, irrespective of its ideological affiliation, this aspect has been relegated to the background. A comparative study of the election manifesto of the various parties of 1998 mid-term poll on this specific point clearly confirms this. At present nearly one million Indians are working in the United States and sons and daughters of the political elite and outstanding Indian intellectuals, civil servants are important component of this Indian intelligentsia working in the United States. Why this brain drain is taking place in India and not in two other major Asian countries *i.e.*, Japan and China? The answer to this question is to be found in the system.

The Indians who migrated to developed countries did not get job satisfaction and career promotion opportunities in their own country. The problem is further aggravated by the high standard of living available to them in other countries.

Quite apart from these factors, prolonged domination of British colonial system, perhaps weakened the roots of the Indian educated middle class from the soil of their own motherland. Consciously or unconsciously, they look up to the Western models and electronic media has further reinforced this trend.

This aspect is being highlighted to underline how the middle class in the Japanese model of industrialisation has played an important role. We have already discussed earlier, how Japan has made systematic changes, both in its educational system and periodical training of workers at every level. Quite apart from security of service, the prospects of promotion through periodical training, give the workers and middle classes a sense of commitment to production and productive forces. This needs to be examined more deeply because it will have direct bearing on making, for instance, Indian public sectors more productive.

Let us now examine how the middle class in Japan has played a very significant role in country's industrial development.

The development of modern industrial society of Japan has been analysed earlier. What stands out is that Japan has utilised the whole arsenal of means accumulated by its society in order to smooth over the conflict between the enormously grown productive forces and the nature of private ownership of social relations, as well as to prevent political destabilisation and social upheavals. From all available indicators, it appears that traditional conflict between labour and the capitalist does not appear with intensity. To say this does not mean that trade union movement and Left-wing political trends in Japan are weak. The role which Japan Socialist Party plays clearly reflects this. Japan's Communist Party polls nearly 10 per cent votes. Therefore the trend should be examined with an open mind.

One of the most widespread theories of classless society in modern Japan is the concept of middle class, new middle strata, and so on.

Objective shifts in the class structure of society and a certain improvement in the financial position of the working people should not be ignored.

Japanese scholars engaged in the studies of middle class problem maintain that a mass and homogeneous stratum of middle class society has its own social and economic implications. Though there is no unanimity among social scientists of Japan about class conflict, and the existing criteria are vague, it is possible to distinguish several of the most frequently met indicators of a belonging to the middle class. Among these are the status of wage-and-salary earner, inconstancy of social status, the rather high incomes received by the representatives of the middle class which guarantee them equal access to material benefits and finally people's subjective appraisals of their social and financial positions. In other words, the middle class in the interpretation of Japanese scholars, is a certain intermediate community uniting people according to the above mentioned indications. Thus, one of the zealous advocates of the middle class theory, Prof. K. Tominaga of Tokyo University maintains that the middle class is a community of wage-earners or people without any permanent social status. According to him the overwhelming majority of Japanese society belongs to this strata.

On the other hand, there are other scholars who point out that this concept is based on a subjective interpretation of the post-war changes taking place in the class structure of Japanese society. It may be interesting to compare the conclusion of Tominaga, with the stand of Japanese specialists who adhere to the analysis of the class structure of modern capitalist society. The estimates of the latter, based on the results of national population censuses throw light, both on the class structure of Japanese society and on the nature of shifts taking place in it in the post-war period.

The serious changes taking place today in the economic and political life of Japan, over and above all the scientific and technological progress and the increasing domination of upper crust of industrialists, cannot but affect the structure of Japanese society. The expansion of the boundaries and the numerical growth of the working class are the most important changes, which have taken place in Japan.

According to some researchers, the numerical strength of the Japanese working class increased from 13,888,000 in 1950 to 38,009,000 in 1980, that is from 38.3 per cent to 66.6 per cent respectively of the able-bodied population. The explanation is that at the early stages of industrial development the overwhelming majority of wage-and-salary earners consisted of workers engaged in physical work in the sphere of material production, the so-called blue collars, whereas in modern Japanese society the working class incorporated an ever increasing army of wage-and-salary earners engaged in intellectual work, the so-called white collars. In 1950 there were 7,267,000 production workers, or 20 per cent of the able-bodied population, while 1,552,000 people or 4.3 per cent were engaged in unproductive labour. The figures for 1980 were 16,267,000 or 28.5 per cent and 7,056,000 or 12.4 per cent respectively. The percentage of white-collar workers among middle strata is simultaneously increasing. Although the industrialists grew in absolute figures, from 681,00 in 1950 to 2,701,000 in 1980, they constituted, as previously, an infinitesimal section of the country's able-bodied population—4.7 per cent in 1980. These objective changes taking place in the structure of modern Japanese society are very significant. The steep increase in the number of white-collared workers in the 1990s has changed the social structure of Japan and it has become a productive force in Japan.

This is a specific feature of Japan's socio-economic structure though no comparative study has been made in this regard with other developed societies. In pre-war Japan, a person with high income usually had a high social status, whereas in modern society such inter-dependence has been broken.

It has another dimension also. In pre-war Japan a person with high income usually had a high social status. But now the situation has changed. A judge, a state official and a university lecturer are people whose social status is traditionally considered to be prestigious. However, before World War II the representatives of these professions simultaneously boasted of high income whereas in modern society they have become financially far less well-off than the representatives of such traditionally unprestigious trades as proprietors of small-scale enterprises or retail shops. This phenomenon eliminates the difference between representatives of prestigious and unprestigious categories. This has its social consequences. The phenomenon of non-coincidence of a person's income with his social status can be explained more simply and comprehensively if it is subjected to analysis. Scientific and technological advancement and the development of industries in the Japanese economy which gave rise to such branches as radio electronics, robotics, biotechnology and mecatronics, greatly enhanced the demand for skilled brainworkers, while the profound changes in management required more administrative personnel. The profession which used to be the prerogative of the representatives of middle strata for example those of a judge, state official and university lecturer have become commonplace. The work of the bulk of intellectuals, employees, professionals and technical specialists though has a special position in productive forces; they are brain-workers, even though highly-skilled.

About their economic standing they have come closer to the working class as regards living and working conditions. Therefore, if formerly quite a number of brain-workers were a part of the middle strata and, consequently, had their own business, in modern society intellectuals usually constitute a part of the working class and are compelled to sell their labour in order to earn their living, according to another Japanese school of thought.

From this viewpoint, it is interesting to compare the dynamics of changes in the number and percentage of wage-and-salary earners belonging to the working class and to the middle strata. Between 1950 and 1980 the category belonging to the middle strata of the population more than doubled but constituted only 1.4 per cent of the able-bodied population. At the same time, the category belonging to the working class, grew more than three-fold during this period, reaching almost a quarter of the entire able-bodied population (23.2 per cent). In other words, today the bulk of brain-workers—representatives of prestigious professions are not the part of middle strata but of the workers whose number is steadily growing owing to an intensive process of class differentiation observed also among brain-workers, these scholars argue.

Thus, an attempt to explain the phenomenon of non-coincidence of income with the status of a worker by a certain democratisation of the system of criteria, offer new approaches to this phenomenon, and to conclude on this basis that the existence in Japanese society, of an intermediate community of wage-and-salary earners or holders of a changeable social status, is quite arbitrary. It is based on subjective approach and only confuses the matter. Several Japanese social scientists have vividly described this fact.

Regarding the inconstancy of social status phenomenon as important in principle for analysing the structure of modern society, some scholars think that its emergence shows the untenability, of the theory which interprets too narrowly the modern capitalist society as based on antagonistic contradiction between the industrialistic and the working class. In other words, they maintain, that the rise in Japan of an intermediate community means an obliteration of society's class structures, or at least a tendency towards the creation of a homogeneous society in which the worker and the manager of a major corporation are wage-earners, that is, have equal opportunities.

The idea of replacing the class structure of modern Japanese society by a unified intermediate community is shared by Prof. Y. Murakami of the Tokyo University, a leading advocate of the middle class theory. In an attempt to substantiate this theory Y. Murakami, like K. Tominaga, proceeds from the thesis on the untenability of the theory of capitalist society.

These two conflicting theories, equating brain-workers with industrial workers are being hotly debated in the academic circles of Japan. Nevertheless, in modern Japan white-collared workers are playing a significant role in industrialisation. The existence of a certain managerial elite which come from the middle class and whole representatives automatically turn into ordinary workers, being deprived of their managerial elite is understood as a group of people running the country, a corporation an enterprise, etc., then, it is perfectly obvious that even having been deprived of their managerial functions, they continue to act as representatives of the powers that be. Besides the acknowledgment that a managerial elite in modern society has emerged clearly brings out the role of a new middle strata. Many Japanese scholars of oppose the replacement of the concept of the class structure of the modern society with the theory of an intermediate community or a homogeneous middle class.

Prof. S. Kishimoto, of the Yokohama University, maintains that in reality there exists only a middle class which occupies an intermediate position between the two diametrically opposed classes—industrialists and workers. According to him, less than 10 per cent of the country's entire population belongs to such conventional middle class. He stresses that only those living on the terms of their own business, that is, those possessing capital, can be attributed to a middle class proper or to be more exact, to the middle strata of the population.

The middle class theory in Japanese sociology does not, however, boil down to understanding it only as a concept of intermediate community of wage-and-salary earners, or people of changeable social status. This theory takes not only the social status and class, but also economic aspect into consideration. Its advocates are trying to create an illusion of the rise of a certain consumer community in Japan whose living standard is high enough to ensure them equal participation in the distribution of material wealth. The origin of such a consumer community is being associated by Japanese scholar with—considerable improvement in living standards as a result of high economic growth rates.

In Y. Murakami's opinion, this issue manifests itself in a considerable narrowing up of the gap in the incomes of different classes and social groups, improvement of the social security system, overall growth of educational levels, general availability of consumer durables etc. He maintains that all this indicates to the existence of a middle class which is highly homogeneous in its ways and styles of life.

Indeed, the rapid development of the Japanese economy in the past three decades, the period of the so-called economic miracle characterised by unprecedently high economic growth rate could not but bring about a certain improvement in workers' standard of living. This manifested itself in the growth of incomes, higher levels of the consumption of durables and services, improvement of leisure and recreational activities and higher educational level of workers.

According to official statistics, the nominal annual income of workers and employees increased from 59,557 yen in 1965 to 359,353 yen in 1984 per family. But this fact alone does not yet mean that a considerable reduction of difference in the incomes of various strata of the population is taking place in the country.

According to research conducted by some other scholars, despite a certain reduction of difference in incomes, personal savings, consumption of durables, etc. among various categories of Japanese wage-earners families, the overall size of the gap in all the above-mentioned parameters remain enormous. It must also be borne in mind that no matter how high the workers incomes or consumption level of durables may grow they are the result of workers personal labour inputs, whereas a small section of the population, which wields, the means of production and capital, appropriates the labour of the former. Noteworthy in this connection is the viewpoint of Japanese economist M. Ozawa, who examines the middle class issue in close interrelationship with the problem of personal consumption. From her well founded viewpoint, in the late 1970s and early 1980s when as a result of skyrocketing prices, real income growth rates considerably slowed down, the main factor affecting the purchasing capacity of consumers was capital and not income as it was the case in the 1960s. On the basis of official statistics showing that a considerable gap between income and capital still remains among various social groups of the population of modern Japan, she draws the conclusion that assertions of the existence of middle class in Japan are unfounded. In Ozawa's opinion two diametrically opposed poles exist in the country-owners of capital who consume top quality goods, on the one hand, and those who live on personal incomes and are compelled to be content with low-quality goods, on the other. Therefore, she believes, the existence of middle class is an illusion.

The attempts by some Japanese scholars to substantiate the emergence of a unified and homogeneous intermediate consumer community, proceeding from their thesis on a considerable rise of living standards actually ignoring such a major factor as the ways of earning income, are in the final analysis seen as nothing but an attempt to conceal property inequality and, subsequently, any class differences in an industrial society. It is also wrong to conclude that there exists an intermediate community, taking as a basis such phenomenon as general availability of consumer goods and services, higher educational level of the population and improvement of the social security system. Whatever successes might be achieved in these spheres, they cannot conceal that inequality still exists and is growing in Japan.

Besides, even the existing improvement in workers living standards does not correspondent to the present stage of the country's progress and the development level of productive forces. Describing the living conditions of the Japanese today Prof. S. Kishimoto notes that among the persons who rank themselves among the middle class many receive low income, are burdened with debts and do not have normal housing conditions. In such leading newspapers as Asahi and Mainichi one can read the following reports: Ninety per cent of the entire population consider themselves as belonging to the middle class.... but their standard of living is infinitely far from it. Thus 20 per cent of all those who regarded themselves as middle class are compelled to work overtime in order to support their families. The wives of 40 per cent of such people work. Sixty three per cent have to settle loans for the construction of their own houses.

Then how can we talk about a unified intermediate consumer community or equal access to material benefits? Yet according to official statistics from 80 to 90 per cent of Japanese rank themselves among the middle class.

The situation is explained by the peculiar psychology of a middle Japanese. Typical for the overwhelming majority of the Japanese is a superficial and subjective appraisal of their social and financial position. They strive too hard to be like all others in everything, not to stand out against the general standard and so on. Naturally, this cannot but back the middle class concept. At the same time it is obvious that the subjective realisation of belonging to the middle class and objective existence of such a class are utterly different categories. Thus according to sociologist M. Naoi, the subjective ranking of the Japanese among the middle class and objective existence of this class is far from being one and the same thing. Using the results of the national population census in 1975, she comes to the conclusion that a large section of the population which think, they belong to the upper stratum of the middle class and those believing to belong to its lower stratum (49.7 and 3.8 per cent) at the same time rank themselves among the working class and not among the middle strata or capitalists. Nevertheless the fact is that during official polls the overwhelming majority of Japanese working people, owing to their subjective desire to look like all others, rank themselves among the middle class. Many rank-and-file Japanese, inexperienced in the subteleties of political economy, rarely think of their attitude towards the means of production or the ways of earning icome. They believe that if their life has become better than before and is at first sight, just as good as that of their neighbours then they are part of the middle class. Sometimes an ordinary Japanese does not see the difference between the notions middle class and middle strata. Therefore, assessing his standard of living subjectively, he ranks himself among a certain middle class. According to sociologist K. Kusaka, many Japanese count themselves among the middle class as they believe that they meet purely outward signs of belonging to the middle strata of the population, higher education, private car, a rather big, at first sight income, and so on. The idea of turning the entire Japanese people into a well-to-do middle class was reflected in the programmatic documents of the ruling Liberal-Democratic Party of Japan (LDP).

In the midst of this controversy in the academic and political circles of Japan about the characteristics of the middle class, what clearly stands out is that in terms of socio-economic structure, Japanese society has already undergone a major change. Where does the Japanese middle class stand? What is the role of the white-collared workers? What is the perception of the intelligentsia of Japan about these changes? Above all, where does the new managerial class stands in the different layers of the Japanese society? All these are relevant questions and have been investigated by scholars, economists and social scientists. However, these do not fall in the realm of this study, which is mainly devoted to the socio-economic factors, which have led to the emergence of Japan as a super economic power. Nonetheless, the answers to these questions are moulding the politics of this country and thereof the changes in the co-relation of political forces is taking place rapidly. If one leaves aside the controversy about the nature of the middle class in Japan, it has to be admitted that if this middle class made a major contribution in the economic development of Japan and now is increasing in numbers, in the coming decades in stimulating both the technological and industrial revolution, this strata of Japanese population will become a strategic factor. In the final analysis, the fate of both these revolutions, which are intertwined, scientists, technocrafts, skilled and semi-skilled workers would play a crucial role. This clearly stands out by an objective study of Japan's industrial development.

The development of high technologies on the basis of national fundamental research calls for centralised state management, more state allocations for R&D, and a greater role for the state in the exploration of sources of financing. But the calls made at different levels in Japan for increasing the state's share in R&D expenses have not met with tangible response, according to industrialists. Japanese science and technology continue to develop, chiefly, thanks to the private sector's financial and manpower resources. However, strategy of Japanese private industrial companies and the activity of universities are substantially changing in the new conditions which necessitate reliance on national fundamental research.

Along with governmental institutions, Japanese private companies have, in recent years, been also intensifying fundamental research into the development of various high technologies. For this purpose, many companies open laboratories, institutes, and even research centres. This process was pioneered by electro-technical companies. Quite a number of research institutions were established in Japan's electro-technical industry in the early 1980s. At that time Mitsubishi Denki opened nine research laboratories and Nippon Denki comissioned six.

Companies operating in the food, textile, chemical, pharmaceutical and other traditional Japanese industries also decided to open new research laboratories and provide them with the latest equipment and high-flight researchers. To enliven their business activity they launched research, often involving financial risks into ultramodern technologies.

Biotechnology is today one of the most attractive spheres for private investments. For instance, Mitsubishi Kagaku Kogyo, Asahi Kagaku Kogyo, Ajinomoto, and other companies earmark vast resources for fundamental research with the view of boosting the production of artificial proteins and new medicinal preparations.

In early 1987, Ajinomoto and Kirin Brewery set up new fundamental research centres. Kyowo Hakko, a major manufacturer of alcoholic liquors, amino-acids, condiments, and petrochemical products also conducts large-scale research in a number of biotechnological fields. In 1986 the company allocated 13 billion yen for biotechnology projects. These projects include the output of interferons and fish-raising hormones by genetic engineering methods. In one of his interviews, the director-general of the company's research programmes said that work on these projects would continue though, in his view, not all programmes would be implemented with equal success.

Most of the pharmaceutical companies expenditures on research programmes are rapidly growing. In 1987 Daiichi Seiyaku, Chugai, and Yamanouchi increased their research allocations by 10 per cent or more compared with the previous year. They also plan to spend more to expand the existing research laboratories and to set up new ones.

Sankyo, Ono Pharmaceutical, Green Cross, Sumitomo Pharmaceutical and Santori are also actively developing fundamental research in the sphere of biotechnology. Santori, a well-known manufacturer of alcoholic liquors, added pharmaceutical to its activities and in the spring of 1988 opened a fundamental medical research centre in Chiyoda. Morinaga Milk allocated 10 billion yen for the construction of an institute in Zama (Kanagawa Prefecture) so as to transfer its food and biological laboratories there to ensure a better organization of biotechnological research. Japan's biggest textile company, Torei Industries, became the leading manufacturer of an interferon used in cancer therapy which shows that this area of research is highly promising. According to the head of the Torei Industries pharmaceutical department, new lines bring the company the greater part of its profits.

A boom in the establishment of new research laboratories also took place in Japan in the 1960s. But those laboratories specialised in applied research. Today, much more attention is devoted to research the results of which may be materialised in marketable products only in ten years and even later. In the 1970s the central laboratory of the Toshiba company devoted over 75 per cent of its research to applied problems and today more than 50 per cent of it has no direct bearing on commercialisation of products.

In the late 1970s and early 1980s Japanese companies increasingly relied on long-term approaches to market competition. Japanese managers consider it necessary to consolidate their companies' position in competition as distinct from American businessmen who try to maximise current money earnings. The term of recoupment at Japanese companies is much longer than that of US firms. Japanese electronic and other companies conduct R&D non-stop and are persistent in attaining their goals. A long preparatory period has ensured the rapid progress of Japanese electronics in the last ten years.

Qualitative shifts are now under way. Having reached a high level in the applied branches, leading Japanese companies can increase allocations for fundamental research. Private sector experts also see the growing difficulties in purchasing new advanced technologies abroad. According to the Nippon Denki President now Japan has no one to emulate in developing technology. Private companies have in recent years accelerated their own fundamental research to rank among the leaders in the most promising hi-tech fields. Japanese private companies now focus on the development of national technology on the basis of fundamental research and not on the improvement of the existing types of imported technology. But rapid progress in new areas of science and technology is making it more and more difficult for industrial companies to keep pace with the times.

Therefore, Japanese industrial companies have to search for ways of cooperation in fundamental research with national and foreign universities. But, unlike in the United States, ties between industrial companies and universities in Japan are rather weak. Traditional distrust of national universities compelled some Japanese companies to make direct investments in R&D in the United States and some other foreign countries. For example, the Massachusetts Institute of Technology annually carries out research work worth 3.5 million dollars under contracts with Japanese companies.

Japanese private companies face acute shortage of skilled research personnel when developing new high technologies. This is especially true of electronics, electrical engineering, mechanical engineering, and bio-technology. In an attempt to solve this problem, some companies send their experts for advanced training abroad, mainly to the United States. As many as 243 Japanese experts worked at the National Institute of Health in the United States in 1984. Italy ranked second (107) and Britain was third (94) in the number of foreign research personnel at that prestigious scientific centre. In only five years the number of Japanese exports at the institute's laboratories increased by 65 per cent.

Many Japanese companies establish and actively develop their research branches in the United States. For instance, Kyosera set up a research centre in Washington with a mixed Japanese-American staff. Sony, Hitachi, and Matsushita Denki also have their laboratories in the United States. According to the Vice-President of the Sony branch in the United States, work on products for the American consumer would have taken much more time and involved higher costs in Tokyo. The development of R&D in their branches in the United States enables Japanese businessmen to collect more information on the latest scientific and technological advances. Direct contact with American companies prevent Japanese corporations from falling behind their American rivals.

Hiring foreign experts is a new practice adopted especially by Japanese medium private companies and ventures. The ventures being set up in Japan, most of them medium-sized, face an acute shortage of skilled personnel since college graduates try to find jobs in major companies.

Several years ago Nippon Software, a leading Japanese software manufacturing company, started hiring Irish specialists who, according to its president, are more skilled than Japanese college graduates. Two dozen foreigners, including four Chinese, are presently working for Nippon Software and form the backbone of the company.

The director-general of the Fujitsu electronics company said in an interview that hiring a group of foreign experts is the company's urgent task. Fujitsu officials sent requests to 25 universities in the United States and Western Europe. In this way Fujitsu bosses intend to stabilise R&D and ensure the company's subsequent prosperity. Managers of Matsushita Denki, Sumitomo Denki, Furukawa Denki, Meiji Milk Products, Honda R&D and some other Japanese companies are also going to break the tradition of hiring laboratories. But the language barrier remains a serious obstacle.

The foreign mass media, particularly American, express growing dissatisfaction with the unilateral benefits allegedly derived by Japan from international scientific and technological cooperation. They urge closer contacts not only with Japanese universities but with research laboratories and centres owned by private firms. So Japanese private companies desiring to hire foreign experts will, probably, meet with active response abroad, especially in the United States.

In Japan foreign technology and equipment have played a tangible role in R&D. While intensifying their own fundamental research, Japanese companies continue importing foreign know-how. Today, they not only sign license agreements but increase direct investments in the research of American and West European private companies. Dozens of Japanese companies have shares in small American firms or conclude agreements on joint research. Such agreements are usually of great help to small Western firms and, at the same time, enable Japanese companies to manufacture and sell their products in international markets.

From 1980 to 1983 Japanese genetic engineering companies alone signed 188 cooperation agreements with small American firms. Many sided contacts between companies are being extended. The bulk of them is made up by licence agreements on the manufacture and sale of products worked out by small American firms. As distinct from their West European counterparts, which conclude agreements on acquisition of foreign firms, Japanese companies preferred to sign contracts on R&D.

In recent years Japanese scientists have been increasingly involved in American R&D under contracts on joint research or under agreements allowing the Japanese independent fundamental and applied research at US universities and laboratories of private companies. American analysts in the field of scientific and technological progress fear that such access to their research may give Japan the upper hand in its competition with the United States. But the flow of scientific and technological information and the derived benefits are not unilateral. Such American companies as IBM and Burroughs establish branches in Japan, and American experts conduct research under contracts at Japanese companies.

Research associations specialising in definite fields have in recent years become quite widespread in the Japanese economy. They are established by private companies and are encouraged by Japanese ministries. These associations function under the law on research associations, which allows joint research without violating the existing anti-trust legislation. New quasi-governmental organisations are also set up under the aegis of leading government bodies to develop R&D in key areas of scientific and technological progress.

These associations proved their efficiency in conducting research and elaborating basic technologies. Experience shows that they are one of the most promising forms of research. But at subsequent stages of research the associations are disbanded and former partners become rivals. This is the state's strategy: government bodies help pool the companies' efforts at the research stage and turn them into rivals at the development and application stage to achieve better results.

Private companies working on new materials and engaged in biotechnology expect fruitful cooperation between their research associations and government bodies, as was the case with the elaboration of computers and very large integrated circuits. But private companies are unhappy with the fact that the greater parts of joint research is appropriated by the state, which enjoys all patent rights. Because of this private companies often decline invitations from government bodies to participate in joint projects.

In view of the accelerated development of new high technologies on the basis of national fundamental research, Japan is restructuring the educational system particularly at the college and university levels. In

1984 a supreme commission on general educational reform was established under the Prime Minister's office. It incorporated academics, industrialists, journalists, teachers and young people.

The system of education in Japan does not meet society's need in creating scientific personnel. As a member of the commission put it, the training of skilled personnel is an urgent problem. In recent years Japanese political leaders and businessmen have voiced growing concern over the country's dependence on foreign science. They agree with the view of foreign observers that Japan is a consumer and not a generator of scientific ideas. The Japanese blamed their universities for such a state of affairs. Many Japanese universities are isolated from the mainstream R&D while their American counterparts are active generators of scientific ideas. This does not refer to some Japanese state universities. But about 80 per cent of students in Japan study at private universities which are not as well equipped as the state universities.

The intensive development of national fundamental research in Japan demands a greater role for universities. Formerly this role mainly boiled down to the training of scientific personnel. But of late, research especially at laboratories and institutes run by universities, has been acquiring growing importance. High-energy physics, geophysics and the latest trends in biology medicine, and genetic engineering feature prominently in fundamental research at universities.

A system of extra subsidies for original research has been approved in Japan to promote progress in this field. A special commission has been set up to select the most promising individuals or collective research works to provide them with additional financing—a research encouraging system has been adopted to attract scientists under 35 and update their skills.

The Japanese press insists on raising state's share in the expenses on R&D, first of all subsidies to university experts who undertake fundamental research.

The Ministry of Education backs R&D at universities as well as fundamental research at specialised state-owned institutes: it allocates funds for specific projects, most of which go to state universities. The Ministry of Education has established three types of subsidies for research: special subsidies for outstanding research, special subsidies for long-term research and subsidies for purpose-oriented projects. The third typed is unusual for Japanese science and makes it possible to bring quite a number of researchers from different institutes to work on a single project. In 1986, for instance, Sezuro Ebashi of the National Institute of Psychology headed 38 scientists from 20 institutes researching into the functions of the vascular system. Allocations for the first year of research totalled 190 million yen. Subsidies for special long-term research now go to four major fields: cancer, natural calamities, the environment energy and thermonuclear fusion. Every year between 500 and 2,000 million yen are earmarked for special research into 100-200 projects in these fields. Though priority spheres are mapped out by the ministry, most projects are approved on scientists recommendations nation wide. Not only researchers but university and college instructors also may take part in these projects.

In the early 1980s Japanese universities started inviting foreign lecturers. However, despite its obvious significance, this practice has not yet become widespread due to rigorous budget limitations.

In recent years US universities, on their part, have increasingly sought to conduct joint fundamental research at integrated centres in Japan. Eight leading American universities intend to establish a research centre in Kyoto. The Massachusetts Institute of Technology and Nihon University are to open in Tokyo an integrated institute of international research into new fields of science and technology. According to Prof. Richard Samuels of the Massachusetts Institute of Technology, American-Japanese links are mainly developing in the sphere of advanced technologies.

Since the early 1980s R&D has been developing on a large scale through the joint efforts of industrial companies, state institutions and universities. The aim of such cooperation is to come out with final products or technological processes for industrial use and also to carry out fundamental research accelerating the accomplishment of practical tasks. In 1982 the Administration on Science and Technology published a report stressing the need to assist private companies in their research by extending the contracts concluded with the state. It also urged universities to play a more active role in the cooperation between private companies and state organisations by elaborating new and strategically important high technologies. In the same year a liason committee was set up to carry out joint comprehensive research by universities and private companies (Sogo Kenkyu Renraku Kaigi). It includes twenty representatives from academic and industrial quarters and defines the subjects trends and organisational principles of R&D.

According to press reports, cooperation between Japanese research and educational institutions and private companies has in recent years been intensifying. Between 1983 and 1986 their joint research programmes increased from 56 to 272. In 1987 Toyama, Kobe and Kumamoto universities set up special centres to take up the orders of private companies. The Japanese Ministry of Education, in turn, revised its stand on relationship between universities and the business world. The universities were allowed to include in their curricula courses partially financed by private companies. This is expected to facilitate the flow of scientific data from universities to industrial companies and ensure the training of students with due regard for private firms' urgent needs. But, despite closer links between higher educational institutions and private companies, the drawing of Japanese universities into major research projects still remains a key task.

The Japanese government hopes that a research centre in Tsukuba, near Tokyo will considerably consolidate national fundamental research. It took more than ten years to construct and was in the main completed by the 1980s. The centre comprises more than 40 research and educational establishments. Here Japanese experts conduct large scale research into high-energy physics, nuclear and space technology, MHB generators, biotechnology, and new materials. Considerable attention is paid to the training of experts from among gifted young people.

The Japanese government intends to use and develop Tsukuba's experience in establishing technopolises in the suburbs of 19 major cities. The idea of technopolises was first advanced by the Ministry of International Trade and Industry in March 1980 in a document titled 'Trade and Industrial Policy' in the 1980s. The Law on Industrial City Development approved in April, 1983 provided for the accelerated development of the region incorporating hi-tech processes. A programme for the development of technopolises in 14 regions (15 Japanese prefectures) was published on the basis of this law in October 1983. The idea is to establish cities that would ensure the simultaneous development of production, science and the social sphere. Technopolicies are aimed at ensuring independent and viable regional economies, at strengthening Japan's technological independence by creating favourable conditions for R&D and hi-tech production and improving the regional distribution of the country's economic potential.

These facts clearly bring out that after having achieved a high-level of technological and industrial development, Japan has embarked on the path of becoming a highly technologically developed country. In fact, by the end of the present century it has touched a new height in technological development. If this trend continues in the beginning of the 21st century Japan, in certain areas of science and technology, may become a leading country. Nonetheless, Japan has become technologically an independent country. During the last two decades a qualitative change has taken place in this area. A country which used to import technology and transform it for mass production, now has become a centre for development of technology independently and that too of a very high quality. This is how Japan has already become one of the most important centres in the world of technological revolution.

9

Economic Relations between China and Japan

With the emergence of Japan as a super economic power its economic relations with the countries of the Asia-Pacific region are undergoing certain basic changes. In the previous chapters we have critically examined the various factors which have contributed to the rapid industrial growth of Japan and its technological revolution. Now let us look how Japan's relations with China are developing. This is of far reaching significance in more than one sense. Undoubtedly China is the biggest nation on our planet, with vast human and material resources. According to all predictions and economic indications, in the beginning of the 21st century, economically, politically and militarially China will become a superpower. Seen in this context, the new direction of economic relations between Japan and China will become a major factor in the new world economic order, which has yet to take shape.

China is today most secure from external military threat and better placed for economic development than at any other time in the last two Centuries. There are no two opinions about it. There is something more to it.

China has access to the best banks, the best technology and the best export markets. It occupies a pivotal position in the United States-Sino-Russian relations. It has better relation with Russia than ever before. In fact, it will be correct to say that Sino-Russian relations are becoming a key factor in the new developing situation in the Asia-Pacific region. On the other hand, the US, on its part, is willing to provide China with some of the most advanced dual-use technology in the world. In the recent past Russia and China have taken a series of steps to ease the situation on their long borders. Sino-Russian borders have become more peaceful than ever before. This has created a most favourable condition for foreign investments in China. There is yet another factor which should be kept in mind in assessing the new thrust of economic relations between China and Japan.

Japanese strategists have always been sceptical about China's ability to modernize its socio-economic structures. They long ago concluded that China's size and inability to make hard choices between partial capitalism, political reforms and centralized socialism would inevitably lead to a political and economic turmoil. But these predictions have gone wrong. China has embarked on the path of economic liberalisation, which has surprised even its most bitter critics. Its theory of "socialist market economy" and "two systems and one state" clearly brings out that China has evolved its own model of regeneration of economy and no more sticks to old dogmas.

The policy makers of Japan perhaps were fast to grasp the real significance of these changes. Japanese policy makers do not hesitate to emphasize that they want a most prosperous China. This explains why Japan's relations with China have been expanding rapidly.

It is relevant to mentioned here that since the 1980s, Japan's foreign direct investments have been showing an upward trend. According to the 'Business Facts and Figures' published by the Japan External Trade Research Organization (JETRO) in 1994, total Japanese Direct Investments abroad were worth 34.1 billion US dollars and net assets abroad were equal to 513.6 billion US dollars, which represented just 1 per cent and 14.6 per cent of Japan's GDP in that years. What is important to note in this connection is that Japanese investments in China have been steadly registering on upward trend. In 1980-82, Japanese investments in China were $ 56 million and in 1992-94, they increase to $ 5326 million. These statistics are startling revelation in themselves. During these 15 years, though there was a period, following the Tiananmen incidents in China when these investments registered a decline.

It is pertinent here to mention that between 1979 to 1990, Hong Kong accounted for 58.5 per cent of foreign investments in China (26480 million dollars), next to it came the United States and Japan. The investments by the US accounted for 9.9 per cent of the total foreign investments and from Japan 8.1 per cent. This implies that in this period the investment made by the US and Japan in China together came to 18 per cent. This is a significant economic indicator, reflecting deep economic interests both of the US and Japan in China. Though some economists have challenged these figures the fact remains that after Hong Kong the largest investments to China came from the US and Japan.

However, the recent trends are more revealing. Of late these investments from Hong Kong, Taiwan and the US to Japan have shown a declining trend. On the other hand the investments from Japan to China have increased. It is for instance, claimed by some economists that Japan's investments to China were in 1993, 0.1 per cent. In 1993 China was the largest recipient of Japanese foreign investments in Asia. However, this does not mean that the direction of Japanese investments in the US and Europe has changed. Till early 1990s Japanese investments in the US and Europe were very high. According to one estimate Japanese investments in the early '90s to the United States were 40.5 per cent and to Europe 20.7 per cent. As against this its investments in China were as low as 5.1 per cent. This fact is being mentioned to bring out that Japan's economic relations with the US and Europe stand on a different footing as compared to China, which is still on a low priority of Japan with regards to foreign investments.

This, however, does not mean that one should ignore the growing tendency in Japan to make investments in China. Quite apart from this aspect one has to take into account the Japanese investments in Hong Kong. This alone will give us a clear picture about Japan's economic interests with China because Hong Kong now is a constituent of the main land China. In fact, both the US and Japan have made huge investments in Hong Kong and China. In the light of such huge investments, one gets a clear picture of the new pattern of economic relationship between these two countries.

In order to get a more exact estimation of Japanese investments in China, one should include Japanese FDI in Hong Kong since after 1997 this island has become a part of China. Since 1970s, Japan has been the second largest overseas investor in Hong Kong. By 1989, the USA had invested 9,290 million Hong Kong dollars or 31.2 per cent of total FDI while Japan had invested 8,642 million Hong Kong dollars or 29.1 per cent of total FDI in Hong Kong which was estimated at 29,734 million Hong Kong dollars. In 1986, the Directory of Japanese Business in Hong

Kong listed 465 branches, subsidiaries of, or joint ventures with, Japanese companies. These included manufacturing units, banks, airlines and leasing companies.

According to another estimate by Prof. Shri Prakash the number of new Japanese companies established in Hong Kong between 1960 and 1979 were 1.63 per annum and between 1980 and 1990 this figure increased to 3.7 per annum. This steep increase by 127 per cent is significant.

Japanese investments in Hong Kong have another aspect. Some of these units are assembling base for final product and others are export oriented. This implies that in the coming period Hong Kong will become an economic link between China and other countries, Japan in particular.

What is noteworthy is that Japanese investments in China are dominated by medium and small business which are more labour intensive and whose main market is often in Japan so that the shorter distance to China is an advantage for them. The big Japanese companies have yet to invest in China on a scale comparable to their investments in North America and Europe.

According to another report, the average amount of Japanese Investment in China in recent years has increased only from US dollars 1.34 million in 1990 to US dollars 1.45 million during January-September, 1992. These figures conceal more than what they reveal. If one goes by the analysis of Japanese economist, he can easily understand this fact that the Japanese Government has focused his attention of these two factors. Firstly, Japan is closely watching the nature of China's new economic policy. Secondly it has yet to watch the results of industries set up in Hong Kong on the markets for its goods.

These changes between Japan and China in the area of economic cooperation have a history behind them. The Kishi cabinet's hostile policy towards China met with growing resentment in Japan in the 1950s. However, some influential figures in various circles were seeking ways to break the stalemate in Sino-Japanese relations. Inejiro Asanuma, Leader of the Japanese Socialist Party, Tanzen Ishibashi, former Prime Minister and Kenzo Matsumura, a renowned political figure, paid successive visits to China in 1959. Chinese leaders stressed that the Japanese government should respect China's sovereignty and not get involved in "two" China theory. This is how Sino-Japanese relations developed and intergovernmental talks were conducted. It was emphasised that China was not against strengthening of Japan-US relationship but it hoped that such a relationship would not hamper Sino-Japanese relations, and that the deadlock in Sino-US relations should not hinder Sino-Japanese friendship either. China also underlined that the wounds in the relations between China and Japan over the past four decades should be healed rather than aggravated.

In June, 1960 when Hayato Ikeda became the Prime Minister of Japan, he said that he would follow an independent policy towards China. Therefore, there was change for the better in Sino-Japanese relations. In August, 1960, Kazuo Sauki, Special Director of the Japan-China Trade Promoting Association, paid a visit to China. To seek greater progress in the relations between the two countries in a new situation, the Chinese side, put forward three principles regarding trade with Japan, namely, promotion of China-Japan trade through three channels: governmental agreements, non-governmental contracts and special consideration for individual cases.

During this period, increasingly active were the exchange and cooperation between China and Japan in such fields as the economy, culture, science and technology. The volume of their two-way trade in 1981 broke through 10 billion dollars, 10 times that of 1972, when the two countries established diplomatic ties. Being roughly one quarter of the total volume of China's foreign trade, this figure put Japan at the top of the Chinese list of foreign trade partners. The total volume of the bilateral trade in 1984 reached 12,728 billion dollars, accounting for 25.5 per cent of the total volume of China's foreign trade, and further went up to 16.44 billion dollars in 1985, 27.3 per cent of the total volume. According to the customs statistics issued by the Japanese Ministry of Finance, the volume of Sino-Japanese trade in 1985 accounted for 6.2 per cent of the total volume of Japan's foreign trade, thus ranking China as second among Japan's trade partners.

The two countries also made progress in the fields of capital cooperation and technology transfer. The Japanese Government furnished its first batch of low-interest government loans to China in 1979, and the second batch came in 1984 which totalled 470 billion yen (about 2.1 billion dollar). The Japanese side agreed in December 1984 to provide the Chinese side with a second batch of loans for energy development to the amount of about 2.4 billion dollars. According to statistics, from 1979 to

1984, Japan only had 57 joint ventures in China with a total investment of 110 billion dollars amounting to 8.5 per cent of the total foreign investment in China. However, in 1985 alone, Japan started 101 Joint ventures in China with a total investment of 220 million dollars, accounting for 7 per cent and 11 per cent of total foreign investment in China in terms of project number and volume. There was also new progress in Sino-Japanese cooperation in the field of offshore oil exploration. The two sides signed five contracts, with an aggregate Japanese investment of US dollar 800 million. With a view to promoting and ensuring smooth growth in economic cooperation between the two countries, the two Governments signed in 1983 the Sino-Japanese treaty on avoidance of double taxation. The ever closer Sino-Japanese economic cooperation was a strong boost to the economic development of each of the two countries, bringing both of them huge benefits.

The traditional friendly contacts between China and Japan enjoyed continued growth, with their cultural interflow and scientific technological and other fields of cooperation becoming ever richer in content and more diversified in form. The two Governments signed an agreement on cooperation in atomic energy in 1985. Non-government personages of the two countries held regular meetings, and sister relationship was established between 93 pairs of provinces and municipalities. In addition, Japan gave China some free aid such as the Sino-Japanese Friendship Hospital.

In the development of Sino-Japanese relations, there were also many problems to be solved. There were problems about China's huge trade deficit with Japan, slow pace of Japanese investments in China and a passive attitude of Japan on technology transfer to China.

Japan should further open its market, and reduce its restrictions by lowering tariffs, increasing import quotas, etc. China suggested to rectify the trade deficit situation. On its part, China agreed to improve the quality of its products so that they may better meet the requirements of the Japanese market. China also hoped that the Japanese side will do more to encourage and promote investment in and technology transfer to China.

China's overall strategy for foreign trade development visualises country's specific policies towards developed countries. In recent years, China's trade with countries such as Japan the United States and Western Europe had developed fairly rapidly. China's trade with other developing countries has developed at a slow pace, though it wants to promote south-south cooperation. It now wants to tap the great potential in importing some primary products from developing countries for processing and export. It wants to export farm products to these countries as well as textile and other light industrial products which can be exchanged for equipment and other goods.

In the past few years, China has purchased a large quantity of cotton and synthetic fibres from the United States. The United States, however, has unreasonably imposed restrictions on textile imports from China violating the principle of reciprocity. China therefore wants to take appropriate counter-measures.

During the sixties and the mid-seventies, China imported technology and equipment from Japan and Western Europe for use in the oil, chemical, metallurgical, mining, electric and precision machine building industries, of which a number of items were purchased on credit extended by the sellers. These imports increased the production capacity of some important sectors of China's economy and filled some gaps in China's industry as well.

In principle, China does not reject foreign capital. But there were times in China, when, with Left ideology holding sway, utilizing loans granted by international financial organizations and governments of other countries and accepting direct investments from abroad were regarded as a forbidden zone in foreign economic relations. During that period China took pride on being a country with neither internal nor external debts. This was in fact a reflection of "Leftism". Especially during the cultural revolution, things were pushed to such extremes that the use of foreign capital was actually labelled as worshipping things foreign and fawning on foreigners a characteristic of the comprador bourgeois ideology. This inevitably led to the practice of binding China hand and foot against making use of foreign funds—a practice which could only produce adverse effects on the country's economic growth.

But strategic change was brought about after the Third Plenary Session of the Eleventh Central Committee of the Communist Party of China. The elimination of the Left idelogy and the initiation of the policy of opening up to the outside world and invigorating the domestic economy have made possible the utilization of foreign capital.

The soundness of this strategic shift is proven by the remarkable success China has had in this field in recent years. China's success is evidenced by its boldness in making use of foreign funds, and its capability to use them in a variety of standard ways.

The first method consists of direct investments made by foreigners in one of the following four ways :

1. Joint Oil exploration

This is a form chiefly used, at present, for prospecting and exploring offshore oil.

Beginning from 1979, the Oil Ministry signed nine agreements successively with 48 oil companies of 13 countries such as the United States, Britain, France and Italy for carrying out geophysical prospecting in the Yellow and South China Seas. In a little more than a year's time, general seismic surveys were completed in these waters and detailed reports submitted. Based on the results of the survey, the China National Offshore Oil Corporation concluded contracts with oil companies of Japan, France and the United States for the prospecting and exploration of oil resources in the Bogai Sea, the Beibu Gulf, Bay of the South China Sea and part of the sea area of Yinggehai. By the end of 1983, China had signed five such contracts, and foreign investment involved amounted to more than one billion US dollars.

2. Joint Ventures

This is a form in which investments are jointly made by enterprises of China and other countries, and profits and risks are shared among partners in proportions to the size of the investments.

To date, 83 joint ventures, of which 35 are in the four special zones in Guangdong and Fujian, have been set up in which the capital contributed by investors from Hong Kong, the United States, Japan, West Germany, Switzerland and some other countries amounts to 140 million US dollars. These enterprises, with foreign investments accounting for a minimum of 25 per cent to a maximum of 40 per cent of the total capital, are distributed in about 15 provinces, municipalities and autonomous regions, and are engaged in various lines—in foreign trade, machine building, electronics, electrical appliances, foodstuffs, pharmaceuticals, textiles and other light industries, food-processing and wood-procession trades, animal-breeding and plant cultivation, tourism and computer and oil-rig services.

Some of the enterprises have already become operational and their products are being sold on the world market.

3. Joint operation (contractual operation)

With the exception of a few firms, which are independent economic entities enjoying the status of corporate bodies, all the enterprises are run jointly by domestic and foreign partners and with the foreign partners cooperation limited only to production and operation. Sites and housing are usually provided by the Chinese side while technical equipment is provided by its foreign counterpart. Profits and other incomes are shared out between them according to the ratios laid down in the contract.

So far, 790 of such enterprises have already been approved by the Chinese government, and the foreign investments involved amount to 700 million US dollars. The majority of these enterprises are in Guangdong Province and many of them are restaurants, residences, or are firms engaging in tourism, fishery, building trade and taxi service. Outstanding examples in this respect are the White Swan Hotel at Guangzhou, the Lido Hotel at Beijing, the China Scientific and Technological Exchange Centre and the Oil Palm Plantation at Chengmai, Hainan Island.

4. Compensation trade

In compensation trade, foreign investment in an enterprise is paid back in direct products or in other products approved by the government.

Contracts have so far been concluded for 869 items, and the value of equipment imported stands somewhere at 700 million US dollars. The Common Rubber Tyre Factory at Guangzhou, and an antimony mine whose equipment is supplied by Romania are both examples of enterprises run under compensation trade contracts.

The second method of the use of foreign capital is for the foreign governments and international financial bodies to provide long and middle-term loans. By the end of 1982, over 30 agreements had been reached in this connection, and the sum of loans had reached around 6 billion US dollars. They include the 1.16 billion dollar energy loan granted by the Japan Import and Export Bank for the exploration of oil and coal; the 529 million dollar loan from the World Bank for teaching facilities for key Chinese universities, for the construction of ports for containerships, and for agricultural development; the 759 million dollar loan granted by the International Monetary Fund under special drawing rights for use in balance of payments. In addition, there were other long-term, low interest loans and donations provided by the governments of Belgium, Kuwait, Denmark, Italy and Australia.

From China's experience of the recent years, we can see that foreign capital has played a positive role in the following respects.

1. The use of foreign capital has speeded up the exploitation of energy resources and the construction of ports and railways.

The area for prospecting of offshore oil opened jointly by China and other countries has reached 420,000 sq.km, and altogether 470 promising oil-bearing structures have been found indicating favourable conditions for future exploration and exploitation. Working in cooperation with Japan and France, China has succeeded in drilling three high-yield oil-gas wells in the Bohai Sea and the Beibu Gulf of the South China Sea. Two harbours (Qunchuangdao and Shijiusuo) are being constructed in China with capital supplied by Japan's Overseas Economic Coordination Fund. On completion of these projects, China will be able to transport 35 million tons of coal every year.

2. The use of foreign capital has provided support to projects whose construction had been suspended or postponed and to enterprises which had been ordered to close down or suspend production. Loans obtained from Japan's Overseas Economic Coordination Fund, the Japan Import and Export Bank and non-governmental sources have made it possible for the first phase of the construction work of the Daqing Petrochemical Factory and the Baoshan Iron and Steel Works to continue. Investments jointly obtained by the China International Trust and Investment Corporation and the Textile Ministry have restarted the construction of the Chemical Fibre Factory at Yizheng, Jiangsu, and the low interest loans granted by Kuwait have given a hand in the completion of the Ningguo Cement Plant of Anhui and the Fertilizer Factory in Urumqi.

3. The use of foreign capital has promoted the technical transformation of small and medium sized enterprises. The import of 36 million US dollars worth of equipment by Shanghai through compensation trade has pushed the technical transformation of textile and other light industries forward with the result that the variety of products has been enlarged, the quality of products improved, labour productivity raised and twenty thousand more people employed. The import of the freezing ferment technology and advanced equipment by the Sino-French Brewery at Tianjin has given an impetus to the innovation of the technology of distilling grape wine in China as a whole.

4. The use of foreign capital has helped raise the level of production management. Through the joint ventures set up in recent years, China has

been able to introduce and learn the production techniques, and operation and management methods of foreign enterprises.

This shows how China's economic relations with the developed countries, with Japan in particular have contributed to the regeneration of the economy of this country. From whatever angle you look the economic relations between China and Japan, including Japanese investments in China and import of technology from it, in the next century will become an important factor. Therefore, the prospects of further economic cooperation between these two countries are bound to grow. This in turn will boost economic development of China. Nevertheless, China is moving forward to become a major player in the economy of the world.

China continued fast growth in foreign trade in 1997, according to state statistics Bureau, total volume of export and import in 1997 reached 325.1 billion US dollars, up by 12.1 per cent over the previous year.

Of the total, the volume of export was 182.7 billion dollars, up 20.9 per cent and that of import was 142.4 billion US dollars, up 2.5 per cent, resulting in a trade surplus of 40.3 billion US dollars.

The import and export by foreign funded enterprises rose by 11.3 per cent. Export of general trade showed strong momentum of growth and its share in total export rose from 41.6 per cent in 1996 to 42.7 per cent in 1997.

The export of processing trade continued to grow fast and the structure of import and export commodities was further improved. The share of mechanical and electrical products in export rose from 31.9 per cent to 32.5 per cent, continually making up the largest category of export commodities.

In terms of import, significant increase was seen in the import of technology intensive merchandise and resources commodities, said the report.

Further progress was made in the development of multimarket strategy for foreign trade. The volume of trade with Africa and with Latin America rose by 24.5 per cent and 40.6 per cent respectively, 12.4 per cent and 28.5 per cent higher than the average growth of foreign trade. The precedence of China in the world with respect to foreign trade rose from the 11th to the 10th, according to the reports.

China scored average annual economic growth of 11 per cent from 1993 to 1997, or 7.3 per cent higher than the world's annual average for the same period, according to official figures. China's social and economic achievement for the year 1997 indicate that it rose to 7th in the world in GDP. The gap between it and the other major developed countries has been narrowed further.

From 1993 to 1996, China stayed in 1st place in cereal grain, cotton, rapeseed, meat, coal, cloth, cement and TV output and ranked high in power, chemical fertilizer, sugar, and crude oil output. It produced 101 million tonnes of steel in 1996, bringing it up to 1st place in the world from No. 2 in 1995.

It did 325 billion dollars worth of foreign trade in 1997, putting it in 10th position in the world. It introduced 64 billion dollars worth of overseas investment, a 64 per cent increase since 1993, putting it in 2nd place after the United States.

China's foreign exchange reserves stood at 139.9 billion dollars by the end of 1997 putting it in 2nd place after Japan. Its Hong Kong special administrative region ranked 7th in foreign exchange reserves in 1996 and 3rd in 1997.

However, it will be simplistic to jump to the conclusion that there are no irritants between Japan and China. China for instance, has expressed its concern over the question of Japan's stand on Taiwan. China has the apprehension that Japan would adhere to its promise of protecting Taiwan under the framework of US-Japanese security alliance.

10

Economic Triangle of US-Japan-China

In the previous chapters we have attempted to analyse how economic relations between the United States and Japan, China and Japan and China and the United States have either undergone certain basic changes or are passing through a new process of change. In this sense, it will not be incorrect to say that in the Asia-Pacific region, a new economic triangle of the US-Japan-China appears to be taking shape. Notwithstanding the fact that economic relationship between these countries cannot be put at par with their relations with each other and these relations have their own specific characteristics and contradictions, in a period of globalisation of economy and when new forms of economic cooperation have begun to shape themselves, it is also a fact of life that in the Asia-Pacific region, this new development cannot be ignored. In fact if this economic triangle of continues to grow and firm up on the basis of economic interests, it will have a far reaching economic significance for this region in the 21st century. Economic experts in all these three countries have begun to critically analyse the likely emergence of this triangle. Any study about the emergence of Japan as an economic superpower will be incomplete without taking into account the emergence of this new trend and how the experts in these countries look at it. That is what has been attempted in this chapter.

Disintegration of the Soviet Union and the changes in East Europe and the end of the Cold War have ushered in profound changes affecting the balance of power in the Asia-Pacific region. This new triangle has already begun to shape up the power equations, including in the economic field. What impact it will have on other countries, especially on Russia and India cannot be predicted at this stage because the relationship in this triangle is still in the formative stage. It is more so because in today's world, economics and politics are more closely interdependent than ever before.

However, what is new in the situation is that the possibility of military conflict among these three countries appear to be remote in the foreseeable future. To say this does not mean that there are no conflicting perceptions among them. For example, the United States and Japan may have common interest on containing the rapid development of China and may thereby coordinate their strategic policies. However, China's rapid rise is fast becoming a reality. Both the United States and Japan have economic interests in China particularly after Hong Kong has become a part of China. Hong Kong is more important for Japan because the economic linkages of Japanese industries with it are very close.

There is yet another aspect of this problem. Both the United States and Japan, sooner or later, perhaps sooner than later will have to depend on the fast emerging Chinese market. Compulsions of their internal economies is already pushing them in this direction. In fact Chinese economists predict that US-Japan conflict will grow in view of fast changing situation in this region.

The United States in an attempt to maintain its hegemony over the world is seeking to turn the Pacific rim into a launching pad to sustain its economic growth. This is why its objective is to transform the Asia Pacific region, a region of the next century, which comes under its economic domination. Japan on the other hand no longer is willing to play the role of a junior partner with its existing economic strengths. In one of the earlier chapters, we have examined the new frictions and conflicts which are developing between the United States and Japan. However, Chinese scholars opine that in view of the economic growth of the Asia Pacific region and its economic potential, these contradictions will sharpen. They do not leave at that.

Both the United States and Japan cannot ignore the pace of economic development in China, particularly the model which the Chinese leaders have evolved for speedy economic growth of their country. Both the United States and Japan have evolved their own strategies to meet this challenge.

The United States in an attempt to maintain its hegemony over the world, seeks to turn the Pacific rim into a pivot for its sustained economic growth. Thus attempts are being made to turn the future Pacific century into a US century. Japan, however, wants to gain the status of a world political power supported by its formidable economic strength. In the estimate of Chinese experts US-Japan alliance will witness new tensions because of emergence of Japan as a super economic power and its expanding economic relations with the countries of Asia Pacific region.

However, both the United States and Japan have a peculiar attitude towards China's rise. On the one hand, they dream about flooding Chinese markets with their products. In fact, they have spared no effort to penetrate the world's potentially largest market. On the other hand, they are reluctant to see China as their competitor. Thus there is a duality of relationship, capture the Chinese market and yet not allow it to become another super economic power. Nevertheless Japan being an Asian power and pragmatic in its economic relations with the countries of this region is likely to be more flexible, if trends of development of Sino-Japan relations are any indication.

Japan and the United States have different agendas. From a strategic view point, the United States still feels the need to check Japan and, for that purpose, uses China's influence. Japan, although sharing the common goal with the United States to contain China, avoids nonetheless, being in the forefront of a confrontation with China and intends to benefit from Sino-US quarrels, some Chinese scholars think.

Quite apart from China, the United States and Japan, there are other countries such as Russia and the Association of South East Asian Nations (ASEAN) which constitute major players in regional security affairs. India, too, has its own position in the region for variety of factors such as its geography, size and population and above all its economic potential.

In the early 1990s, Russia disillusioned with the West, made major adjustments to its once pro-Western foreign policy. The tens of billions of US dollars promised by the West never came and it turned out that the United States treated Russia not as an equal. Even when much-weakened Russia no longer constituted a threat, the US-led West still refuses to loosen its hold on Russia. They are attempting to expand their sphere of influence in almost all the countries around it. These grim realities prompted Moscow to build up ties with Asia as a counter measure against the West. Predictably, with the domestic situation tending to stabilize and the economy recovering, Russia will seek stronger ties with the Far East and the entire Asia at large. However, the main thrust of the Russian foreign and economic policy will remain in handling relations with the Commonwealth of Independent States, Eastern and Central Europe and the West. This implies that Russian-Japan and Sino-Russian economic cooperation will expand.

ASEAN is a regional interest group which is playing the role of a major balancing force in the rivalry between the region's major powers. With rising economic clout, ASEAN is assuming an increasingly important position in Asia.

In making an assessment about changing equation in this triangle, one should also take into account the changes which are taking place in the polity and economics of Japan.

Japan is now in the midst of a new round of great historical changes, purposefully to succeed the Meji Reforms beginning in 1868 and the post-World War II reforms after 1945. On the basis of the political heritages handed down by its predecessors, the Japanese leadership is going all out to promote its programme of reforms in the fields of administration, finance, etc. in an attempt to perform a surgical operation on the nation's structure of 1950 and structure of 1955, on which Japan's post-war economic development and political stability have rested for so long. Aiming at raising Japan's international strategic status, Japan's leadership has also begun to practice Eurasia diplomacy to inject new vitality into the body of the nation at the turn of the century.

It is self-evident that, the three Pacific-rim countries while making efforts to carry out their respective trans-century strategies for economic and social development, will also pay great attention to the circumstances in their adjacent areas and the world, especially to the trilateral and bilateral relations among and between themselves, on which hinges to a great extent success or failure of their master strategies. It should be noted that both the Sino-US relationship and Sino-Japanese relationship have just extricated themselves from a dangerous trend of rapid decline and are now at the crossroad. China is keen to improve its relations both with the USA and Japan. One can see herefrom the weight of Sino-US relations and Sino-Japanese relations in China's foreign relations today.

At the present historical turn of the century, there are two opposite tendencies in Japan with regard to its relations with China. These two tendencies can be deemed as two parts of the strategic contradiction which are being faced by Japan. On one hand, Japan would like to make a positive historical adjustment to the quarter-of-a-century-old relationship with China since the establishment of their diplomatic ties with a view to making it more comprehensive in content and more far-reaching in coverage, as well as with more political flavour and more far-sighted visions. In the words of the Japanese themselves, they want to have a Japan-China relationship in the context of Asia-Pacific or a Japan-China relationship in the context of the world.

On the other hand, however, there is another tendency which places China as the main target of the Japan-US security treaty. In this sense, the treaty means in essence a strategic reserve force with China as its main object of attack. In this context, it would be natural for Japan to choose the US at the expense of China when it is compelled to make a strategic choice between the two—as a matter of fact, Japan's alliance with the US is the cardinal axis of the country's foreign affairs and is of great realistic and historical importance to the country's future development. That is the reason why some leaders of Japan insist on expressing explicitly that there could be no modification to the basic framework of the Japan-US alliance even when it is seeking China's understanding for the revision of the guidelines for Japan-US defence cooperation. It is noted that Japanese political circles and foreign affairs department have declared that Japan-China relations are as important as the Japan-US relations, but it would be very hard for Japan to put the two relationships on an equal footing when it has to make a strategic decision.

To speak plainly, as some Chinese scholars have put it, an attempt to keep an apparent balance between China and the US, Japan has been showing more of the positive side of its China policy. Since the beginning of 1998, Japan has been laying more emphasis on taking the initiative in its own hands in handling a series of international issues such as human rights, Hong Kong's return to China, political strife in Cambodia, financial crisis in Southeast Asia etc.

Significantly in the recent past particularly in 1997 there were indeed certain substantial advances in Sino-Japanese economic and trade relations. First, significant progress was made during their bilateral talks over China's entry into the WTO. Secondly, the two countries successfully concluded their talks on fishery with an agreement. Thirdly, Japan provided China with new credits of nearly 1.7 billion US dollars (about 2023 billion Japanese yen), with an average interest rate of 2.3 per cent. Thus far, Japanese credits to China have totalled 20.5 trillion Japanese yen, ranking it first among all foreign creditors of China. It can be said that so far as the past is concerned including the issues relating to recognizance of history, suspension of economic aid and the Diaoyu Islan, Japan has basically restored Sino-Japanese relations to its previous level, and has hence ushered in a peaceful relationship between them. But if the future of the bilateral relations is taken into consideration, one can not but say that there are still areas of difference between the two countries.

In Asia's history, there has never been such a precedent as the co-existence of a strong China and a strong Japan. The phenomenon has appeared against the backdrop of a changing security pattern in Asia-Pacific. Here it is proper to point out that between China and Japan, there are objectively a number of identical strategic interests, which dictate that the two neighbouring countries must come to terms with each other and have stable diplomatic relations. Their latest agreement on exchange of top-level visits will be a new starting point for them to open up new relations in the next few decades. It goes without saying that the road ahead will be a long and arduous one. Fortunately, however, Hashimoto reached a series of agreements with China during his visit in the end of 1997. Besides the regular exchange of top level visits, there were also those for promotion of intercourse and dialogues between the two countries on security matters and for furtherance of contacts between Chinese and Japanese parliamentarians. All this can be regarded as the first step towards establishing an effective framework of good-neighbourliness and friendship between the two countries, the significance of which can never be over estimated. Last but not the least, Chinese Premier Li Peng paid an official visit to Japan in November, 1997, which had a far-reaching impact on Sino-Japanese relations by laying emphasis on consolidating their cooperation on the basis of not only friendship and mutual benefit between themselves but also peace and stability in Asia-Pacific as well.

This is how Chinese scholars look at the emerging trends in the evolution of Sino-Japan relations. Just like Sino-Japan, relations between US-Sino are also tending towards stabilization after a period of precarious times. A consensus of opinion is being gradually reached within the US on how to deal with China. Although there are still a section of people in the US who continue to refuse to take into consideration the changed circumstances, Sino-US relations have by and large passed over the dangerous schools of confrontation and have created conditions for establishing and developing a strategically cooperative relationship between them, according to Chinese experts.

It is worthwhile to recall here that after the collapse of the former Soviet Union, China policy of US experienced a rather long ordeal of readjustment and reexploration in order to redecide the policy's status, nature, keynote and orientation. However, there is now emerging a framework of policy that may be able to govern the country's relations with China for a considerable time to come. The main mode of the framework is temporary or conditional engagement or temporary or conditional containment. That is to say, engagement is the means or manner, but not the policy itself; containment is the installation (the fixed part) of the policy; and the aim is to integrate China into the international community, which will be the end of one process and the beginning of another. In a certain sense this is such a process of policy-making that aims at regulating the future and such a kind of strategic thinking that centres on predicting the results.

Among these two big Pacific-rim countries there are, on the one hand differences in national interests and degenerating factors to destabilize their relations: but on the other hand, there are also a number of common interests between them, which demand the two countries to actively cooperate with each other. So today's Sino-US relationship can be depicted as a complex and many-faceted, one that embraces all kinds of key elements of international relations, including conflict, cooperation, competition, dialogue, etc. This is the actual condition of their bilateral relations at the present stage. What is needed now is a spirit of mutual trust and a political will to actively promote further development of their bilateral relations. Then it would be possible to end the stagnant state that has been prevailing since the beginning of the 1990s, which was characterized by a cycle of conflict-negotiation-recovery.

China's strategic objectives under the present international circumstances are to strive for an international environment favourable to its economic construction and to avoid any direct military conflict with the US. In fact, its relationship with the US is the main shaft of its foreign policy or the leading factor that affects its relations with all other countries. For the development of Sino-US relations China has adopted a fundamental policy, to enhance confidence, decrease troubles, promote cooperation and avoid confrontation. It has also put forward four principles for the same purpose, namely, to improve mutual understanding, broaden consensus of opinion, promote cooperation and jointly create a bright future. All these reflect China's strategic thinking in connection with Sino-US relations at the present stage. To take a view from this angle, the orientation of China's US policy has a rather thick common bottom line with the US policy toward China. To develop their mutual relations on the basis of this bottom line would not only serve well their respective national interests, but also afford a great potential for furthering their relations.

President Jiang's state visit to the US is a significant step forward for ending the seven year-long stalemate of Sino-US relations. Proceeding from a far-sighted long-term strategic point of view, he had fruitful discussions with American leaders and reached important consensus with them on a framework for the development of Sino-US relations in the future. This signifies that a new epoch has dawned on the relations between the two countries.

There are, however, still numerous troubles, contradictions and hard nuts to crack in the relations between the two countries. Nevertheless, now that the direction of the way to go has been made clear, all difficulties would be easier to handle. Chinese experts now openly admit that these relations are of primary importance to the security in the whole Asia-Pacific region.

This shows that relations in the triangle, between Japan and China, US and China and Japan and US have already taken a new direction. The exchange of visits between top leaders of China, Japan and the US as well as the positioning and redefining of the bilateral relationships between these countries have greatly promoted interactions among them. Some of the visits have already yielded results of win-win games, but some other have left behind some negative affects of a zero-sum game. The bilateral relationship between the US and Japan is now no longer the one between a winner and a loser; the relationship between China and Japan has been defined by the Sino-Japanese peace treaty; and China and the US are striving to build a constructive strategic partnership. But in the tri-lateral structure, there may appear, or rather has already appeared a configuration of 2:1, with the latter one representing the imaginary object of strategic deterrence of the former two. The US-Japan joint declaration on Security issued on April 17, 1996 and the newly revised Guidelines for US-Japan Defense Cooperation signed in September, 1997, have set the tone for the trans-century strategic cooperation between the two countries. Where their strategic cooperation directs against is known to every body, for there has never been a military alliance in the world without any target of attack, this broadly is the thinking of the Chinese experts.

What perhaps is of far reaching importance for all the countries of Asia-Pacific region is that a proposal to hold a Japan-China-US dialogue on Asian security has already been put foreward. What will be India's stand and role in this is unpredictable at this stage.

striving to build/re-constitute a strategic partnership. But in the bi-lateral structure, there may appear, or rather has already appeared, a tendency of 2+1, with the latter one representing the imaginary object of strategic attention of the former two. The U.S.-Japan joint declaration on security issued on April 17, 1996 and the newly revised Guidelines for U.S.-Japan Defense Cooperation signed in September, 1997, have set the tone for this ... strategic cooperation between the two countries. Where their strategic cooperation is directed against is known to every body, for there has never been a military alliance in the world without any target to attack, this broadly was the thinking of the Chinese experts.

What perhaps is of far reaching importance for all the countries of Asia-Pacific region is the proposal to build a Japan-China-U.S. dialogue on Asian security has already been put forward. What will be India's stand and role in this is unpredictable at this stage.

11

Russian-Japanese Relations

Russian-Japanese relations, particularly their economic relations have begun to unfold certain new trends. After the collapse of the socialist regimes in the Soviet Union and Eastern Europe, major Western nations had begun to evince interest in developing economic relations with Russia. However, Japan initially had certain reservations. Before the demise of the Soviet Union, the total volume of Soviet-Japanese trade had touched US dollars 6 billion in 1989. In fact, at that stage, Japan was the third largest partner of the Soviet Union next to West Germany and Finland, and unquestionably the most important trade partner in Asia. Unlike the US, Japan granted the most-favoured nation status to the Soviet Union. Thus, it can be said that in economic terms Soviet-Japanese relations were more advanced than Soviet relations with the US or any other major Western country except West Germany and Finland.

Diplomatically, despite generally chilly relations, both countries had maintained correct relations. In fact, in terms of economic, political and cultural relations, Soviet-Japanese relations were more advanced than any other relations between Soviet and other Asian countries except perhaps with Soviet's socialist allies and India. Thus it must be stressed that Russian-Japanese relations are not bad so as to threaten peace and stability in the region. Neither are their any signs to indicate that these relations are deteriorating. Moreover, there are some important signs of improvement in relations.

Nevertheless it must be recognized that Russian-Japanese relations are not improving as rapidly as Russian relations with other major Western countries. Abnormality of the relations is obvious, when one remembers that fifty-two years since the war, Japan and Russia have not concluded a single peace treaty. It is precisely in this sluggish pace with which both countries are moving in improvement of relations that their relationship gives the impression of sourness and stalemate. This situation is creating negative consequences. Japan vetoes the Russian entry to GATT (General Agreement on Tariffs and Trade) and other international economic organizations. It played a major part in the Ottawa summit in 1988 to persuade the other Western leaders to accept that the cold war was not yet over in Asia, and in its opposition to West Europeans' proposal Japan contributed to foiling the West's unified aid policy to the Soviet Union at the Houston summit in July, 1990. Furthermore, Japan stands as a major stumbling block for the new Russian Asian policy as Japan frustrates any Soviet arms control initiatives. Economic development in the Russian Far East, the sine qua non for Russian entry into Asia-Pacific economic activities, is impossible without Japanese cooperation which the Japanese government has refused to offer. It has become clear by now to the Russian leaders that without significant improvement of relations with Japan, they will not be able to the integrate their economy with the world, particularly when Japan has already become a super economic power.

The obvious cause for the stalemate in relations is the northern territorial dispute, a dispute over the four islands off Hokkaido-Etorofu, Kunashiri, Shikotan, and Habomais—which the Soviets seized at the end of World War II. Both sides claim that the islands rightfully belong to their side historically as well as legally. Japanese government has insisted on iriguchiron (Entrance Theory) by which it makes the return of the four islands a precondition for improvement of relations including a peace treaty, as opposed to deguchiron (Exit Theory), which advocates the return of the territory as the end result of piecemeal improvement in relations in other areas of cooperation. To the Japanese, the northern territories symbolically represent the humiliate status Japan was subjected to during the occupation period immediately after World War II. Despite the unquestionable economic global status it has attained unless these islands are returned, sengo (post-World War II era) is not over for them. It is understandable, therefore, that the Japanese have been sticking to their stand, insisting that as far as they are concerned, the cold war is not over, unless their inherent territory they perceive as illegally seized by Stalin is returned to them.

The dispute between Russia and Japan over these islands has a long history spread over centuries. The history of the territorial dispute is extraordinarily complex. The conflicting claims of Japan and the Soviet Union, now Russia, are based mainly on differing interpretations of a series of agreements and treaties which go back to the mid-19th century.

To the Russians the islands are simply the southern most islands of the Kuriles, a chain of Russia-held islands that stretches a thousand kilometres between Hokkaido and Kamchatka Peninsula. These islands were part of the Russian Empire under Czar.

On the other hand the Japanese insist however, that the southern most islands are distinct from the Kurilies, and that the Russian claim is illegitimate. As trade developed with the Ainu people in the interior, the Japanese gradually made their way into the southern part of Sakhalin and the Kuril Island, where they came into conflict with the Russians. In 1875 Japan concluded the Treaty of St. Petersburg with Russia and gave up the southern part of Sakhalin in exchange for the Kuril islands, Japanese claim.

In April, 1991 Mikhail Gorbachev became the first Soviet leader to visit Japan. The long-anticipated visit was thus, in itself, a highly significant event. It was also highly successful as a public relations exercise. He made a strong positive impact on the Japanese people. He addressed the Diet, held more meetings with Prime Minister Kaifu than scheduled and as expected signed a number of agreements on bilateral exchanges and cooperation.

But on the issue which dominated the summit, little, if any, progress was made. That issue was the long-standing and bitter territorial dispute between the Russia and Japan over a number of islands which the Japanese call the Northern Territories and the Russians refer to as the southern Kuriles.

The Russians had long claimed that no dispute existed, the islands were Russian territory and thus not subject to negotiation. The fact that the territorial question absorbed 80 per cent of the meeting time of the Tokyo summit, and that the names of the disputed islands were mentioned for the first time in an official Japanese/Soviet document, were clear signs of progress. But despite the long hours of discussion no agreement was reached on how the conflict might be resolved.

In a way, the Russians are paying the high price for the accumulated mistakes and short-sightedness in the past in dealing with Japan. To begin with, Stalin's decision to seize the islands for geopolitical gains irrevocably predetermined, the conflicted nature of relations with Japan. The Soviet decision not to sign the San Francisco Peace Treaty in 1951 was a major miscalculation that prevented the Soviet Union from setting the territorial problem with Japan once and for all, when Japan was forced to abandon its insistence on the four islands, giving up the claim to the larger two islands, Kunashiri and Etorofu. Although the Soviet Union agreed to return the smaller two islands, Shikote and Habomais, in 1956, when both countries normalized relations, this promise was unilaterally abrogated by Khrushchev in 1960, when Japan renewed the security treaty with the US. According to a Soviet journalist, having unilaterally violated the intergovernmental agreement, Moscow demonstrated its unreliability and its ill-will towards Japan. When Prime Minister Tanaka came up with massive economic aid for Siberian development in the early 1970s, Brezhnev promised to open up the territorial issue, but when Japan concluded a peace treaty with China, the Soviet government began to backtrack and held that the territorial dispute did not even exist between the two countries.

The last chance the Soviets had to offer a substantial concession to Japan was during the end of 1986 and beginning of 1987, when Gorbachev's visit to Japan was planned. Gorbachev could have made a bold concession to Japan, at least to restore the 1956 promise. But his trip was cancelled and the chance to reach a compromise with Japan without provoking serious domestic opposition within the Soviet Union virtually disappeared.

The past Soviet mistakes and miscalculations underscore the low priority they have accorded to Japan. Until recently the Soviets treated Japan with disdain as a second-rate country with no military significance which blindly followed US foreign policy. However, in the 1990s, the Soviet Union and later Russia began to treat Japan with more sophistication and civility. At that stage Japan's trade with the Soviet Union represented only 1.3 per cent of the total volume of Japan's trade.

It is important to recognize that the Soviet-Japanese relations were improving, albeit at a slower pace than Soviet relations with other major powers, since Gorbachev's accession to power. Soviet-Japanese relations, which had been placed in a deep freeze after the Soviet invasion of Afghanistan, began to improve after Shevardnadze's visit to Japan in

January, 1986 and after Shevardnadze's second visit to Tokyo in December, 1988 the momentum picked up further. Soviet opinion leaders outside the government began voicing various constructive proposals for solution to the territorial dispute. The Soviet government dropped its intransigent position that there existed no territorial dispute, and accepted the existence of the dispute itself. Both governments agreed to establish a working group to prepare for the conclusion of a peace treaty, whose most important task would be to find a solution to the territorial dispute.

It became obvious by then, at least to the specialists on Japan and Asia, that Japan provided a key entry ticket for active partnership in the Asia-Pacific region, and that the failure to achieve rapprochement with Japan will make it virtually impossible to implement the new Soviet Asian policy.

Two developments are significant to note in the 1990s: first, the LDP leaders began to take an active part in the formulation of Japan's policy towards Russia, and second there were signs of a softening attitude within the Ministry of External Affairs.

It was remarkable that such influential, mainstream LDP politicians as Abe, Kanemaru, and Ozawa were voicing their strong opinions favouring rapprochement with the Soviet Union.

The Japanese government has taken the position called *kakudaikinko* (expanded equilibrium) by which it intends to improve relations piecemeal despite the absence of resolution of the territorial dispute. In July, 1989, the Japanese government presented a ten-point proposal to improve relations. This is a virtual abandonment of the *iriguchiron*, and adoption of *deguchiron*. If so, the differences between the Soviet position and the Japanese position had considerably narrowed. Thus in the late 80s and in early 90s, relations between the two countries began to show a new trend. This conclusion is confirmed by the various developments which took place in 1997 and in early 1998. However, we will come to this aspect later on.

Although Japan's trade with the Soviet Union had reached its record high in 1989, it represented merely 1.3 per cent of Japan's foreign trade, a sharp decline from more than 2.5 per cent share it used to hold in the early 1970s.

Nevertheless, the future of Russian-Japanese economic relations will not be determined by politics but rather depend on the success of economic reforms in Russia itself.

Many problems still persist in preventing Russian-Japanese rapprochement. These problems—the territorial dispute, economic incompatibility etc. are all difficult problems that can not be easily resolved. Behind these differences there are accumulated distrust and suspicions. And yet, a cautious optimism is finally warranted that in the years ahead both Japanese and Russian politicians will be able to muster political courage and wisdom to achieve a major breakthrough on the territorial dispute and move the relations for the first time since World War-II, beyond the stalemate. However, a wind of change has begun to blow over these two countries. Let us examine this change in concrete terms.

As we have analysed above, in the new historical conditions, there was a market change in the attitude of both Russia and Japan in the late 80s and early 90s. This trend gained further momentum during the last two years. This conclusion is confirmed by a series of developments which took place in 1997 and early 1998. In the last week of May, 1997 Japan's Foreign Minister Yukihiko Ikeda visited Russia. He negotiated with Russia's President Boris Yeltsin as to how the relations between the two countries can be upgraded. He handed over to the Russian President a letter from Japanese Prime Minister Ryutaro Hashimoto. This letter underlined the importance of elevating bilateral dialogue to the highest level. It was decided during this visit that a Russian-Japanese summit should be held during the G-8 Summit in June, 1997. The most important aspect of this visit was that it was decided that delicate issues of bilateral relations including the territorial problem and the conclusion of a bilateral peace treaty should be taken up. This was followed by a visit by Russian First Vice Premier Boris Nemtsov to Japan in the second week of June, 1991. In this meeting Japan agreed to use 400 and 500 million dollar credit lines, which was extended to Russia earlier. Besides this, Russian leader emphasised that Japan should make direct investments in Russia. This paved the way for direct economic relations between Japanese and Russian businessmen.

When Japanese Prime Minister Ayutaro Hashimoto met Russian President Boris Yeltsin at Denver on the occasion of the G-8 Summit, both the leaders agreed that contacts between the leaders of the two countries should be more frequent and more intimate. Within three weeks after this meeting on July 1, 1997, Russian President spoke to prominent

Japanese politicians who were in Moscow. Japanese leaders emphasised that the fact that Russia had become a full-fledged member of G-8, would go a long way in enabling it to play its rightful role in the international economic affairs.

During his visit to Japan in the last week of July, 1997 Russian Foreign Minister Yevgeny Primakov highly assessed new principles of mutual relations with Russia advanced by the Japanese government. He went out of his way to highlight that the principles of "trust, mutual advantage and long term relations" announced by Prime Minister Ryutaro Hashimoto deserve high appraisal. It was during this visit that it was decided that Russian President and Japanese Prime Minister should hold a summit meeting. Again Chairman of the Federation Council Yegor Stroyev articulated the same viewpoint about the significance of new trends in Russian-Japanese relations when he visited Tokyo on October 30, 1997. He pointed out that the "new approach" of Japan towards Russia in essence boils down to "intention to build", the relations between the two countries on the "principles of trust, mutual benefit and long term perspective" without "tough linkage" to the territorial problem. According to him this approach will open up "new vistas" for the development of trade and economic cooperation between the two countries. This will be in the interests of both the countries.

All these developments culminated into Russian-Japanese Summit at Krasnoyarsk on November 2,1997. Russian President described this Summit as a "massive breakthrough". This Summit adopted documents, the most important among them was the "Yeltsin-Hashimoto Plan" which would be like a "tree" germinating other decisions. The document provides that Japanese government in the period until 2000 in cooperation with the Russian government will be implementing measures in three areas, what is most important is that the two leaders had a "very serious" discussion on the conclusion of a peace treaty. This treaty could be based on the 1993 declaration which was concluded during Boris Yeltsin's visit to Japan. This perhaps marked a turning-point in Russian-Japanese relations.

There is yet another aspect of this development. Russian Foreign Minister Yevegeny Primakov announced in Tokyo on November 13, 1997 that the idea of creating a "mechanism of consultations" among Russia, the United States, China and Japan for Asia and the pacific should be discussed for peace, security and cooperation in this whole region. According to him, this idea has a "positive content" because the stability and security in the Asia-Pacific region largely depend on these countries. This idea was advanced by the former Prime Minister of Japan Yasuhiro Nakesone to the Russian Foreign Minister.

On the eve of second summit between the Russian President and Japanese Prime Minister in April, 1998, Japan's Foreign Minister Keizo Obuchi met Boris Yeltsin in Moscow on February 23, 1998. In this meeting, a review was made about the implementation of the various accords signed between the two countries in November, 1997. In this connection, Russian President and Japan's Foreign Minister emphasised the special importance of the "Yeltsin-Hashimoto Plan", which lays down long term basis for expanding the entire range of bilateral ties and cooperation, trade and economic cooperation between the two countries.

Significantly, both the leaders expressed confidence that the second summit will become another milestone in developing relations between the two countries. Ad-hoc Russian-Japanese Commission, which has been set up for peace treaty is expected to play an important role in this respect.

However, Ryutaro Hashimoto-Boris Yeltsin summit in a resort south-west of Tokyo on April 19,1998 further stimulated the normalisation of relations between Japan and Russia, notwithstanding the fact that on the question of resolution of territorial dispute between the two countries and thereby paving the way for signing the peace treaty they could not make much headway. The obvious reason for this was the internal political situation in Russia arising out of the conflict between the Duma (lower house of Russia) and the Russian President over the appointment of the Prime Minister. It has to be admitted that expectations for a major breakthrough were low from the very beginning. Japanese as a matter of fact did not expect any immediate solution to the dispute. They hope that greater economic ties would eventually lead to mutual trust and a favourable solution on the return of the islands.

It is relevant to recapitulate here that trade between the two nations still totals less than one per cent of Japan's world wide trade, while Japanese investments in Russia are estimated at 330 million US dollars, just one per cent to two per cent of the foreign investments in Russia.

But one new significant development in this summit took place which conceals more than what it reveals. Though neither side ever mentioned sovereignty over the disputed islands, Russian President proposed that Japan and Russia build a large scale fish processing facility together on the disputed islands. But Hashimoto responded to this proposal by pointing out that Japan would only consider this proposal along with efforts towards a peace treaty, according to the official sources in Tokyo.

This stood as a contrast to the long "chilly" relations between Japan and Russia which have only slowly thawed since the collapse of the Soviet Union.

Japanese media, including *Tokyo Shimbun* has disclosed that Japanese Prime Minister proposed to the Russian President during this summit that their two countries should draw a new demarcation line north of four disputed islands. This in itself shows that new proposals are being discussed with zeal between Russia and Japan to resolve the territorial dispute.

From all indications, it appears that Russia's response to the new proposals was positive, though full details of these proposals have not been spelt out. Russian President Yeltsin, for instance, commented that "Hashimoto's plan" was a serious new proposal towards a peace treaty to be finalised by the end of the present century.

The crux of the problem is that this proposal, if it has been designed, "side steps" opposition in Russia to any explicit compromise on the sovereignty issue, while effectively guaranteeing Japan's control over the islands. The main content of this proposal is that a border be drawn north of the four small islands of the tip of Japan's northern most main island of Howkkaido.

Whatever may be the element of truth in these officially leaked reports, one thing is certain that after a dreary past of more than five decades, Russia and Japan have begun serious discussions to resolve their territorial dispute. The leaders of the two countries, however, cannot ignore the mood of their people on sensitive questions of claims and counter-claims on disputed territories.

Nevertheless, one thing is certain that economic interests of both the countries demand that they should strengthen economic relations in their mutual interests. If Russia needs capital investment and technology from Japan, it also provides huge market to Japan's industries, which are facing

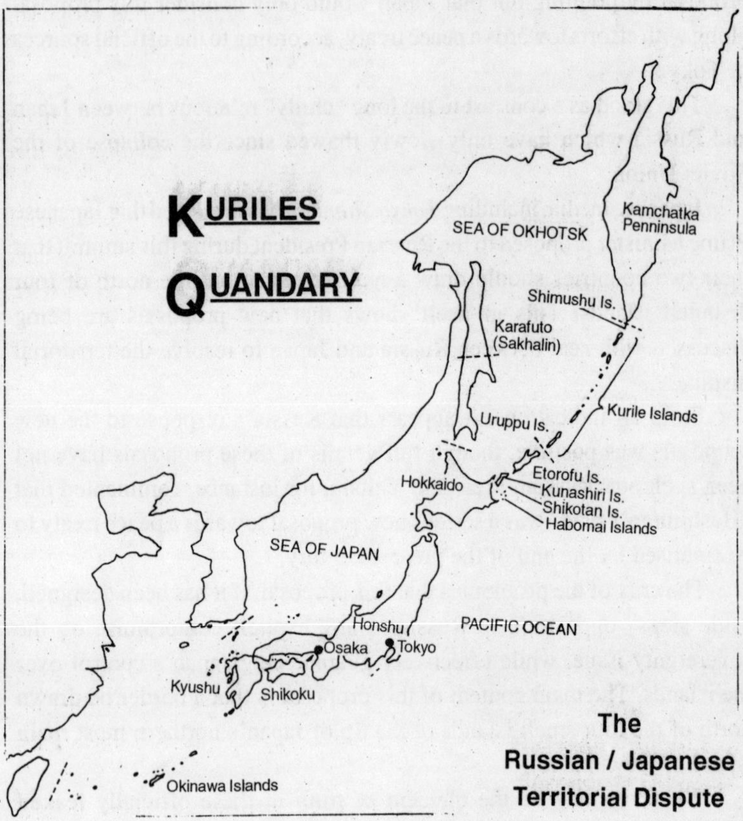
KURILES
QUANDARY
SEA OF OKHOTSK
Kamchatka
Penninsula
Shimushu Is.
Karafuto
(Sakhalin)
Kurile Islands
Uruppu Is.
Etorofu Is.
Hokkaido
Kunashiri Is.
Shikotan Is.
Habomai Islands
SEA OF JAPAN
Honshu
PACIFIC OCEAN
Osaka
Tokyo
Kyushu
Shikoku
Okinawa Islands
The
Russian / Japanese
Territorial Dispute

new pressures from the United States and other industrialised countries of Europe. But there is something more to it than meets the eye.

Japan has to play her rightful role in the world economy in a period of globalisation of economy, it is not enough for her to play an effective role in the international financial institutions such as World Bank. The fact of life is that Japan is emerging as the centre of world finance and the leading capital exporter, much as Great Britain did at the height of its power in the nineteenth century and as the United States did in the heydays of the Pax Americana immediately after World War II. Seen in this context, it is in Japan's own interests, its people, its economy and the industrialists to put its economic relations with its Asian neighbours including Russia on a higher pedestal. This is the need of the hour.

12

Indo-Japanese Relations in 21st Century

Indo-Japanese economic relations during the last two decades have developed rapidly and seem to have already entered a new phase. To understand this new trend, one has to recognise the fact, as Japanese scholars have been underlining that the main concern of their country have been "high current account trade surplus; the ageing composition of its population; and the reorientation of its industrial structure to knowledge intensive industries and its moving towards a surplus oriented society". After India embarked on the path of liberalisation of its economy, trade between India and Japan constituted less than 1 per cent of Japan's overall imports and exports. However, there has been considerable improvement in economic relations between the two countries. Japanese bilateral aid to India was 39 billion yen in 1985, 48 billion yen in 1986 and 68.5 billion yen in 1987. If one adds 29.5 billion yen as drought assistance given in 1986, this figure comes to 98 billion yen. The increase in ODA (Overseas Development Assistance) to India is part of Japan's response to a variety of pressures from its Western allies that it was dominating "unfairly" the world trade balance and not contributing enough either in the economic or strategic defence fields, as Japan's scholars perceive.

India is preparing to enter the next century through medium term plans which, by the beginning of the next century, aim at eliminating poverty, creating near full employment and meeting the basic needs of the people for food, clothing, shelter, education and health. India also intended to attain a degree of modernisation and utilise new technologies which would bring about improvements in both industry and agriculture. The development scenario for India assumed an investment rate of 25 per cent of its GDP which could be jeopardised if there was a deterioration in the security environment. Developing countries like India would need greater access to international capital markets.

The following fields are suggested by Indian experts.

1. The application of bio-technology to agriculture and of genetic engineering in medicine and environmental control.
2. Micro-electronics, the use of sixth generation computers in inventory control, communication and transport network.
3. Different aspects or components of the information revolution.
4. Exploration of new sources of energy and of space.
5. Urban development and its ramifications.

This raises certain pertinent questions. India feels that Japan's greatest contribution to the developmental process is to explode the European myth that a country could modernize only if it adopted Western institutions and values. In its earlier economic revolution Japan could ignore certain elements in the social modernization process such as equality, trade unionism and democracy. Today there has to be a balance between the technological and economic aspects of modernization and its social, cultural and political ones. It is not possible for developing countries to adopt the Japanese model. The present problem is that technological change is much faster than man's capacity to make appropriate institutional adjustments, to preserve essential and basic values. A vision of the future and planning are needed to ensure all this.

Japan has to play an international role commensurate with its power, albeit economic and not military. Japan's predominance in Asia's economy is much greater than that of the developed world as a whole in comparison with the developing. Yet, there is great asymmetry between its economic strength and the manner in which Japan tries to influence the Asian and the world economy. Doubling its external assistance in terms of Japan's growth rate represented a minimal and not a quantum increase. A much greater Japanese role and bolder initiatives would be more appropriate.

A question is raised as to what Japan should do if its present per capita growth rate continued at between 4 and 5 per cent, as it has been for a century. On a per capita basis it would have risen 55 time or to half a million dollars by the twenty-first century. How would Japan cope with this situation?

Seen in this context, it is in the interest of both India and Japan that their economic cooperation should be given a new momentum. It is relevant in this connection to mention that India had fulfilled three basic requirements of economic growth : capital formation, creation of a pool of skilled scientific and technical manpower and the production of wage goods. Above all, India has not only become self-sufficient in production of foodgrains but now is in a position to export it to the other countries.

That being the position, Japan cannot afford to ignore the harsh reality of the Asian societies in the sense that it could not remain an "Island of prosperity in a depressed ocean".

India and Japan are bound together by strong historical and cultural linkages and it would be in their common interests to explore the manner in which they contribute together to the restructuring of the international economic order. The various agreements between India and Japan including in the fields of shipping, trade, aviation, science and technology and inter-organisational links and transfer of technology have already laid the basis for expansion of their relations.

It should be noted that Japan had achieved extraordinary economic growth falsifying the pessimistic forecasts of eminent economists in the fifties. Some idea of this progress can be had from the following facts : life expectancy was 80 for females and 75 for males by 1984; the gap between the rich and the poor had been reduced; Japanese per capita GNP was expected to be around 90 per cent of the US figure and Japanese GNP had risen from 3 per cent of the world total in the sixties to 10 per cent today. Japan was expected to increasingly internationalize its financial and capital markets and instead of concentrating on national development, it would harmonize its policies with the rest of the international communities. It would promote joint technological development, the sharing of profits with companies in other countries and the expansion of joint ventures. There would be interstructuring with a more pronounced shift to knowledge-intensive industries and a movement towards a service-oriented society. Japan was committed to increase its official development assistance in the coming period.

India was preparing to enter the next century through medium-term plans. Japan had made phenomenal national progress, it could play a more active and important role than it had hitherto, and take initiatives befitting its economic strength and share in global GNP. While welcoming the increase in Overseas Development Assistance the India feels that even this was inadequate commensurate with Japan's capacity.

In this context, let us examine the development of economic cooperation between India and Japan in the 1990s. This will give us an idea how in the next century more concerted and coordinated attempts will have to be made to fully tap to potential of economic cooperation between the two countries on the principle of balance of interests of these two Asian nations.

Until 1991, overall amount of FDI (Foreign Direct Investments) flowing into India from Japan was lower than even that reaching the Philippines and Thailand, which are much smaller economics compared to India. According to the report of the Asian Development Bank, between 1987 and 1990, India received 730 million dollars worth of FDI, whereas Thailand alone got 2,336 million dollars. However, from the standpoint of the similar structure of the Chinese and Indian economies which are both big in terms of market potential and requirements of development it is necessary to analyse the trends of FDI being received by them. In this context, since the start of economic liberalisation in 1991, India has seen a marked rise in the total of FDI being received by it.

Taking the for years 1990-1993, Japanese investments into India ranked number five in a total list which actually includes 10 countries, the NRI's plus others, 13 categories. What is significant is that Japanese investments at 300 million, although substantially less than the investments from the USA, were ahead of Britain, Germany and Holland, which may be considered as long-standing, traditional, European investors. In aggregate terms FDI received by China is far ahead of the amount going to India. During the same period, 1990-1993, China got 188090 million dollars worth of FDI which is 32 times the figure for India and 6402 million dollars US worth of FDI from Japan which is still 21 times more than what India received. However, in proportional terms Japan was the fifth largest investor in India and among the first four in China.

According to list of 249 Japanese investments in India in collaboration with Indian companies between January 1991 and March 1994, 66 per cent or 165 cases were of technical collaborations, 71 or 29 per cent were financial, 10 or 4 per cent were in collaborations in drawings and designs, and 3 or 1 per cent were mainly to provide foreign publicity, according to a study by Prof. Shri Prakash. Indian industry is mainly interested in getting technical knowhow and technical advice to upgrade its existing production system and quality of products. At the same time, through such technical agreements, many big Japanese companies have gained a foothold in the Indian market and Indian industry which could be useful for future expansion. JVC, Hitachi, Mitsubishi, Sony, Sanyo, Suzuki, Yamaha, Honda, Toshiba, Nissan, Shimadzu, Sumitomo all big names have collaboration agreements with Indian companies.

Collaboration between Indian and Japanese companies has already led to expansion of business by various organizations. Recent examples of such expansion are Yamaha's new venture with Escorts Ltd. to make motorcycles; Sony's 100 per cent self-financed company for making TV picture tubes; Honda Motor Company's decision to pick up a majority stake in a joint venture with Siddharth Shriram's SIEL Ltd. to make automobiles in India.

The Japanese government is helping in this process directly. It has decided recently to offer a yen 2.6 billion loan to India to support a plan to build the country's largest ever industrial city to be called Industrial Model Town in the Gurgaon region of Haryana state in northern India. The project has been jointly planned by the Haryana State Industrial Development Corporation and three Japanese trading houses—Mitsubishi Corporation, Mitsui and Company and the Marubeni Corporation.

Japanese companies are encouraged by the grand success of Suzuki's joint venture with the government owned Maruti Udyog Ltd. in making medium sized fuel efficient cars. Over a period of 13 years or so, Maruti-Suzuki has come to command a share 74 per cent in India's growing car market producing the right product at the right time and using Japanese management techniques. A recent report by the Hitachi Corporation's Research Institute entitled "Reassessment on the Indian Market and Opportunities for the Hitachi Group" quotes the example of Maruti-Suzuki with enthusiasm.

However, Japanese industrial houses at the present stage are more interested in making investments in China than in India for various reasons. They argue that Japan should attach priority to China, where it already has many branches and business plans under negotiation. Nevertheless, in some fields in which India has an advantage like software, consumer goods industry such as automobiles and household electronics, Japan wants to utilize Indian market in its global strategy.

Japan's foreign aid is known as Overseas Development Assistance (ODA). It is divided into grants and loans. Grants are outright aid packages not to be repaid. Loans are for 30 years with a grace period of 10 years and on a concessional rate of interest, which since 1988 has been lowered to 2.6 per cent per annum for the developing countries.

Since 1989, Japan has been the largest aid donor in the world. According to one study, 46 per cent of Japan's ODA during the decade of the 1980s was received by five Asian countries viz. Indonesia, China, Philippines, Bangladesh and India. Indonesia and China received much more than the other countries.

Japan has been India's top donor, for certain period between 1988 and 1992, with about 30 per cent of India's foreign aid coming from Japan. The amount of Japanese ODA to India has shown greater fluctuations, but still has recorded an overall increase. The 1,612 million dollars India got between 1991-93 was 18.53 per cent more than what it got between 1980-82 and 191.77 per cent more than its level in 1985, according to the data compiled by Prof. Shri Prakash.

The post Cold War period and India's open door policy have created a new situation for expansion of Indo-Japanese economic cooperation.

In order to understand the economic interdependence which is developing between Japan and India, one has to analyse the volume and composition of their bilateral trade.

When one examines the bilateral trade between India and Japan, one notices that though the trade between the two countries is growing, there is a fluctuation in the pattern of trade. In a significant study, A.G. Leonard has examined various facets of the trade relations between India and Japan from 1950 until 1985. According to the data collected by him from Government of India publication one gets the following picture of the balance of trade between India and Japan in the 1980s.

Balance of Trade between India and Japan

(In Rupees crores, Indian)

Year	*Value of Exports*	*Value of Imports*	*Balance +/– (In India's favour)*
1977-78	504.64	427.28	+77.36
1978-79	594.18	516.24	+77.94
1979-80	641.92	609-40	+32.52
1980-81	596.89	748.77	-151.89
1981-82	703.76	886.47	-182.71
1982-83	833.08	1078.90	-245.82
1983-84	828.31	1446.91	-618.60
1984-85	1024.57	1240.02	-215.45

Source: A.G. Leonard, India's Trade Relations with Japan: An Economic Analysis (Indus Publishing Company, New Delhi, 1993) pp. 206/215.

If we compare the value of India's trade with Japan then we see that in 1977-78 it was Rs. 931.92 crore or at the 1990 US dollar rate (1 dollar = Rs. 17.5), 532.5 million dollars. By 1987, it had reached 3487 million dollars and by 1993, it was 3087 million dollars. The increase in the value of Indo-Japanese trade after 1987 has been much more than the value of Japanese FDI into India. Further, when we examine the commodity composition of trade between India and Japan, we further find that India's exports to Japan are not related to Japanese FDI in India.

The value of diamonds in India's exports to Japan between 1992 and 1994 went up from 25.5 per cent to 26.5 per cent; that of shrimps and prawns from 11.7 per cent to 18.3 per cent; and of textiles from 10.7 per cent to 10.9 per cent. None of these commodities have seen any noticeable Japanese FDI. In this respect, the increase in India's export to Japan is taking place independently of Japanese direct investments. India imports industrial machinery which accounts for the bulk of imports. This shows how Japanese technology is helping to further industrial modernisation in India. Engines-pumps-boilers; other industrial machinery; transport equipment; precision instruments; and semi-manufactured iron and steel at 59.9 million dollars constituted 39.8 per cent of the value of India's imports from Japan in 1992 and at 847.3 million dollars, 41.3 per cent in 1994. Hence we can conclude the Japan's imports from India are driven more by the level of demand in Japan than by any other consideration.

Japanese investments in India in the 90s have increased for various reason. In India, many of the concessions being offered since 1991 for attracting FDI are more liberal than the Chinese ones. To begin with, foreign investors can invest in all areas of the country and in all industries except defence, atomic energy and railways. Even among the six industries reserved for the public sector, private and foreign investor to have a local partner even when he wishes to own less than the company's full equity. No industrial licence is required in India except for setting up a few industries.

Foreign companies are taxable for their income originating in India at the new rates with certain expenses being deductible for tax purposes. However, the effective tax rates are significantly reduced by the other incentives being offered by the Government of India. A five-year tax holiday is given for power projects, for firms engaged in exports, for new industries in notified areas and for new industrial units established in electronic hardware/software parks and units in Free Trade Zones. The Central Government Budget of 1995-96 has extended the five-year tax holiday to companies investing in infrastructure such as building roads, bridges, ports, airports and mass transport systems. Tax deductions are available up to 100 per cent on export profits. A deduction of 30 per cent of net income for tax purposes is available for new industrial undertakings. Deduction of 50 per cent of income on foreign exchange earnings is given to construction companies and hotels. Capital can now, after the introduction of currency convertibility on trade and current account, be repatriated after payment of taxes and dividend income remitted through authorised foreign exchange dealers at market rates. Technical collaboration agreements are automatically cleared and approved.

This shows that during the last fifteen years, significant changes have taken place in the evolution of Indo-Japanese cooperation, irrespective of the political power structure in India. This process began in November, 1985 when late Prime Minister Rajiv Gandhi visited Japan. The pace for developing economic relations between the two countries was set by Rajiv Gandhi and the then Japanese Prime Minister Naka Sone during their high level discussions in November, 1985. This process gained a new momentum, when India initiated economic reforms.

Notwithstanding the recent financial crisis, which some of the countries of Asia, particularly of South Asia have witnessed in 1997 and 1998, it goes without saying that the 21st century will be the Asian century. While it is difficult to predict exactly, how high per capita GNPs will go by the year 2000, it is reasonable to expect that with one per cent population growth in the Asian Newly Industrialised Countries (NICs), their per capita GNP will increase if the industrialised countries help them to overcome their present financial crisis. Japan obvious has a major role to play in this.

The main problem for countries like India for the 21st century seems to be how the increasing horizontal division of labour can promote industrial dynamism. India's developing industrial sector, rich labour resources and huge force of scientists, technocrat, experts in business management and above all its natural resources have created ideal conditions for its industrial development. It is herein that Japanese capital and technological strength can play a major role. The potential is obvious. Rapid industrial development will enlarge that segment of the middle and upper middle class which will become buyers of new industrial products, the consumer goods in particular. This will create a new market. In this sense Japan has a major economic interest in India. Nevertheless, Indian model of industrialisation will be different. However, from whatever way you look at the development of Indo-Japanese economic relations and their future in the next century, both the policy makers and the industrialists in Japan will have to look at India with a new perspective.

Though it will be wrong to draw any historical parallels, the fact of the matter is that at the present stage, if one compares Indo-Japanese and Sino-Japanese relations in the area of economic cooperation, India still occupies a low priority, if one goes by the present economic indicators. This does not mean that Sino-Japanese economic relations should not be strengthened further. The issue under discussion is that India, being the second largest populated country on our planet and with its vast material resources, too, should get a higher priority in the development of Indo-Japanese economic relations. It is this aspect, which needs to be highlighted. May be in the past, there was a communication gap between the political and economic leaders of the two countries. This gap has been reduced in the recent years. Japanese industrialists from their own experience must have seen how attractive their investments have become in India. That being the position, in the next century these two Asian nations, India, the second most populated country with its democratic structure and Japan which has set a model of overcoming its economic backwardness in its own specific ways should evolve new structures and systems of economic cooperation. This will be in the interests of the people of the two countries and of the Asian people. This is the new challenge which the objective reality has thrown up.

13

Japan and the ASEAN Countries

Japan's emergence as a super economic power and weakening of the United States as the "sole superpower" and demise of the Soviet Union, all these major changes have begun to change the correlations of forces in the Asia Pacific region, though slowly but surely. In this context, Japan's interaction with the member-countries of the ASEAN group-Brunei, Indonesia, Malaysia, the Philippines, Singapore, Thailand and Vietnam needs an objective examination. The ASEAN group has been closely associated politically and economically with the West. How has the relative decline of the US as global power affected the ASEAN countries and Japan's ASEAN relations? Has there been a significant erosion of the effectiveness of international trade and security regimes in the region? Have Japan's policies towards the group compensated for the US decline? What problems and constraints exist in Japan's relations with its ASEAN neighbours? All these have become relevant questions.

Japan's policies towards the ASEAN member countries are probably more indicative of the nature of Japan's evolving international role in the new historical conditions.

Japan's Prime Minister Toshiki Kaifu, in May, 1991 in his speech during his visit to ASEAN, underlined that Japan had made ASEAN a focus of its foreign policy and worked for closer cooperative relations with these countries in all fields. With the changes in the international situation. ASEAN having grown far stronger than ever before is ready to set new and loftier goals for itself and to move for still closer and more diversified cooperation. Japan and ASEAN are becoming mature partners, able to look seriously at what can be done for Asia Pacific peace and

Direction of ASEAN Trade (in value terms)

(in million US dollars)

		Value of imports from			Value of exports to			Total trade value		
		1988	1992	+/-over 1988 (per cent)	1988	1992	+/-over 1988 (per cent)	1988	1992	+/-over 1988 (per cent)
1.	World	99167	191318	+93	102016	171590	+68	201183	392501	+95
2.	Japan	23207	45520	+96	43589	87500	+101	66796	133020	+99
3.	USA	15602	29749	+91	24107	33611	+39	39709	63360	+60
4.	China (PRC)	3457	5177	+50	2513	4242	+69	5970	9419	+58
5.	Intra-ASEAN	18046	29279	+62	25202	32234	+28	43248	61613	+43
6.	India	602	1460	+143	1614	1392	-14	2216	2852	+29
7.	Pakistan	115	217	+89	369	698	+89	484	915	+89
8.	Hong Kong	6919	9534	+38	7079	13023	+84	13998	22557	+61

N.B. : The ASEAN countries here include Indonesia, Singapore, Philippines, Malaysia, Thailand and Brunei. (The data for Brunei refer to 1984 and 1989 respectively).

Source: International Trade Statistics, Trade by Country Yearbook, UN Vol., 1, 1994, pp. 488-489.

Courtesy: Strategic Analyses (April, 1997) and Prof. Shri Prakash.

Direction of Trade Statistics, 1970-85

Country	*Trade as Per-centage of GNP (%) 1983*	*Percentage of exports to Japan (%) 1970-85*		*Percentage of imports from Japan (%) 1970-85*		*Percentage of exports to US (%) 1970-85*		*Percentage of imports from US (%) 1970-85*	
Indonesia	43	41	49	29	28	13	23	18	14
Malaysia	99	18	25	17	23	13	13	9	15
Philippines	33	40	19	31	14	42	36	29	25
Singapore	302	8	9	19	15	11	20	11	13
Thailand	41	25	13	37	26	14	20	15	11

Source: IMF, Direction of Trade Statistics Year book.

These benefits are not inconsiderable. Japan's trade with the ASEAN group grew extremely rapidly in the 1950s and 1960s, both as a percentage of ASEAN imports as well as a percentage of ASEAN exports. By the end of the 1960s, Japan had become the first or second largest trading partner of most of the countries. This trade relationship was based on the purchase of natural resources products by Japan as it had an enormous appetite for raw materials and primary products from Southeast Asia as has been mentioned earlier. It sells in return manufactured goods that displaced traditional imports from the United States and Western Europe. Undoubtedly, Japan's growth as a market for the primary products of ASEAN countries has been an important factor in their export earnings and growth.

Two factors have significantly changed the pattern of ASEAN export growth to Japan. The first is the reduced growth of demand in Japan for ASEAN primary products, a consequence of a much slower Japanese growth rate after 1973, structural change in the Japanese economy away from resource-consuming industries and toward less resource-intensive service and high-technology activities, and the success of energy and raw materials conservation efforts within the industrial sector. A second factor has been that as manufactured goods have become increasingly important in ASEAN exports. The ASEAN export structure has apparently become less complementary with Japan's import structure.

Both factors have been a source of friction in Japan-ASEAN trade relations and, from the Southeast Asian perspective, have caused ASEAN doubts about Japan's value as worthy economic partner.

The first factor and its consequences for trade relations are illustrated by Indonesian petroleum, the largest single ASEAN export to Japan. Japan's trade deficit with Indonesia, mainly because of petroleum, has been so large (7.7 billion in 1982, 6.9 billion in 1983) that it has overwhelmed its persistent surpluses with Thailand and Singapore, giving Japan an overall deficit for ASEAN as a whole (4.7 billion in 1982 and 2.3 billion in 1983). Because of recession and energy conservation, crude and partly refined petroleum imports from Indonesia have been decreasing in both value and quantity terms. Japan's petroleum imports from Indonesia decreased from 37.4 million kilolitres in 1977 to 36.66 million in 1981 to 29.4 million in 1983. The effect on export earnings was further magnified by the sharp decline in prices.

In the longer run, Japan's value as an ASEAN market will be increasingly judged in the ASEAN states by its purchases of manufactured products, and here is where the second factor comes into play. All of the ASEAN countries have adopted to varying degrees, export promotion based industrialization strategies, modelled after the successful policies of the newly industrializing countries. Manufactures now account for 25 per cent or more of ASEAN exports for all countries whose exports of manufactured goods have been suppressed until recently. Like the other ASEAN countries, however, Indonesia believes its longer-term growth prospects depend on the fortunes of its manufacturing sector, and it is now emphasizing diversification of its exports into relatively unsophisticated processed or manufactured goods such as textiles and plywood.

Japan's imports of manufactured goods from ASEAN are low, and they have not been expanding nearly as rapidly as industrial goods are expanding as a percentage of ASEAN exports. As a consequence, following a pattern established in the case of Japan's trade with more industrialized Taiwan and South Korea, Japan's share of total exports is declining for those ASEAN countries whose export structures are rapidly becoming more industrialized. This is in contrast to the United States and Western Europe, whose shares of ASEAN exports in the past fifteen years have remained about the same or even increased, primarily because these other advanced countries are large importers of labour-intensive manufactured goods from the ASEAN. We will come to this aspect later on.

The post-war Japanese efforts to establish an overseas economic role, however, began considerably earlier. Japan has had long-standing economic and political interests in this region, which is significant to Japan as a source of raw materials, a market for Japanese manufactured goods, and an area through which many of Japan's fuels and products are transported. In the early 1980s, the ASEAN countries accounted for approximately 15 per cent of Japan's imports, including most of its natural rubber, tropical timber, and palm oil, about half its liquid natural gas and one-sixth of its petroleum. The region purchased about 10 per cent of Japanese exports. It stands astride major trade routes connecting Japan with fuel suppliers in the Middle East and iron ore suppliers in western Australia. Politically, the future ASEAN member-countries were the first in the developing world in which Japanese influence and presence was reasserted after the war. In the post-war period, Japan did not assert her independent role and preferred to work under the leadership of the United States, the change came after it became economically strong.

Nevertheless the Japanese and ASEAN governments have had complementary interests in a stable regional order in East Asia, including the preservation of the basic social, economic and political framework of the ASEAN societies. Changes in the international environment forced a more explicit recognition of these interests. American pressures as well as uncertainties about the US regional role have raised the question of whether Japan must assume a more prominent regional role if it is to achieve its economic and political goals. Japan has become an important regional actor and its fundamental foreign policy—priority in its relationship with the United States has ensured that its activities in ASEAN generally have been supportive of the previously established political and economic order in the region, Japan's scholars feel.

However it is useful to review the power disparities between Japan and ASEAN. Clearly Japan is a much larger power than any of the individual ASEAN countries. Japan's greatest advantage lies in its economy which is nearly six times that of all the ASEAN members combined. Although the rate of economic growth in most of the latter exceeds Japan's, projections made for Japan's Economic Planning Agency suggest that even in the year 2000, the ASEAN gross national product will be about 750 billion dollars in today's dollar terms, still, only a third of what will then be as 2.18 trillion dollars Japanese economy. Because of the large economic disparity, ASEAN leaders know that theoretically Japan's military power could also be expanded to about the same range of difference.

In the late sixties, the United States and Western European countries remained the main sources of both tangible assistance and psychological support for the ASEAN governments. The governing elites in the ASEAN societies were, however, deeply disturbed by what seemed to be a steady retreat of their major allies after 1966. Some milestones along the way were—the 1967 British announcement that it would withdraw it military forces from Singapore; the 1969 Guam (or Nixon) Doctrine, which stated that the United States would look to its allies to take the primary burden in dealing with internal insurgencies; the United States Vietnamization policy; the 1973 Paris Peace Agreements ending US military intervention in Vietnam; the 1975 fall of the Lon No 1 government in Cambodia and the Thieu government in South Vietnam and the 1977-78 US plans to withdraw ground forces from South Korea. To these must be added the significant rapprochement in Sino-American relations, whose implications were variously interpreted but which was frequently regarded in Southeast Asia as an effort by the United States to cover its retreat from the region. Finally, another disturbing element for some of the ASEAN governments was the growth of human rights concerns in the United States in the mid-1970s at times accompanied by harsh political rhetoric directed precisely at the elites and governments that looked to the United States for support.

These events, of course, seemed to Southeast Asian elites to be the regional manifestations of a more general external and internal decaying of the post-war US hegemony. The broader context included the visible social conflicts within the United States, the years of stagflation, the collapse of the post-war monetary system, the growing signs of protectionism, the inability of the United States to respond effectively to the Arab oil embargo, the decline of US support for foreign aid, the ability of the Soviet Union to establish strategic parity with the United States and the collapse of bipartisanship in US foreign policy.

As Japan's economic strength grew, it came under growing pressure from the United States to play a more aggressive economic role in support of free world political goals, but in contrast to the later Japanese emphasis on comprehensive security, the economic-political connections were downplayed. Japan's regional initiatives, including its prominent role in the establishment of the Asian Development Bank, its joining of the Asian and Pacific Council (ASPAC) and its initiative in establishing a series of Ministerial Conferences for the Economic Development of Southeast Asia, heavily emphasized economic cooperation. Tokyo was especially sensitive to the charge, both domestically and abroad, that these initiatives were designed in collusion with the United States to build an anti-Beijing axis along the Pacific rim.

Several dramatic events in the 1970s demonstrated that the underlying conditions had changed and that new foreign policy approaches might be required. Apart from the shift in the US posture in Southeast Asia, these events included the serious textile dispute with the United States in the late 1960s and early 1970s, which was the first major post-war US-Japan trade conflict, and the Nixon shocks, the opening to China and the floating of the dollar. These called into question the degree of Japanese dependence on the United States. Another important event was the 1973 Arab oil embargo. Japan had developed a particularly energy-intensive pattern of industrialisation and it relied heavily on petroleum imported from the Middle East for energy. The embargo's short-term effects were enormous, bringing Japan's economic growth rate down from 9 per cent in 1973 to zero in the following year. It brought home the fragility of Japan's economic base and illustrated the helplessness of Japan's principal ally—the United States—to help it cope with this resources crisis.

The changing structure of the international environment thus strengthened the affinity of interests between the Southeast Asian governing elites and their counterparts in Japan. Japan was one logical place for Southeast Asian governments to seek new sources of support. It was already the principal trading partner and aid provider for most of the ASEAN group, and although the growth of Japan's economic presence had created some resentments, it had become a major supporter of the economic development programmes that, by the late 1960s, had been initiated by the ASEAN governments, although the ASEAN governments were making accommodations with China and Vietnam.

At the end of February, 1976, at the first ASEAN summit conference, political cooperation among the member-countries was formally initiated and the economic ministers were elevated to a role in the organizational structure more or less equivalent to that of the foreign ministers. Shortly afterward, Japanese foreign Ministry officials concerned with Southeast Asia met in Hong Kong and agreed that Japan should assist ASEAN in developing its own resiliency and encourage peaceful co-existence between the ASEAN and the Indochinese countries. In October, 1976, Foreign Minister Zentaro Kosaka spoke publicly of Japan's interests in promoting an ASEAN-Indo-China dialogue, and at the end of the year, Prime Minister Takeo Fukuda spoke of Japanese—ASEAN ties as being a little alienated and said that he would like to make amends as soon as possible.

Japan's Southeast Asia policy was formally enunciated in August, 1977 when Prime Minister Fukuda visited the ASEAN countries and attended the second ASEAN summit in Kuala Lumpur.

The Fukuda Doctrine is regarded as a major turning point in postwar Japan-ASEAN relations in that it provided what Japan regarded as a statement of its political interests in the Southeast Asian region.

On the concept of Pacific economic cooperation, ASEAN political sensitivities quickly asserted themselves. The initial reactions in ASEAN in 1979 and the early 1980s were cautious and fears were expressed that a broader regional grouping would dilute ASEAN cooperation or would be dominated by Japan and the United States. Yet there were groups of some influence in the ASEAN region who saw an advantage for ASEAN in the enthusiasm for the concept in the more advanced Pacific Basin countries could be translated into increased attention or aid. In 1984, at the initiative of Indonesian foreign minister Mochtar Kusumaatmadja, the ASEAN countries agreed that the annual Foreign Ministers meeting with their advanced country counterparts could include Pacific Basin economy cooperation as a specific agenda item. By putting Pacific Basin economic cooperation in the ASEAN dialogue framework, the ASEAN governments co-opted the government-to-government discussions of the dialogue and asserted their own control on the pace and substance of progress.

The ASEAN governments have looked on their economic relations with Japan as vital to their economic growth and political survival. In this, the ASEAN group was outstandingly successful until the early 1980s. Between 1960 and 1982, per capita income increased at an average annual rate of between 2.8 per cent for the Philippines (the lowest) and 7.4 per cent for Singapore (the world's fastest growing economy after Saudi Arabia in these years). The three other major ASEAN economics grew at per capita average rates of between 4.2 per cent and 4.5 per cent annually, Economic growth has been accompanied by rapid structural change, with the industrial sectors accounting for an increasing share of production at the expense of agriculture. Although the larger ASEAN economies are relatively resources rich, they are also labour rich and a process of continued expansion of more labour intensive industries can be expected in years to come. This process is supported by demographic trends. All the ASEAN countries have achieved remarkable reductions in fertility rates but the labour force increments through the year 2000 will remain high. Thus, despite their good economic growth performances, the ASEAN governments have never felt economically secure. Fears of serious economic problems or of unmet expectations with attendant serious political implications are always present, as the recent developments have shown.

Japan regards the economic development of the ASEAN group as important to Japan's political and economic interests in the region. Japanese concerns about political instability in ASEAN have tended to focus more on potential internal political and economic failures than on external threats. Because of this, Japanese government officials believe that Japan's trade with ASEAN, its investments in the region, and especially its aid programmes have important political implications. Moreover, Japan's definition of its evolving international role in a more general sense, including its support for the comprehensive security of developing countries, centres around economic policies.

However, in the later half of the seventies, East and South East region for the first time in several years witnessed its output growth decline sharply. These countries are passing through a financial turmoil. This in turn have forced the IMF to revise its earlier growth projections for the global economy by 1 percentage point from 4.3 to 3.5 per cent in 1998. Although the United States and West Europe have remained unaffected by this development in financial markets. However, Japan is facing its impact with falling equity prices and nil growth was recorded in 1997 after 3 per cent rise GDP in 1996. This implies that Japan's poor performance in 1997 and modest recovery expected in 1998 will have the effect of slowing global growth. According to some economists, the intensification of financial problem in Japan and South Korea will not only have a negative impact on short term outlook for Asia as a whole but also spread to other countries. Notwithstanding the forecast that these countries will overcome this crisis and again embark on the path of recovery, short term outlook perhaps will remain bleak for some of these countries.

Significantly, China was less affected in 1997 by the negative developments in the region. It decided not to devalue its currency yuan but to take other measures to improve the competitiveness of its exports and attract continued large foreign investments. China has maintained its strong growth performance in 1997 despite tight macro-economic policies, while inflation has remained subdued.

This development has created certain new economic problems for Japan, particularly in the area of its economic cooperation with the ASEAN. In this context, world's major economic powers kept up the pressure for "decisive reforms" by Japan. It was emphasised, for instance, at G-7 meeting in third week of April, 1998 that Japan should strengthen its banks and implement structural changes. It was underlined that Japan needed a fiscal boost to achieve a "sustainable economic recovery". Since Japan is facing a "classical liquidity trap", a fiscal injection is required that can achieve a recovery, it was argued by the British Chancellor of the Exchequer Gordon Brown.

German Finance Minister Theo Waigel said proposed Japanese tax cuts should be more effective in strengthening domestic demand than additional spending programmes. The challenge Japan now faces is to stabilise its banking system and to implement structural reforms which will permanently strengthen the conditions for growth, he said. Even Malaysia's Finance Minister said that Japan's latest stimulus package announced in the second week of April was not strong enough.

These developments clearly bring out that both the present level of economic development of the ASEAN countries and pressure of other developed countries to open its internal market have begun to change the relations between Japan and the ASEAN at least in the economic area.

The pattern of industrialisation in East and Southeast Asia has been equated by some Japanese economists to flying geese. They do call into question whether Japan, despite its position as the lead goose, is helping the industrialization efforts of the others much in terms of providing demand for their principal export growth sector manufactured goods. The whole pattern of export-oriented growth appears to depend largely on markets outside Asia, principally in the United States and Western Europe. The point is that in recent years the evolving ASEAN export composition appears to be moving in a direction more complementary to the import composition of countries both developed and developing, other than Japan.

Japan's relative share of ASEAN import markets has also tended to decline since the early 1970s as ASEAN importers have diversified sources of supply. Therefore, both export and import figures suggest that Japan's importance as a trading partner has declined in the ASEAN region, particularly for those countries where there is a strong upward trend in the share of manufactured goods in total exports.

Japanese trade friction with ASEAN is likely to continue into the future primarily over issues of ASEAN access to the Japanese market and ASEAN efforts to locate more higher value-added processing and manufacturing facility in their countries. Frustrated with the slow process of overcoming Japanese protection that escalates with the degree of processing, the ASEAN countries are increasingly resorting to blunt means of forcing exports of processed goods. The case of logs and plywood is an instructive one. To encourage their domestic industries, the ASEAN countries have progressively restricted log exports. As early as 1976, the Philippines limited unprocessed exports to 20 per cent of total log harvest. Indonesia has introduced similar restrictions and provided an incentive for logging companies to install plywood-making equipment. Malaysia banned all log exports from the peninsula in 1985.

Though economic relations between Japan and the ASEAN have undergone a change, the ASEAN countries, unlike the United States or Western European countries, feel that they can ill-afford to antagonize Japan. They are aid recipients and depend largely on Japan for technology and investment funds. ASEAN governments can, however, be expected to be more aggressive than in the past in insisting on access for their industrial products because as industries in their countries grow, they also acquire political power. These industries will increasingly lobby their governments to pressure Japan to provide more access, particularly if other markets look less hopeful. Above all, trade frictions with Japan mostly represent future opportunities rather than actual jobs in the economy that workers believe are being lost to foreign imports.

14

Present Phase: Japan in 21st Century

India has economic and strategic interests in the Asian economy. That explains why in February, 1998 India expressed solidarity with the South-East Asian Nations struggling to overcome their economic crisis. India's Foreign Secretary told the senior officials of the ASEAN nations that Indian-ASEAN cooperation was of top priority. However, what is being debated both in the official and academic circles is : what will be the role of Japan in the 21st century. It is this question which needs an examination.

The young Japanese scholars foresee a world dominated by a new economic system, increasing interdependence and free trade, the decline of nationalism and military spending, and the emergence of a peaceful world order. The most advanced societies were leaving behind a militant phase and evolving a new industrial phase. Coercive, regimented, hierarchical societies were being tansformed into open, democratic, commercial, and peaceful ones, they argue. This analysis needs serious examination at present when the world is still "unipolar".

For Japan, it indeed is a formidable task because it entered the age of industrialisation rather late and now has become an industrial giant, at least in Asia.

The specific feature of Japan's road to industrialisation is that it built new industrial structures on a feudal society, without sharp conflicts as has been mentioned earlier in this book. However, today, the advantages and opportunities of late development are largely over. Having caught up, Japan no longer has the old image of its future, of speedy technological development. Nor will Japan have the advantage of the problems, mistakes and shortcomings of Western social development from which to learn. It has, therefore to evolve its own course. This is what Japan's experts are attempting to achieve.

Japan finds itself in the 1990s in an unaccustomed position. As a pioneer, with no one to follow, it is seeking to formulate the future course of economic, technological, and social organisation. The term most often used in Japan to sum up the bundle of ideas and images about the future is information society which is widely regarded as the next stage of universal social evolution. "All industrial societies, writes a senior researcher at the Nomura Institute, including Japan are expected, without exception, to move toward an information-centered society in the coming years. New theories are being evolved with growing emphasis on what is called 'softnomics'.

A variety of ambitious and highly visible projects receiving official encouragement and sponsorship have caught the national imagination and become symbols of the drive toward an Information Network System (INS), a new telecommunication network pushed by Nihon Telephone and Telegraph Community Antenna Television (CATV); and the Character and Telephone Access Information Network (CAPTAIN) to provide vast amounts of information in the home. The fifth-generation computer has received international attention. A far more ambitious project is the plan of the Ministry of International Trade and Industry (MITI) to develop 14 technopolises as a means of diffusing the most advanced technologies in to regional centers as the backbone of the Japanese economy in the twenty-first century. This is the new perspective which Japan seems to have set before itself. Japan wants to be a leader in this realm long before America and West Europe embark on this road.

The question of Japan's readiness for world economic leadership and for a role in the governance of the international system is on the minds of Japanese leaders. In 1984, Japan requested, and ultimately was granted, the position of second largest shareholder in the World Bank after the United States. In terms of voting power on the bank's executive board, it moved from fifth to the second spot, ahead of Britain, Germany and France. MITI's 1984 White Paper appear to envision Japan's emergence as the centre of world finance and the leading capital exporter much as Great Britain did at the height of its power in the nineteenth century and as the United States did in the heydays of the Pax Americana immediately after World War II. Such a role is seen as resulting inevitably from recurrent Japanese trade surpluses because of such inherent structural strengths as technical innovation, productivity and high savings that will always give Japanese manufacturers an edge over those of Japan's trading partners.

What would be the implications of Japan's achieving world economic and technological leadership and pioneering in the development of a new stage of social evolution? The relative decline of US power raises serious questions about the governance of the international system. The Pax Americana system is about to be forced to undergo a reorganization because America's reliability is no longer absolute in the economic field, point out Japanese scholars.

A differentiation of world leadership might take place with different countries specializing in different functional areas. Some Japanese experts go beyond this. They point out that since monopoly of nuclear power has broken down and nuclear weapons can only be used for pressure, the world leadership cannot be concentrated in one country. There will be many centres of powers.

Along with the concern about Japan's readiness for leadership in the world system comes anxiety about the psychological reaction of the United States, on which Japan must rely for its security. The comprehensive National Security Study Group, an advisory committee appointed by the late Prime Minister Ohira, hinted at this problem in its July, 1980 report. The report acknowledged that US-Japanese cooperation will be difficult since Japan's per capita GNP is likely to overtake that of the United States; and Japanese manufactured products will by and large be more competitive on the international market, and Japanese exports will continue to expand faster than US exports. In this sense the positions of the two economies are being reversed, and this itself will entail difficult psychological problems. A highly popular science writer and senior researcher at the Nomura Research Institute, Masanori Moritani, put the matter less delicately. He wrote in 1982 that Japan's vast technological strength had come to be feared and the source of mounting frustration. And if things continue unchanged, that fear will explode into anger. If this were not a nuclear age it is possible that bombs might be falling on Japan even now. He concluded that restraint and caution or looking out when you're number one, were essential.

However, many leaders have sought to soften Japanese expectations and ambitions that their nation might soon exercise a decisive role in reshaping the world order, in light of the US decline. In particular, some official spokesmen stress international cooperation and closer ties with the United States as a matter of national interest. They argue that Japan should play a number two role and urge Japanese to model their role in governing the international system as that of an assistant to number one or as that of a vice-president. History shows, they argues that world leadership requires that a nation possess the following attributes: (1) military and economic power; (2) a set of ideals with universal applicability; (3) a rational and exportable system through which it can realize its ideals; and (4) a distinct, viable, and transferable culture. They also point out that although Japan may be equal to the United States in terms of economic power, in other respects the time is far from ripe for gracing Japan with the title of Number One. They conclude that whether we like to admit it or not, there will be no free world and no free trading system if the United States does not preserve them for us...The best Japan can aspire is to be the vice-president. For its own sake, it must recognize this and conduct itself with the tact and discertion befitting its real position in the world community. These scholars are concerned that Japanese pretensions to international leadership stirred by the recent success story will inflame US suspicions.

Thus there are two conflicting trends among Japanese scholars about the role of their country in the next century.

The concept of an information society: pioneered by Japan and representing a new historical stage in human social evolution poses profound problems for the Japanese. At the heart of the matter is their ambition for global leadership in economic and technological development and the implications of this for governance of the international system. Japan's economic power has come to be perceived as disruptive and challenging to the existing international order. French foreign trade minister Michel Jobert remarked in 1982 how quiet and peaceful the world would be without the Soviet Union and Japan.

The issue of the role of this economic power in political and strategic affairs remains unanswered and the source of great debate and soul searching. Many influential Japanese profess to believe that the importance of military power in international relations is declining because of the advent of nuclear weapons, increased economic interdependency, and a growing global consciousness. For the moment, at least a section of Japan's elite believes that Japan must continue to work closely with the United States, deferring to its overall leadership of the alliance. New conditions and new attitudes are, nevertheless forcing the Japanese to rethink the assumptions that have guided their postwar foreign policy.

There are various trends among Japan's scholars and policy makers about its role in the world. This is not the scope of this study to go into them. However, there is a powerful trend which has been described as "new nationalists". What sets the new nationalists apart from other trends is their belief that Japan should exercise an independent role in world politics. As the sociologist Ikutaro Shimizu, undoubtedly the new nationalist who has attracted the most attention, wrote in his sensational book, *Nippon yo, kokka tare* (Japan, become a state) published in 1980. On the one hand, Japan must encourage friendly relations with the United States, the Soviet Union, and all other countries, but at the same time we must not forget for an instant that Japan is alone. In the end we can only rely on Japan and the Japanese.

The confidence that Japan is capable of an independent role is supported by an immense pride in Japan's socio-economic and technological achievements. In the judgement of a number of contemporary observers, the Japanese have mastered the skills of organizing a modern industrial society with greater success than any other people. Scores of books have been written about the reasons for Japanese success; their common theme is an emphasis on the unique characteristics of the Japanese and their culture. Japan has, outstripped the economic performance of other industrial countries, goes the usual explanation, because its historically formed institutions have proved more productive and competitive than those of other countries. More than one writer drew this conclusion.

It was inevitable that the US occupation, its reforms, the war crimes trial and the postwar self-criticism was subjected to revision. Many writers, have scrutinized the procedures followed in drafting and imposing the constitution. They have emphasized the censorship, the manipulation of popular opinion, and the "alien and utopian" nature of its provisions. The result was a constitutional system that deprived Japan of sovereign rights fundamental to a nation-state, they have argued.

The basic goal of US occupation policy, wrote Eto, was to destroy the greater Japanese empire, which had styled itself as unparalleled among national and to create an ordinary Japan. Ironically, the Occupation gave birth to a Japan that is, in an entirely different sense, unparalleled among nations. Without the right of belligerency, which was renounced in Article 9, Japan could not be a free, sovereign nation, master of its own fate. Yoshida accepted this servile status and built Japan's postwar system to suit it. For Eto, so long as we continue to set up Yoshida politics as the legitimate conservative politics, we Japanese will not escape from the shackles of the postwar period, and the road to self-recovery will be closed. Since the administration of Prime Minister Ikeda, Eto believes the government has shelved the constitutional issue, concentrated on economic development, and offered flexible interpretations of the constitution as the need arose. Eto maintains that a tacit understanding exists between the conservatives and the progressive to leave the issue unresolved but during the last two decades, particularly the ninties, a sea-change has taken place in the dominant thinking of Japan's ruling elite. There are three main factors responsible for it. Firstly, and primarily Japan's rise as an economic power. Secondly, the demise of Soviet Union, Thirdly, decline in the economic and political influence of the United States.

But the time has come, some Japanese scholars argue to confront the issue and restore Japan's right of belligerency so that Japan can prepare to defend itself should the need so arise. Americans, for their part, must face up to the new situation as well. They must admit that Article 9 was the result of their distrust of Japan and their fear that Japan might some day again attack the United States. If there were among the American people the determination to wipe away completely their distrust of Japan, to tolerate a more powerful and less dependent Japan and to form an alliance to coexist with such a Japan, then the future to Japan-US relations would indeed be bright.

It seems that Japan is now well-positioned to play the central role in third world development, while the United States is on course to reduce its overall commitments in this field. This is one of the areas where Japan may have to have some kind of surplus capacity to be a co-leader in a plural leadership structure with a collective leadership or with a basically functionally differentiated structure, argues Prof. Akio Hosono. What kind of global leadership sharing between the United States and Japan is most likely in this field having in mind recent tendencies in development assistance and international cooperation of the United States and Japan, he has emphasised.

This kind of analysis should be made not only at global level but also at regional and sub-regional levels. For example, possibilities of such shift or new scheme of shared leadership should be examined regarding development assistance to Latin American countries where the United States have been the major traditional donor.

Japanese economic capacity and political will to provide development assistance to the third world is obvious at least in terms of financial value or quantity of aid. In 1989, Japan was the number one donor. Although in 1990 and 1991, the country's ODA was slightly below the US level, its relative share in the total of DAC countries ODA increased. In 1994, the ODA of the United States and Japan corresponded to 40 per cent of the total. The amount of Japanese ODA disbursed in 1994 increased to 13,240 million dollars (22.9 per cent of the total DAC countries ODA), while that of the United States decreased to 9850 million dollars (17.1per cent). Moreover, it should be mentioned that in the case of Japan, its official financial cooperation to the third world is almost twice the value of its ODA, if the finance made through the programme of Recycling of Capital started in 1987 (the name was changed later: International Cooperation Programme) is included.

Japanese cooperation to the third world has been increased substantially and systematically according to previously established programmes. Since 1989, the amount of Japanese ODA was doubled in five years. At the same time the wide range Programme of Recycling of Capital was implemented with special emphasis to help highly indebted developing countries.

After the successful implementation of the fourth five year outline that called for doubling ODA and of the Programme of Recycling of Capital, the government of the then Prime Minister Kiichi Mayazawa unveiled during the Tokyo summit of the seven industrial nations in June, 1993 the fifth five year ODA outline that called for increasing Japan's ODA by 20 per cent to 70-75 billion dollars during 1993-97. The midterm scheme also envisages earmarking about 120 billion dollars globally during the same period for the International Cooperation Programme, by expanding the scale of the previous Programme for Recycling of Capital into developing countries, in addition to the 50 per cent increase of ODA.

The Japanese programme is gradually taking into account certain political principles shared by most of the donors, especially the United States. In this sense the major shift in Japan's policy occurred in 1991, when Japan, under Prime Minister Toshiki Kaifu, announced that it would take into account arms spending levels, moves towards democratization and market reform and human rights considerations in determining a country's aid level. It did signal a major break with Japan's policies, at least in a dejure sense in the past. This shows that a convergence in concept between the United States and Japan is taking place.

In terms of support of democratization and shift to market economy, significant assistance was made for Mongol, Combodia, Vietnam, Central Asian Countries, Palestine, the Republic of South Africa, etc. On the other hand, problems of human rights, freedom, difficulty in democratization, military spending, trade of arms and so on were considered in case of Sudan, Guatemala, Myanmar, Nigeria, Kenya, Malawi, Sierra Leone, Haiti, India, Pakistan and China, according to the White Paper on Japan's ODA 1994.

However, the US aid programme has been heavily centered on the projection of strategic goals, although it is moving gradually in the direction of becoming more attentive to US economic interests. In contrast, the Japanese Programme is formulated almost exclusively on the basis of considerations regarding economic development of the recipient countries such as level of development according to Japanese scholars.

(i) Outright grants are extended chiefly to nations with the lowest per capita income; (ii) Concessional credits are extended to countries with per capita income lower than a certain level, complemented by grants; (iii) Various kinds of economic cooperation among other direct loans from the Export-Import Bank of Japan are extended to other developing countries complemented by concessional credits normally related to environment concerns in case of these countries and grants.

The regional distribution of Japanese ODA is now much more diversified than before. The share of Asian countries in the total amount of Japan's ODA decreased from 98.2 per cent in 1970 to 59.5 per cent in 1993. On the other hand, the financial cooperation under the Programme of Recycling of Capital (debt reduction related finance under the new debt strategy of the Brady Plan and other direct loans of the Export-

Import Bank of Japan) has been mobilized to non-Asian countries, particularly heavily indebted Latin American countries.

Therefore, Japan's ODA and Other Official Financial (OOF) cooperation to the third world has been getting much more diversified in terms of its regional distribution and increasingly more complementary to the United States Programme. In case of some countries or regions, Japanese cooperation is substituting the US's aid.

Furthermore several efforts have been already made to coordinate the two countries assistance, or to implement jointly, development projects in recipient countries. For example, the United States and Japan cooperated in the project of Agricultural Development Programme of North-East Thailand, Higher Education Project of Indonesia, Graduate School of Agronomy in Bangladesh, Partnership for Democracy and Development in Central America, etc.

Japanese strong support for development cooperation through international organizations, especially such organizations where the United States active role is widely recognized, could mean a kind of leadership sharing as well as burden sharing between the two countries. Examples of such international organizations are the International Monetary Fund, the World Bank and the Inter-American Development Bank. The Japanese government disbursed a large amount of funds through such joint schemes as co-finances with these international financial institutions, especially cofinances for structural adjustment programmes, according to Prof. Akio Hosono.

However, Japanese scholars do not fully share the concepts of World Bank. In fact before the recent financial crisis in some of the ASEAN countries, this aspect was underlined by the scholars of Japan. For instance, a Study of the Japan Centre for Economic Research on the Role of Institutions and Policies in Japan's Modern Economic Growth and their Applicability to Developing Countries, a study commissioned by the EPA in 1994, offered interpretations certainly different from that of the World Bank study.

The most prevalent development policy at present is the one based on a mechanism of market economy. But the government also has a place to play its role in development policies, most important being a role to supplement possible deficiency of the market economy, this report points out.

Nevertheless, the EPA's 1994 paper made the following interesting statements regarding conditionalities of international financial institutions: In the light of failure of import substitution industrialization strategies in many developing countries under state enterprises policy, and of developing countries' troubles with budget deficits: and worsening balances of payments, the World Bank and the IMF have added structural adjustment loans to the assistance menu since the 1980s. Conditions for these loans are based on neoclassical economic models. They call for eliminating government intervention and regulation as much as possible, letting market mechanisms operate, and creating conditions where the private sector is free to operate unhindered, and the developing countries are expected to make these changes-deregulation, liberalization, privatization and decentralization. To the developing countries, meeting these conditionalities means that the barriers arising from too much government intervention and so on are removed, and in general, it is thought that such change is necessary. On the other hand, there have always been problems meeting these conditionalities, and in addition, the development models which require these are theoretical ones based on neoclassical economics and do not appear to take into consideration the relationship between policy changes in the country concerned and conditions for policy acceptance, as defined by relations between the government and the private sector, level of the private sector vitality, state of the infrastructure, development of the factor market of production-capital labour, parts availability and so on. This indeed stands as a complete contrast to the American perception.

Japan claims that it has made a significant contribution to debt alleviating schemes to solve prolonged debt problems of developing countries. It was Japan, not the United States that first proposed substantial debt relief scheme with participation of industrial countries government. The Japanese proposal was made as Miyazawa proposal in the annual meeting of the IMF and World Bank, in September, 1988. This proposal was not supported by the United States. Curiously, six months later (March 1989), the Brady proposal, very similar to the Miyazawa proposal, was announced. Japanese concern regarding financial problems of developing countries was expressed again when it proposed a scheme to issue SDR for a new fund to be mobilized to developing countries in April, 1991. But it was again not supported by the United States.

Nevertheless, in the decision making process, Japanese initiatives were not necessarily supported by the United States. On the contrary, Japan fully supported the Brady Plan proposed by the United States.

Quite apart from this aspect there appear to be differences between the United States and Japan over economic policies in the Asia-Pacific region. As is well known, three fundamental pillars of APEC are liberalization of trade, facilitation of trade and investment and cooperation for development. The United States and Japan are two major donors in APEC, their partnership is crucial for successful "cooperation for development" among APEC countries.

Nevertheless, it should be recognized that certain differences in the approach exist between the US and Japan regarding development cooperation in the APEC.

Japan emphasizes the importance of development "cooperation" in APEC while the United States appears to put the highest priority on "liberalization". This difference is better understood when we compare APEC and NAFTA/FTAA. These three initiatives are regional integration of both industrial and developing economies. But the approaches to the "North South relations" in their respective regions are significantly different.

The Bogor Declaration reiterates the simultaneous process of attaining the above-mentioned three targets of APEC-liberalization, facilitation and cooperation. The Declaration stresses further more that APEC's objective of strengthening cooperation for development of societies of the Asia-Pacific region would enable the attainment of sustainable growth and equitable development of APEC economies and efficient utilization of human and natural resources of the region in order to diminish economic differences and improve economic and social welfare of people of the region.

In comparison with this concept of the Bogor Declaration, the Miami 'Summit of the Americas' Declaration of Principles adopted in December 1994, one month after the Bogor Declaration, did neither express any commitment to strengthening cooperation for development among countries of the region nor emphasised explicitly that cooperation is as important as liberalization.

Nevertheless, the Miami Declaration of Principles recognized that "investment is the main engine of growth in the Hemisphere". Such investment should be encouraged by cooperating to build a more open, transparent and integrated market. Moreover to advance economic-integration and free trade it is necessary that financing from the private sector and international financial institutions should be promoted to create a hemispheric infrastructure. This process requires a cooperative effort in fields such as telecommunications, energy and transportation. The differences in these regional processes relations reflect the differences between the US and Japan regarding development cooperation in APEC.

These differences were made more explicit in the APEC Osaka meeting. Japan had been proposing since 1994 the creation of Partner for Progress (PFP) in order to implement effectively the development cooperation in APEC. But, the proposal to establish a PFP Centre was not supported by the United States. The US representative expressed that it would mean over-dimension of APEC organizations. This shows that the United States was rather reluctant of Japanese initiative to strengthen the cooperation among countries of APEC in the field of promotion of small and medium enterprises. The United States was not very much in favour of Japanese leadership in this field.

It is expected that rapid economic growth will be sustained in East Asia, but in this process it is considered indispensable to construct an economic and social infrastructure, for which financial cooperation from industrial countries is crucial. The World Bank estimates that 1,200 billion to 1,500 billion dollars of investment in infrastructure should be done in the coming ten years in order to cope with the rapid growth in East Asian countries. Technical cooperation should also be necessary in a variety of fields in this region.

However, Japanese experts feel that inspite of differences between the US and Japan in their approaches the development cooperation is one of the most promising areas where US and Japan would be able to collaborate very closely sharing both leadership and burden, for the following reasons: i) the APEC process has already started with its clear target of trade liberalization, while development cooperation is considered one of its three fundamental targets; ii) US and Japan are two major donors of the region and there is expectation among countries of the region that they play leading roles in this area; iii) several practical organizations and mechanisms for implementation of cooperation as well as for consultation and coordination for cooperation are now being established in the APEC process.

A new approach for development cooperation: "Shaping the 21st century: The Contribution to Development Co-operation" was adopted by High Level Meeting by the DAC, OECD in May, 1996. This approach was endorsed by the G-7's Lyon Summit, when G-7 leaders agreed to implement the New Global Partnership for Development. Behind the new initiative there are several factors which characterise the recent development of the world economy. First of all it should fully take into account the irreversible tendency of globalization accompanied by simultaneous regional processes all over the world. The globalization is not yet clearly defined and its real impact in individual countries especially developing countries, is not comprehensively analysed. However, its importance is widely recognized among economists and political leaders. While the G-7 leaders consider that the globalization provides great opportunities for the future, referring to its many positive aspects, recognize that it also poses challenges to societies and economics. However, its benefits will not materialize unless countries adjust to increased competition. In the poorer countries, it may accentuate, inequality and certain parts of the world could become marginalized. The adjustment needed is, however, imposing rapid and sometimes painful restructuring, whose effects in some of the countries can temporarily worsen the employment situation. Globalization of the financial markets, which requires all countries to pursue sound economic policies and structural reforms, can generate new risks of instability, underline some Japanese scholars. The second factor is the increasingly wider appreciation of the East Asian success by not only orthodox policies but also by a series of other policies which differ among high performing Asian countries. To what extent the latter policies are responsible for their success is yet to be more deeply analysed. But the interest regarding East Asian success is now really widespread and a number of organizations are proceeding researches on this subject, some of them searching for a new paradigm of development strategies taking into account the Asian experiences. The recent crisis in some of the ASEAN countries such as Indonesia and Malaysia have brought into sharp focus this aspect of the problem.

The third factor is the growing global concern about several problems related to the past developmental processes. The foremost among them is the relating to the deterioration of the environment. The persistent phenomena of poverty and social inequality are also getting to be one of the major concerns of the world leaders. In other words, the values other than growth and efficiency such as environment conservation, equity, participation, poverty reduction, good governance, etc., are now increasingly considered to be of high priority.

In this regard, the New Global Partnership for Development agreed upon at the Lyon Summit could be an important approach: This new partnership should set its sight on enabling all developing countries whatever may be their stage of development, to share and participate in the benefits of globalization. To that end, it should take the achievement of sustainable development as its fundamental objective. Goals should include the reduction of poverty and social inequalities, the respect of internationally recognized labour standards, protection of children, a strengthened civil society, protection of the environment, improved standards of health and education etc.

In order to establish a realistic framework for more concerted actions and coordination in US-Japan leadership and burden sharing for development assistance and international cooperation, it seems necessary at least to clarify the following aspects: (i) Would US and Japan be able to share a common vision or principles regarding development of developing countries and development cooperation?; (ii) How two countries would be able to complement each other?; and (iii) To what extent developing cooperation partnership are related to other fields of US-Japan leadership sharing such as security, global economic policy, trade relations and investment, etc.?

These aspects should be discussed both at global and regional or sub-regional levels. Sometimes cross regional or inter regional considerations such as US-Asia and Japan-Latin America could be relevant, according to Prof. Akio Hosono as spelt out in one of his papers at an international seminar in September, 1996.

In 1994, Japan became the world largest donor of Official Development Assistance (ODA) three years in a row with its disbursement of 13.2 billion US dollars. This amount exceeded the traditionally largest donor—the United States by 3.3 billion US dollars. In the environment where the budget difficulties and international environment after the Cold War made most of the donors cut their foreign aid, the Japanese aid level seems to stay stable and high.

This trend in economic terms should be examined in the face of economic-development of Japan.

In 1984 Japan's GNP accounted for 11.8 per cent of total world output and, partly because of the rise in the yen, Japan had the highest per capita national income in the world. The country's growing trade imbalance with the United States led to the Plaza Accord in 1986 and a major appreciation of the yen versus other currencies. This forced a shift in economic emphasis, from one based on exports to one based on domestic demand.

Because of the rising yen and in order to stimulate domestic demand the government maintained a policy of very low interest rates from 1986 to 1989, allowing companies to raise capital at very low cost from the stock market. Low interest rates had the effect of driving stock prices higher, and this was further fuelled by the growing involvement of private investors in the equity market. However, corporates did not use all the capital they had acquired to invest in their business but, rather, used surplus funds to invest in the financial markets. Corporate cash surpluses also led to overinvestment in business operations. Personal consumption also grew rapidly. It did appear that the government's policy of expanding domestic demand had worked, but money supply was growing and there were signs of the economy overheating.

In December, 1989, when the Bank of Japan switched to a tighter interest rate policy, this signalled serious economic situation and of a protracted showdown in the Japanese economy. This was perhaps exacerbated by the introduction of a new three per cent consumption tax in 1989 to finance new expenditures on social security and welfare.

From early in the 1990s land prices, which had appreciated almost without pause during the 1980's, began to turn downwards.

In 1990, the operating ratio of the manufacturing sector fell and corporate profits entered a long, drawnout slump. Industrial corporations and banks were faced with mounting losses on their investments in financial markets and from the consequences of over-borrowing.

In an effort to overcome the slowdown in the economy the government in 1992 again opted for a low interest rate policy, and also introduced a series of emergency fiscal packages, the largest of which was worth 30 trillion yen. However, these measure were not enough to bring about the desired results. While this was partly due to the slump in economic activity elsewhere in the world, from 1994 the advanced overseas economies began to see signs of recovery while Japan continued to idle along, hampered by little or no improvement in the bad debt situation. This was reflected in stock prices in 1996. New York, London and many other overseas equity markets rose to new highs, while Tokyo fluctuated at a level roughly 50 per cent below the high point reached in 1989.

While a partial solution to the bad debt problem facing the banking system has been found by getting the people to foot part of the bill, there remains the larger question of the relevance and suitability of the current economic system. In particular, the competitiveness of the manufacturing sector, the main engine of growth since the war, has declined in the face of yen appreciation, higher labour costs and the growth of emerging economies, particularly in East Asia. The vulnerability of this type of economic system has been clearly shown by, for example, the exodus of production facilities to overseas locations. At the same time, the development of a more knowledge and information-intensive social and economic structure has facilitated the growth of new industries capable of adding value in terms of knowledge and information. However, while manufacturing requires the ability to organize and optimise production, the new information industries require individuality and creativity, two attributes in short supply in Japan.

For Japan to return to stable economic growth the creation of new industries to augment or replace the old manufacturing industries has become imperative. This would involve switching from a manufacturing-intensive industrial structure to a more service-oriented one, and would also require the development of new info-manufacturing industries located somewhere between the two. At the same time the economy's dependence on the major corporations needs to be reduced, and greater attention paid to supporting smaller companies and developing venture capital businesses. This would have significant implications for Japan's commitment to basic research.

The Japanese economy will need a new focus as the switch is made from export dependence. One aspect of this is increased self-reliance on the part of the private corporate sector. For so long under the protection and control of the government, and the revamping of the regulatory structure to allow greater freedom in economic activity. This deregulation is also part of a larger question concerning the way the country is run. The government's huge issues of bonds since 1975 means that it now owes every man, woman and child in the country around 2 million yen. The fiscal problem has intensified in the 1990s since it has been difficult to roll back the budget increase of the late eighties when government revenues were in much better shape.

Japan's gross national product in 1994 was 458 trillion yen, the second largest in the world after the United States. Real economic growth in 1990-94 averaged a low 2 per cent per year. While this was slightly above the growth rates achieved by the other major economies, the 0.4 per cent growth of 1994 was lower. It is becoming increasingly apparent that Japan has been left behind in the recovery which other countries have seen since 1994. The largest component of gross national expenditure in 1994 was private sector, final consumption accounting for 58.6 per cent of the total. Gross fixed capital formation accounted for 29.4 per cent of the total.

Except for the inflation of the two oil crises, wholesale prices in Japan have been extremely low and stable. However, consumer price growth has been uneven: while the stronger yen and rising imports have meant falling prices for foodstuffs and other necessities, higher prices for services and utility mean that, in overall terms, consumer prices have risen slightly since 1990. Nevertheless, since 1990 Japan has still enjoyed the lowest consumer inflation rate of the five major economies.

Wholesale prices rose sharply as a result of the 1979 oil crisis but subsequent stability in oil prices and daily necessities proved a good augur of the wholesale price. Environment in the five major economies remains benign, but this is particularly the case in Japan. In consumer prices, the trend has been generally downward since 1986, when the yen began appreciating and imports began increasing and inflation has been particularly low since 1991.

Nominal GDP by Country

	1980		1990		1995	
	Total (US$ billion)	*Per capita (US$)*	*Total (US$ billion)*	*Per capita (US$)*	*Total (US$ billion)*	*Per capita (US$)*
USA	2,784	12,224	5,522	22,096	7,246	27,799
Japan	1,059	9,068	2,932	23,734	5,110	40,897
Germany[a]	810	13,154	1,496	23,667	2,414	29,644
France	665	12,335	1,195	21,059	1,538	26,496
Italy	453	8,021	1,095	18,993	1,087	19,002
UK	539	9,562	983	17,117	1,057	18,097
Canada	265	11,025	572	21,534	568	19,431
Spain	213	5,635	491	12,609	559	14,286
China	302	303	370[b]	325[b]	522[c]	432[c]
Brazil	235	1,937	479	3,187	507[d]	3,186[d]
South Korea	63	1,643	244	5,693	380[c]	8,540[c]
Maxico	194	2,790	241	2,802	377[c]	4,190[c]
Netherlands	169	11,977	284	18,979	334[c]	21,736[c]
Russia[e]	938[b]	3,532[b]	625[b]	2,160b	364	2,461
Australia	151	10,256	295	17,266	348	19,481

Source : Bank of Japan, Kokusai hikaku tokei (Comparative International Statistics), 1996.

Note : Figures are expressed in market prices. Currencies have been converted using the average rates in IMF, *International Financial Statistics.*

(a) 1980 data is for West Germany.

(b) Gross National Product.

(c) 1994

(d) 1993

(e) 1980 and 1990 data are for the USSR.

Consumer Price Index (1990-100)

Year	*Japan*	*USA*	*UK*	*Germany*	*France*
1985	93.5	82.3	75	93.5	86
1986	94.1	83.9	77.5	93.4	88.2
1987	94.2	87	80.8	93.6	90.9
1988	94.9	90.5	84.7	94.8	93.4
1989	97	94.9	91.3	97.4	96.7
1990	100	100	100	100	100
1991	103.3	104.2	105.9	103.5	103.2
1992	105	107.4	109.8	107.6	105.6
1993	106.4	110.6	111.6	109.8	107.9
1994	107.1	113.4	114.3	112.8	109.7
1995	107	116.6	118.2	114.8	111.6

The following Tables give a comparative picture of Japan's economy in the world, including in Asia.

Real GDP Growth by Country
(change over previous year per cent)

	1991	*1992*	*1993*	*1994*	*1995*[a]	*Average (1991-95)*
China	9.5	14.0	13.3	11.6	10.2	11.7
Malaysia	8.7	7.8	8.3	9.2	9.5	8.7
Thailand	8.5	8.1	8.3	8.8	8.6	8.5
Singapore	7.0	6.4	10.1	10.1	8.8	8.5
South Korea	9.1	5.1	5.8	8.4	-	7.6
Indonesia	7.0	6.5	7.3	7.5	8.1	7.6[b]
Taiwan	7.6	6.8	6.3	6.5	6.1	6.6
Hong Kong	5.1	6.3	6.1	5.5	4.6	5.5
Australia	-1.6	2.6	4.0	5.2	3.1	2.6
Netherlands	2.3	2.0	0.2	2.7	2.4	1.9
USA	-1.0	2.7	2.2	3.5	2.0	1.9
Canada	-1.8	0.8	2.2	4.6	2.2	1.6
Spain	2.3	0.7	1.2	2.1	3.0	1.4
Japan	4.0	1.1	0.1	0.5	0.9	1.3
UK	-2.0	-0.5	2.3	2.2	2.4	1.2

Source : Bank of Japan Kokusai hikaku tokei (Comparative International Statistics) 1996.

(a) Includes projected data.

(b) 1993-95

Components of Real GDP Growth by Country, 1995
(Change over previous year)

	Consumer expenditure	*Government consumption*	*Gross fixed capital formation*	*Increase in inventories*	*Exports*	*Imports*
France	1.1	0.1	0.6	0.1	1.7	-1.4
Germany	0.7	0.4	0.4	0.3	0.9	-0.8
Italy	0.3	0.3	1.0	0.3	2.9	-1.9
Japan	1.0	0.2	0.2	0.2	0.6	-1.3
UK	1.5	0.2	-0.1	0.2	1.6	-0.9
USA	1.6	0.0	0.9	-0.4	0.9	-1.0
Canada	0.8	-0.2	0.0	0.4	4.5	-3.5

Source : Bank of Japan, Kokusai hikaku tokei (Comparative International Statistics), 1996.

These statistics speak for themselves and show how Japan has carved out a place for itself in the world economy and its economic structures are undergoing basic changes.

At the very heart of the debate over Japan's future international role is the issue of Japanese exceptionalism. Everyone involved agrees that Japan has been an exceptional nation-state since World War II, but the issue is can and should Japan continue as an extraordinary nation? Or should and must it conform to new international conditions and become an ordinary nation?

There are no readymade answer to these questions. There are conflicting trends among the scholars of Japan.

There is one school which advocates that post-war Japan had three goals, to build a peaceful state, to establish a free society and to achieve economic prosperity and a standard of living similar to that of Western countries. With regard to the first goal, the Japanese race has gambled its future in a great experiment, the first of its kind in human history, and fortunately till today it has succeeded. Similarly, Japan had succeeded in establishing a free society with protection for human rights and with disparities in income distribution smaller than all but two or three scandinavian countries. Finally, the nation has achieved economic property. But it is important to continue to pursue economic priorities in order to build up social capital for housing, schools and to acquire the benefits of a technological society.

One of the most noteworthy features of this debate is an emergent new sense of nationality, strikingly different from pre-war nationalism.

The social structure and politics of postwar Japan have been greatly transformed. Social and cultural divisions are lessened. Japan's 90 per cent population regards itself as middle class. Japan is overwhelmingly urban, well-educated, perhaps as well informed on international conditions as any nation and thoroughly imbued with the values and tastes of industrial society. It builds on Japan's industrial accomplishments and finds confidence from achieving Western ends by Japanese means.

Moreover, the end of the era of late development is likely to affect the nature of Japanese nationalism. Late development entailed borrowing from the West to supplant traditional wisdom and skills and gave rise to painful cultural dislocations. A key theme in modern Japanese history has been the search for ways to reconcile the conflicting needs of cultural borrowing and national pride, to be both modern and Japanese.

The excesses of Japanese nationalism in the 1930s were partly a result of this failure to solve the dilemma of reconciling cultural borrowing with the need for national pride. The narrow Japanism of that day lead to a war that ended in an imposed conception of nationality that lacked roots in the inherited tradition. In the present era, there is a widespread belief that Japan has reached the Western nations advanced stage of development and that Japan, therefore, has regained control of its own destiny.

There is a pervasive conviction that Japan has caught up not only in a material sense but in the fulfilment of social and political values as well. Furthermore, there is confidence that these goals have been reached by a Japanese—a better cultural route. The goals of Western liberalism have been realized without the social costs apparent in the West because they have been reached by relying on Japanese cultural values and patterns of behaviour.

Discussion of the twenty-first century is probably more extensive in Japan than in any other country. It is remarkable for its optimism about the nature of the projected information society and its belief that the Japanese are best suited for the challenges of this society. One's impression is that there is less concern than in other countries about the loss of privacy, the dangers of unemployment, and the vulnerability of society to control by technocrats. Rather, there is notable self-confidence in facing this brave new world. A blue-ribbon commission of economists and bureaucrats assembled by the Ministry of Finance and known as the Study Group on the Structural Transformation of the Economy and its policy implications concluded that unlike the social systems of the west, Japanese society possesses characteristics well adapted to the new era. For example Japan will be able to deal with the dehumanizing problems of an information society in a better way because the basic characteristic of Japanese culture is that, as shown in the Japanese word that it values relationship between persons. The problem of maintaining a balance between the whole society and the individual, a relationship greatly intensified in the information society, will be better handled in the contextualist Japanese social pattern than in the atomistic nature of Western society.

In the midst of new ferment among Japanese thinker, one thing is certain that in the next century it will be a key factor in the Asia-Pacific region and will assert its independence on the basis of its material base.

Index